Rainer Hoffmann

AF238955

Dynamic Capacity Control in Air Cargo
Revenue Management

Dynamic Capacity Control in Air Cargo Revenue Management

by
Rainer Hoffmann

Dissertation, Karlsruher Institut für Technologie (KIT)
Fakultät für Wirtschaftswissenschaften
Tag der mündlichen Prüfung: 13. Februar 2013
Referenten: Prof. Dr. Karl-Heinz Waldmann,
          Prof. Dr. Andreas Geyer-Schulz

Impressum

Karlsruher Institut für Technologie (KIT)
KIT Scientific Publishing
Straße am Forum 2
D-76131 Karlsruhe
www.ksp.kit.edu

KIT – Universität des Landes Baden-Württemberg und
nationales Forschungszentrum in der Helmholtz-Gemeinschaft

KIT Scientific Publishing 2013
Print on Demand

ISBN 978-3-7315-0003-2

Contents

i

List of Figures

List of Tables

CHAPTER 1

Introduction

Since the US government passed the law to deregulate the airline market in 1978, cost efficiency, operating profitability, and competitive behavior have become crucial management issues (Belobaba, 2009, pp. 1-2). Even though airlines have been free to set ticket prices, increasing competition has forced them to offer low fares. In recent years, being profitable has become difficult for airlines since operating costs, which are largely driven by the oil price and labor costs, have increased. Furthermore, ticket prices have been low since customers have become increasingly price-sensitive, and many low cost carriers have entered the market. Numerous major carrier bankruptcies, such as United, US Airways, Delta, or Air Canada, have demonstrated that profitably operating an airline is challenging. Pilarski (2007, p. 3) even describes the financial situation of the airline industry to be "between disaster and catastrophe". Consequently, airline management actively seeks sources for cost minimization or revenue maximization. For example, in 2012, in order to improve annual profits by over 2 billion dollars, Lufthansa German Airlines introduced a three-year cost cutting program (Lufthansa, 2012).

Traditionally, an airline's strategic focus has been on carrying passengers. Transporting cargo on combination carriers was considered rather as a byproduct. According to Rathert (2006), "cargo has always been the misunderstood and unglamorous step-child of the airline industry". However, due to the described pressure on profitability, airlines have started paying increasingly attention to potential contributions from cargo operations (see e.g. Shaw, 2004, p. 39; Sandhu & Klabjan, 2006; Rathert, 2006; Graff, 2008; Parthasarathy, 2010). In order to improve efficiency and customer service, the International Air Transport Association (IATA) has even funded a non-profit industry group that defines quality standards for cargo supply chains (IATA, 2012). Today, for many airlines, cargo has become an important source of revenue and on average contributes 15% of total air traffic revenue (Boeing, 2013). While all airlines at least sell cargo space on their passenger aircraft to generate additional revenue, many carriers operate an extra fleet of pure freighters to take advantage of demand for air freight. For instance, LAN Airlines generates 39.3% of its total revenue from transporting cargo (LAN, 2012), and for Korean Air, cargo accounts for 29.7% of total revenue (Korean Air, 2012).

While air freight may be up to ten times as expensive as surface transport, it offers the advantage of speed and reliability (Shaw, 2004, pp. 40-47). Typical goods, for which air transport is chosen, are high tech products or perishable goods like fresh fruits (MergeGlobal, 2008). In general, the benefits of speed and reliability are crucial for companies operating global supply chains. Production strategies such as just-in-time and just-in-sequence, which avoid any stock building, increase the importance of a quick and highly reliable transport even further. The increasing importance of air cargo is also reflected in past and forecasted traffic data (see Figure 1.1): Global air cargo traffic grew on average 3.7% per year between 2001 and 2011, with a drop in demand in 2009. Annual growth is predicted as on average 5.2% until 2031, which implies that total air traffic will triple between 2011 and 2031. According to Airbus (2011), the main growth drivers are international trade expansion, especially to and from China, and the development of domestic express freight in China, India, and Brazil. While demand is expected to increase significantly, air freight yields have on average declined at 4.2% per year between 1991 and 2011 (see Figure 1.2), which is owed to, among others, overcapacity and intense competition (Vinod & Narayan, 2008).

In summary, on the supply side, in order to compensate for profit challenges in the passenger business, airlines have started focusing on revenue opportunities

RTKs
in billions

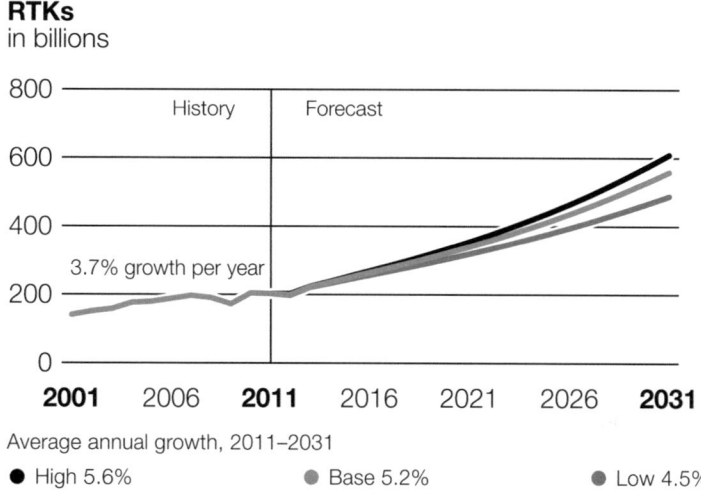

Average annual growth, 2011–2031
● High 5.6%   ● Base 5.2%   ● Low 4.5%

Figure 1.1: World air cargo traffic (Boeing, 2013)

Index
1989 = 1.0

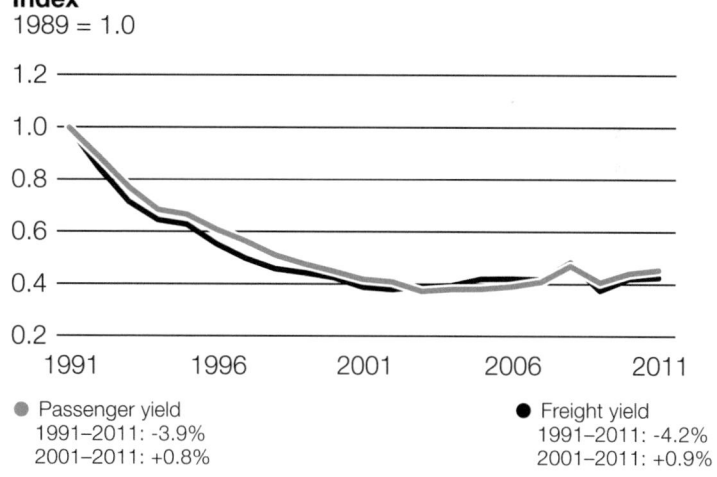

● Passenger yield   ● Freight yield
1991–2011: -3.9%   1991–2011: -4.2%
2001–2011: +0.8%   2001–2011: +0.9%

Figure 1.2: Cargo yields (Boeing, 2013)

from cargo. On the demand side, air freight traffic is expected to increase significantly, but yields are low. Thus, selling the right product to the right customer at the right time is highly important in order to capture market demand and increase yields. This brings along the question of which decision rules to follow when selling cargo capacity to customers. Below, we provide a description of the associated decision problem.

The Decision Problem

Consider a cargo revenue manager who receives short-term booking requests over a finite booking horizon. A request for a shipment type is characterized by the shipment's weight and volume requirement, origin and destination of the freight, and its contribution margin per unit. The aircraft (or multiple aircraft), which connects the specific origin and destination, have a limited weight and volume capacity. When the revenue manager receives a booking request, a decision has to be made whether the incoming request is accepted or rejected. Accepting the request gives the airline the particular contribution margin times the shipment's capacity requirement. Rejecting the request implies that demand is lost, but capacity is saved for later requests. The objective in this decision problem is to determine an acceptance policy that maximizes the overall contribution margin. Since the cargo capacity control problem is one component of the revenue management process, the term 'revenue' rather than 'contribution margin' is usually used despite abusing the terminology.

1.1 Research Questions and Contributions

This work focuses on modeling cargo capacity control problems of airlines and determining decision rules which maximize the revenue from selling available capacity. In general, air cargo space can be sold based on either long-term contracts (allotments) or on a short term basis. We focus our research on managing short term capacity on what is known as "spot market". Accordingly, we attempt to provide revenue-maximizing decision rules for decision makers who have to decide whether an incoming short-term request, for a particular shipment, should be accepted or rejected.

Cargo is 20 years behind the passenger business when it comes to implementing revenue management solutions (Rathert, 2006). According to Kasilingam (2011, p. 179), only a few airlines have actually implemented revenue management systems. Thus, advanced and comprehensible decision support tools, which are easy to implement, are required. However, translating the capacity control problem into a mathematical model and solving it is not straightforward. In comparison to seat inventory control, cargo capacity control is more complex, therefore making most models computationally expensive. This is why, in cargo revenue management, research focuses on solving the decision problem heuristically (see for instance Amaruchkul et al., 2007; Levina et al., 2011). For a system state comprising two capacity dimensions, Xiao & Yang (2010) provide the only study on the exact and analytical-form solution. However, the authors present a capacity control model which is applicable in maritime rather than air cargo revenue management. A similar study for air cargo has not yet been carried out. Given this research gap, the first part of our work analyzes structural properties of optimal solutions for the single-leg air cargo capacity control problem. In particular, our contributions are the following:

- We argue that the basic single-leg capacity control problem, modeled as a Markov decision process, does not feature an optimal monotone control policy, and we provide reasons for this finding.

- Further decision problems are modeled which make assumptions regarding admissible actions and demand. This yields optimal monotone control limit policies, which first, due to their comprehensible structure, are easy to understand for revenue managers, and second, due to a reduced computational complexity, are easy to implement.

- We propose a decomposition heuristic that provides a feasible solution to the basic capacity control problem and offers structured decisions based on switching curves.

- In order to obtain bid prices for weight and volume, a piecewise linear approximation of the value function is proposed. These bid prices are then used to construct a price-directed heuristic. Furthermore, the linear program determining these bid prices provides an upper bound on the maximum expected revenue of the basic capacity control problem.

Controlling the availability of seats and cargo capacity are traditionally two independent tasks. Airlines justify this approach by simply assuming that passenger profitability is higher than the equivalent cargo profitability (Kasilingam, 2011, p. 167). Independently performing the two optimization steps certainly keeps computational complexity manageable; however, it does clearly not maximize an airline's overall revenue. Ideally, according to Kasilingam (2011, p. 167), airlines should control an aircraft's overall capacity based on profitability of passengers versus cargo and thereby set up competition between the two sources of profit. Pilon (2007) even describes an integrated optimization as "the ultimate prospect for revenue management". Graff (2008) remarks that in future, airlines need to be willing to reject passengers in favor of cargo in order to make money even though this contradicts today's business practices. Although the need for an integrated optimization clearly exists, no attempt has yet been made to model the decision problem. Due to the lack of quantitative approaches, the second part of our study proposes and analyzes a model for integrated capacity control both of cargo capacity and passenger seats. In detail, our contributions are:

- We formulate a basic integrated single-leg capacity control problem for cargo space and passenger seats as a finite-horizon Markov decision process and analyze the optimal solutions' structural properties.

- We propose a further decision model that makes specific assumptions regarding admissible actions and demand. This gives us an optimal, simply structured, and comprehensible policy.

- A decomposition heuristic is proposed which gives a feasible solution to the basic integrated capacity control problem and offers a control policy based upon decision rules that are monotone in capacity.

- We propose a further heuristic, which is based on bid prices obtained through a linear program. The solution of the linear program produces an upper bound on the maximum expected revenue of the basic capacity control problem.

Most currently available research regarding cargo revenue management focuses on single-leg problems. There are only four studies about the network problem: These are Pak & Dekker (2004), Luo & Shi (2006), Popescu (2006), and Levina et al. (2011). Only the latter accounts for real-world challenges such as uncertainty in available capacity and shipments' capacity requirement. Furthermore, these authors model an infinite-horizon problem and focus on developing a new value function approximation. However, in a network context, there has not been any attempt to adopt methods, which are thoroughly studied as well as commonly accepted in passenger revenue management, while accounting for uncertainty in both capacity and capacity requirement. Given this research deficit, in the third part of this work, we pursue the question of how methods from passenger network revenue management can be adopted in a cargo network context, where real-world challenges are taken into account. Specifically, our contributions can be summarized as follows:

- By means of a finite-horizon Markov decision process, we model the capacity control problem of a carrier operating flights on a network. Three sources of uncertainty are accounted for: First, uncertain booking request arrival; second, uncertain aircraft capacity; third, uncertain shipment capacity requirement.

- We extend a linear programming upper bound of Amaruchkul et al. (2007) into our network setting and account for uncertain capacity. We further suggest a randomized as well as a partially randomized linear programming upper bound problem.

- An affine value function approximation is proposed to obtain a method which determines bid prices for both weight and volume units on each leg

7

of an air cargo network; we further discuss the structural properties of the resulting bid prices.

• We propose a decomposition approach that builds on those bid prices and show that this method also provides an upper bound on the maximum expected revenue.

• We suggest a piecewise linear approximation of the value function, which accounts for the state of overbooking on each leg.

1.2 Outline

All the decision models analyzed in this work cover problems that are relevant in the field of air cargo revenue management. Hence, in Chapter 2, we provide a comprehensive introduction to this topic. In particular, we describe major characteristics and complexities of the cargo business and provide an introduction to the fundamentals of revenue management. Furthermore, a comparison between passenger and cargo revenue management is provided, and a literature review on air cargo capacity control models is presented.

The theoretical foundations for modeling, analyzing, and approximating the decision problems are outlined in Chapter 3. We introduce Markov decision processes as special types of stochastic dynamic decision processes. In addition, since we analyze optimal monotone control policies of two-dimensional decision problems, the required theoretical concepts like multimodularity are provided. Also included in this chapter is the outline of the linear programming approach to approximate dynamic programming. We use this method to approximate the value function of the Markov decision processes.

In Chapter 4, we analyze optimal decisions of the single-leg air cargo capacity control problem. Additionally, we propose decision models that feature an optimal monotone control policy. Furthermore, heuristics that determine feasible solutions of the basic capacity control problem are developed and tested using numerical experiments. We also propose upper bounds on the maximum expected revenue of the capacity control problem and test their quality using the same experiments.

Chapter 5 discusses a model which simultaneously controls both cargo capacity and passenger seats on combination carriers. We propose a further decision model that features an optimal monotone control policy. Heuristics for solving the original decision problem and an upper bound on the maximum expected revenue are provided. Furthermore, the bound's quality as well as the heuristics' performance are assessed using numerical experiments.

In Chapter 6, we propose a model for the air cargo network capacity control problem that accounts for uncertain capacity and capacity requirement. Since this model suffers from the curse of dimensionality much more than the single-leg model, our focus is on developing heuristics and upper bounds. In particular, we propose a bound and a heuristic based upon bid prices obtained through an affine value function approximation. In order to improve the heuristic and bound, we develop a dynamic programming decomposition approach that uses these bid prices. All heuristics and bounds are tested using extensive numerical experiments.

Chapter 7 summarizes the studies we carried out and proposes some potential directions for future research.

CHAPTER 2

Air Cargo Revenue Management

In this chapter, we provide an overview of air cargo revenue management. In order to get an adequate understanding of how the cargo business works, we describe the basics of air cargo transportation in Section 2.1. An overview of the fundamentals of revenue management is provided in Section 2.2. In particular, we outline the motivation for applying revenue management techniques and a general definition. Additionally, we present an appropriate environment for effective application and describe major components of revenue management. Section 2.3 explores the differences between air cargo and passenger revenue management. The results highlight the need for specific solutions for cargo revenue management. In Section 2.4, we provide an overview of the literature covering topics concerning air cargo capacity control.

2.1 Basics of Air Cargo Transportation

In order to understand the air cargo business, it is helpful to study its supply chain. According to Mentzer et al. (2001, p. 4), a supply chain is defined as "a set of three or more entities (organizations or individuals) directly involved in the upstream and downstream flows of products, services, finances, and/or information from a source to a customer". In the air cargo business, the source of a product is referred to as the shipper, and the customer is denoted as the consignee. The set of entities acting between a shipper and a consignee depends on the particular supply chain concept. There exist two basic supply chain concepts which are depicted in Figure 2.1. In the upper concept, freight forwarders

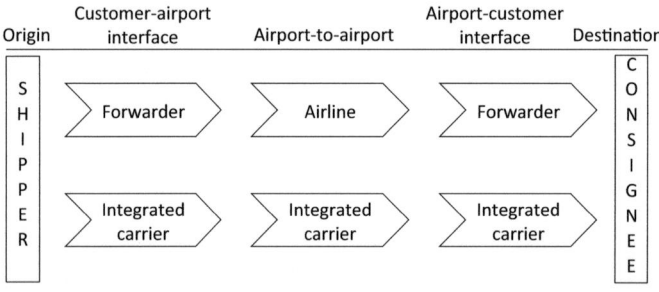

Figure 2.1: Air cargo supply chain concepts (MergeGlobal, 2008)

consolidate single shipments from shippers and purchase aircraft capacity for the accumulated freight. Then, an airline hauls cargo from one airport to another, using either a combination carrier or a pure freighter. Afterwards, forwarders are responsible for transporting the shipments to the designated consignee. Beyond these pick-up and delivery services, forwarders may provide inventory-related activities such as warehousing, commissioning, or handling (Hellermann, 2006, pp. 5-6). For 2011, in terms of revenue, the world's largest forwarders were DHL Supply Chain and Global Forwarding, Kuehne + Nagel, and DB Schenker Logistics (Air Cargo World, 2012). According to MergeGlobal (2008), in 2007, the top 20 forwarders consolidated almost two thirds of total carried freight. This highlights the significant buying power of freight forwarders.

The supply chain concept that is displayed as the lower one in Figure 2.1 is comprised of only one integrated carrier that vertically integrates the business of forwarders and (cargo) airlines. An integrated carrier owns or exclusively controls the assets, employees, and information systems that are necessary to provide a door-to-door service (MergeGlobal, 2008). Most integrators are focused on air mail and package service. Thus, it is not surprising that, worldwide, the biggest four integrators, DHL, FedEx, TNT, and UPS, control more than 80% of the global air package market (MergeGlobal, 2008).

Since we study capacity control problems for all kinds of shipments, the supply chain concept comprising forwarders and airlines is more relevant for us. Note that this supply chain comprises further stakeholders such as ground handling agencies, airport operators, and trucking companies, which we do not consider.

As already mentioned earlier, airlines usually sell their capacity in two sequential steps. First, they sell capacity based on long-term contracts. Second, they decide how much capacity should be available for short-term requests and sell this capacity on the spot market. While long-term allotments are negotiated up to 12 months in advance, short term capacity is available on the spot market from approximately 30 days prior to departure (Hellermann, 2006, p. 15). These two types of capacity allocation reflect the nature of cargo demand: On the one hand, there are customers who can already determine a long time in advance how much capacity they require for transporting perishable and/or valuable goods; on the other hand, another customer group requests express capacity if products need to be hauled in an emergency situation (MergeGlobal, 2008). For instance, in the unforeseen event that some technical spare parts need to be transported from Europe to Asia within one week, air freight is the only option. According to Billings et al. (2003), airlines sell 30 to 75% of their capacity on the spot market. For example, Hellermann (2006, p. 15) reports for Lufthansa Cargo that on average one third of total capacity is sold through long-term contracts. Considering Lufthansa Cargo's 2011 load factor of 69.1% (Lufthansa Cargo, 2012), short term bookings accounted on average for more than 50% of total sold capacity. Thus, the spot market capacity control problem, which we consider in this work, is highly relevant in air cargo revenue management.

When shippers or freight forwarders request capacity, depending on the particular airline, several distribution channels may be available. First, booking requests may be submitted via an airline's own self-service booking portal. Second, capacity bookings may also be conducted via cross-airline online platforms like Global Freight Exchange (Descartes, 2012).

After having provided a short introduction to the air transport business, we now turn to the revenue management fundamentals.

2.2 Fundamentals of Revenue Management

Motivation and Definition

When service firms are constrained by capacity, financial success often depends on the management's ability to efficiently use capacity (Kimes, 1989). The first industry that systematically addressed this challenge was the airline industry. This occurred after the US market had been deregulated in the late 1970s (Kimes, 2005b). A method called *revenue (yield) management* was used to profitably control capacity, which led to a great increase in revenues (see for instance Belobaba, 1989; Smith et al., 1992). More specifically, Boyd (1998) reports that implementing a revenue management system can improve revenues between 2 and 8 percent or even more.

In order to get an understanding of the underlying concepts of revenue management, we outline a simple example from the airline passenger business: Consider an airline that offers two fare classes. The low-fare ticket is associated with a 14-days advance purchase requirement, while the high-fare ticket does not have any restrictions. The airline can achieve the maximum revenue by selling only high-fare tickets to all customers. Since some customers are not willing to pay the high prices, offering only high-fare tickets would yield empty seats which, due to the seats' perishability, represent an opportunity cost. In order to sell these empty seats, the airline offers low-fare tickets to more price-sensitive customers. Further, to avoid price-insensitive customers to book low-fare tickets, the tickets must be associated with an advance purchase requirement. Then, late booking, price-insensitive customers have only the one choice of ticket, which is the high-fare ticket. Early booking, price-sensitive customers can choose between low-fare and high-fare tickets. The airline's objective is to determine the mix of low-fare and high-fare tickets that maximizes total revenue.

So far, we know that revenue management comprises methods and tools for profitably controlling capacity. There are many definitions available in literature, which usually take into account a particular application. Pfeifer (1989) defines yield management in the context of airlines as "the process by which the discount fares are allocated to scheduled flights for the purpose of balancing demand and increasing revenues". A general definition is given by Kimes (1989): "Yield management is a method which can help a firm sell the right inventory unit to the right type of customer, at the right time, and for the right price. Yield management guides the decision of how to allocate undifferentiated units of capacity to available demand in such a way as to maximize profit or revenue". Note that today the term revenue management rather than yield management is used. The reason for this terminology choice is that revenue management techniques are usually applied in capital-intensive industries, and thus additional variable costs for selling capacity are relatively small compared to the opportunity cost of unused capacity (Kimes, 1989). Using the term yield in the airline context may even be misleading. For example, if an airline's objective was yield (profit per seat) maximization, accepting only one single full-fare customer would achieve this objective (Weatherford & Bodily, 1992).

For detailed introductions to revenue management, the reader is referred to Cross (1997), Yeoman et al. (2001), Phillips (2005), as well as Talluri & van Ryzin (2004). Numerous revenue management applications can be found in Yeoman & McMahon-Beattie (2004), Chiang et al. (2007), or Yeoman & McMahon-Beattie (2011). The traditional areas of application are airlines, hotels (see for instance Bitran & Mondschein, 1995; Badinelli, 2000), and the car rental industry (e.g. Geraghty & Johnson, 1997; Haensel et al., 2012). In recent years, many new fields of application have arisen. This includes (examples in parentheses) casino table games (Chen et al., 2012), Internet advertising (Karmarkar & Dutta, 2012), cruise lines (Lu & Mazzarella, 2007), golf courses (Rasekh & Yihua, 2011), car parks (Guadix et al., 2011), retail electricity (Faruqui et al., 2009), restaurants (Kimes, 2005a), and cargo flights (Amaruchkul et al., 2007).

An Appropriate Environment for Effective Application

In order to ensure the success of implementing a revenue management system, the following characteristics are essential (cf. Kimes, 1989). We provide examples for these conditions from the air cargo industry and thereby show that this industry is appropriate for application.

- *Relatively fixed capacity.* If demand changes, it is impossible, at least in the short run, to provide less or more capacity. For example, an airplane's cargo capacity is restricted. Additional capacity can only be gained by operating more aircraft.

- *Perishability.* Products or services which cannot be stored are perishable. This distinguishes the service business from manufacturing firms. In the case of cargo flights, once the plane has departed, unused capacity is irrecoverably lost.

- *Ability to segment markets.* If customers are heterogeneous, a company can segment the market into different customer groups, each with a particular willingness to pay. On cargo flights, the same capacity can be assigned, for instance, to a same-day express shipment or to a standard shipment. According to Sabre (2010), based on different customer requirements, different products are already offered at different prices.

- *Sale/Booking in advance.* Typically, service firms operate reservation systems that offer customers the option to purchase products/services in advance, before actual consumption. This offers the company some security on future revenue, but some uncertainty remains as well, as to whether capacity could be sold more profitably in the future. Cargo capacity can be booked in advance, which holds the challenge of accepting early booking requests or waiting for a more profitable request, which may or may not occur in the future.

- *Stochastic demand.* Capacity providers are confronted with a highly fluctuating demand. If demand was deterministic, capacity would be simply assigned to the customers with the highest willingness to pay. Volatility in demand patterns is named as one of the major challenges in the air cargo industry (Mardan, 2010).

• *Low marginal sales cost and high marginal capacity change cost.* For capacity-constrained firms, adjusting capacity to the demand is associated with significant cost, while selling one more capacity unit creates relatively low cost. Cargo airlines can only increase capacity by changing their fleet which implicates large investments. On the other hand, selling one more unit of capacity generates only marginal handling and fuel costs, which are relatively low compared to the aircraft's fixed operating cost.

Klein & Steinhardt (2008, pp. 10-12) mention a further necessary condition which they describe as *integration of an external factor*. This condition means that an external factor is necessary to receive the product or service. The external factor may be the customer, some object, or information. For example, the service of transporting air cargo can only be provided if freight (which is the external factor) is delivered to the airport. It means, this service cannot be provided before the freight has been delivered. This again distinguishes the service industry from the manufacturing industry, whose products can be produced and stored some time before they are needed.

Components of Revenue Management

Revenue management comprises several problems, all of which have been widely studied. We give a short overview of the ones that are most important in research:

• *Forecasting*: The task of forecasting is to predict demand, cancellations, and no-shows (McGill & van Ryzin, 1999; Chiang et al., 2007). The forecasts' quality is very important since it directly affects the success of overbooking, capacity control, and pricing decisions. According to Pölt (1998), a reduction of 20% in forecast errors can yield a 1% increase in incremental revenue.

- *Overbooking*: This component attempts to avoid unused capacity due to cancellations and no-shows by selling more capacity than is physically available (McGill & van Ryzin, 1999). Thus, overbooking's major task is to determine an appropriate level of capacity that should be sold (in addition to the real capacity). Overbooking has the longest history and most successful practical application of all the revenue management components (Chiang et al., 2007).

- *Pricing*: Differential pricing constructs various products with associated restrictions and prices (Belobaba, 2009, p. 78). Thus, each customer can choose a product according to his or her willingness to pay and corresponding to his or her willingness to accept the restrictions.

- *Capacity Control*: The objective of capacity control is to allocate capacity to the different products so that the expected revenue is maximized (Chiang et al., 2007).

In the above outlined problems, the availability of products is the strategic variable that helps to control capacity. Further, it is implicitly assumed that if the price for a particular product changes, the demand forecast will also change. A different approach focuses directly on the relationship between price and demand and treats price as the strategic variable (Boyd & Bilegan, 2003). This approach is called *dynamic pricing* and is used in newer revenue management applications such as low cost airlines ticket pricing. Dynamic pricing omits the optimization step of differential pricing and varies the resource's price over the booking horizon (Klein & Steinhardt, 2008, p. 178). By adjusting the price, the availability of capacity is controlled. We do not consider this approach in our work because prices of cargo products are traditionally constant. Nevertheless, as the cargo business is continuously developing, in the future, the industry might offer dynamic pricing opportunities. Pilon (2007) even describes it as one of the future challenges in cargo revenue management. For more information on dynamic pricing, the reader is referred to Rajan et al. (1992), Gallego & van Ryzin (1994),

Bitran & Mondschein (1997), Bitran & Caldentey (2003), as well as Elmaghraby & Keskinocak (2003).

The focus of our work is on capacity control, and therefore, we will not discuss the other components any further. However, for the latest forecasting research, the interested reader is referred to e.g. Haensel & Koole (2011), Karmarkar et al. (2011), and Fiig et al. (2012); in case of overbooking, up to date topics can be found for instance in Erdelyi & Topaloglu (2010), Xiong et al. (2011), and Lan et al. (2011); and for pricing, the reader is referred to e.g. Zhang et al. (2010), Westermann & Lancaster (2011), and Zhang & Bell (2012).

2.3 Air Cargo Revenue Management vs. Passenger Revenue Management

The air cargo business may seem very similar to the airline passenger business. Below, we explore the numerous fundamental differences between these two businesses, which all affect the requirements for a revenue management system. This highlights the need for specific cargo revenue management systems since existing solutions from the passenger business cannot be simply transferred.

- *Capacity uncertainty.* While the number of passenger seats is known at every point of the booking process, cargo capacity depends on numerous factors such as the number of passengers, runways, weather, and fuel weight (Kasilingam, 1996). Since some of these factors are random, cargo capacity is random as well.

- *Dimensionality of capacity.* Passenger seats are one-dimensional, whereas cargo capacity is multi-dimensional, i.e. weight, volume, and container positions need to be considered (Billings et al., 2003).

- *Routing options.* Passengers follow their itinerary exactly as they booked it (unless a schedule disruption occurs). On the other hand, cargo can be shipped along any route as long as it arrives at its destination on time

(Kasilingam, 2011). Thus, multiple routing options are available. Furthermore, other modes of transportation can be even chosen, such as trucks (LaDue, 2004). For instance, Slager & Kapteijns (2004) reports that KLM transports the major part of its cargo within Europe by truck.

- *Long-term demand.* Passengers rarely book a seat on a weekly flight half a year in advance. On the other hand, cargo customers reserve allotments on particular flights, based on long-term contracts (Kasilingam, 1996). This space is not available for sale on the spot market, and the carrier has to decide how much space to sell as long-term allotments.

- *Number of customers.* A large number of individuals purchase passenger seats. But since forwarders consolidate the shippers' freight, the number of cargo customers is much smaller (Kasilingam, 2011). Further, cargo is a business-to-business market, and carrying passengers is largely a business-to-customer market (Slager & Kapteijns, 2004).

- *Volatility of demand.* While seasonality patterns in passenger demand occur in roughly the same form each year, cargo demand is much more difficult to anticipate (Billings et al., 2003). Many sources of uncertainty affect the demand for air cargo, e.g. the weather influencing harvest times or production disruptions, which decrease a customer's output (Billings et al., 2003; Becker & Dill, 2007).

- *Show-up behavior.* According to Becker & Dill (2007), air freight deviating from booked capacity is more likely than passengers not showing up at departure. Further, cargo show-up rates can be somewhere between zero and one (or even greater than one), whereas passengers either arrive at the gate or they do not.

- *Priority usage of capacity.* On combination carriers, passengers have the highest priority for using weight and volume capacity, whereas cargo has the lowest priority behind fuel, crew, and passenger bags (Slager & Kapteijns, 2004; LaDue, 2004).

- *Network Utilization.* Passengers usually book a return trip that brings them back to their originating location. On the other hand, air freight is always carried one way which yields an inhomogeneous network utilization (Becker & Dill, 2007).

- *Booking period.* The booking period of the spot market is very short compared to the one of a passenger flight (Becker & Dill, 2007). According to Mardan (2010), most bookings take place within one week to departure.

Further challenges and complexities in air cargo revenue management are described in Pilon (2007) as well as in Becker & Wald (2010). We now turn to an overview of available literature in the field of cargo revenue management.

2.4 Literature Review on Air Cargo Revenue Management

In order to categorize the literature on cargo revenue management, we define the following four major components of the cargo revenue management process (partly based on Kasilingam, 2011):

(i) *Forecasting.* In this step, capacity available for sale, demand, and show-up rates are predicted.

(ii) *Allotment allocation.* The airline determines how much space should be sold based on long-term contracts and decides which allotment requests should be accepted.

(iii) *Overbooking.* The forecasted capacity available on the spot market is overbooked in order to compensate for cancellations and under-tendering.

(iv) *Spot market capacity control.* In this last step, the availability of capacity on the spot market, which is the capacity determined in step (iii), is controlled so that overall revenue is maximized. Here, decision rules for accepting and denying cargo booking requests for particular shipment types are required.

The models we propose in this work focus on the spot market capacity control problem. Thus, we provide a comprehensive overview of literature in this field. For literature on allotment management, the reader is referred to Hellermann (2006), Gupta (2008), Amaruchkul & Lorchirachoonkul (2011), and Levin et al. (2012). Overbooking models for air cargo can be found in Kasilingam (1997), Popescu et al. (2006), Wang & Kao (2008), Becker & Wald (2008), Luo et al. (2009), and Moussawi & Cakandyildirim (2012). To our knowledge, so far, no research paper on forecasting in the cargo context has been published in a scholarly journal.

Early studies on cargo revenue management provide largely qualitative reports on successful implementations by airlines (e.g. Hendricks & Kasilingam, 1993; Slager & Kapteijns, 2004; Nielsen, 2004). Even today, the number of publications on quantitative models is low. While capacity control problems have been widely researched in passenger revenue management, the cargo spot market capacity control problem has not yet gained comparable attention.

The first single-leg model was proposed by Karaesmen (2001) who discusses a static model, which is very similar to a deterministic linear program used to determine bid prices in network passenger revenue management (cf. Williamson, 1992). The author considers requests for shipments that are characterized by continuous weight and volume requirements.

The first network cargo capacity control model was proposed by Pak & Dekker (2004). The authors assume that each request is uniquely defined by weight, volume, revenue, and flights it uses. The problem is modeled as a static multidimensional online knapsack problem and is solved by means of a greedy algorithm (cf. Rinnooy Kan et al., 1993). A simulation study demonstrates that their static bid price policies outperform policies based on bid prices obtained through a deterministic linear program.

Huang & Hsu (2005) present the first dynamic model for solving the single-leg capacity control problem. Their underlying idea is to adapt the model of Lee & Hersh (1993) for air cargo use. In their analysis, they view cargo capacity as one-dimensional. Further, the effect of supply uncertainty on expected revenue is analyzed.

Luo & Shi (2006) study a static stochastic programming approach for modeling the multi-leg capacity allocation problem under normally-distributed demand. Each shipment class is defined by its weight, volume, profit, and legs it uses. The stochastic programming model is transferred to a linear program by means of chance constrained programming (cf. Charnes & Cooper, 1959).

Popescu (2006) models the spot market capacity control problem for multi-leg flights. The unique idea of the author's approach is to decompose the problem into a large and a small cargo capacity control subproblem which both consider weight as the only dimension. While the small cargo subproblem is handled by a probabilistic nonlinear program, the control of large cargo requests is formulated as a Markov decision process.

Amaruchkul et al. (2007) propose a single-leg dynamic capacity control model that uses the number of accepted shipments of each class as the state space. Each class defines the weight and volume distribution of its uncertain capacity requirement as well as a particular fare rate. The authors focus on developing several heuristics and bounds: First, they propose heuristics and bounds based on decomposing the capacity control problem into subproblems of weight and volume. And second, bounds and heuristics based on deterministic linear programs are provided. Our model formulation in Chapter 6 is very close to this single-leg model. We extend the state space to the network setting and allow for stochastic capacity, while in Amaruchkul et al. (2007) capacity is deterministic.

Huang & Chang (2010) present a heuristic that jointly estimates the expected revenue from both weight and volume. In order to reduce computational load, only a limited number of sample points in the state space is evaluated. Thereby, the authors attempt to avoid inaccurate estimates produced by decoupling weight and volume. Only in a few scenarios, this heuristic outperforms the decomposition heuristic proposed by Amaruchkul et al. (2007).

Zhuang et al. (2011) propose a general model considering a random resource requirement which, if only a single resource is considered, can be applied in the field of cargo capacity control. The authors focus on exploring structural properties of a multi-class problem, where the resource requirement of each class is uncertain. Further, the authors describe two heuristics and show in experiments that they outperform other heuristics that ignore random capacity requirement.

Xiao & Yang (2010) analyze structural properties of a continuous-time control model with two capacity dimensions, which they claim is applicable in cargo revenue management. The authors prove the existence of a threshold policy; however, this only applies to a situation with two products consuming the same capacity on one dimension but unequal capacity on the other. Thus, this model is rather applicable in maritime cargo revenue management, where volume is largely fixed by standard containers.

Han et al. (2010) model the booking process as a Markov chain in order to reduce the possible number of scenarios of sold weight and volume. Revenue-maximizing bid prices are then obtained by means of a linear mixed-integer program. The authors show that their approach outperforms the static bid-price policy proposed by Pak & Dekker (2004).

Levina et al. (2011) present a network dynamic capacity control model which accounts for uncertainty in both available capacity and capacity requirement. They formulate an infinite-horizon Markov decision process, which determines capacity control decisions, while an appropriate route for a request is found in a separate subproblem. For learning approximate control policies, a linear programming and stochastic simulation-based computational method are discussed. The model we propose in Chapter 6 is related to this model. While Levina et al. (2011) focus on developing a new approximation of the value function and on the complexities caused by the routing decisions, we assume that a request clearly defines its itinerary. This view is true for small carriers and allows us to use methods that are closer to traditional revenue management methods.

In Chapter 5, we discuss decision models that follow an integrated approach for controlling the availability of passenger seats and cargo capacity. With the exception of some qualitative analyses (e.g. Graff, 2008; Pilon, 2007), there is hardly any work available dealing with this problem. In the field of fleet assignment, Sandhu & Klabjan (2006) propose a model that takes into account both passenger and freight demand. The authors claim that such an integrated optimization efficiently utilizes the overall aircraft space and generates higher overall profit. Further, Blake (2010) reports that increasing cargo demand causes passenger ticket prices to increase. This means, that airlines are aware of the trade-off between passengers versus cargo and obviously, in some way, take advantage of it. However, in the field of revenue management, no quantitative approach for an integrated control of cargo capacity and passenger seats has yet been proposed.

CHAPTER 3

Theoretical Foundations

This chapter provides an overview of the theoretical concepts that we use to analyze and to solve cargo capacity control problems. General challenges of such decision problems are, first, that they require making time-dependent decisions under uncertainty, second, that cargo capacity is two-dimensional, and third, that models are computationally intractable for large problem instances. In the following three sections, we outline the methodology that we use to manage these challenges. In Section 3.1, we introduce stochastic dynamic decision processes. As a special type of decision processes, we consider Markov decision processes, which are used in this work to model cargo capacity control problems. Section 3.2 provides an overview of structural properties that are necessary to ensure optimality of monotone control in two-dimensional problems. In the same section, we also show that two particular problems, which are relevant in cargo capacity control, feature some of these properties. Section 3.3 outlines the linear programming approach to approximate dynamic programming. We use this technique to determine a heuristic solution to large-scale air cargo capacity control problems.

3.1 Stochastic Dynamic Decision Processes

Many decisions in today's business environment do not only require one single action but rather a sequence of actions over time. For instance, a company does not decide on the production output of a machine once and keeps it constant thereafter; it rather has to adjust the output in order to react to changes in the environment such as market demand. Accordingly, decision makers face various complex *sequential decision processes*. *Dynamic programming*, as a collection of mathematical tools to analyze such processes, evolved from the insight that sequential decision processes share several recurring mathematical features (Denardo, 1982, p. 3).

If a system reaches a state with a particular probability which might depend on previous states and actions, it is modeled as a *stochastic dynamic decision process*. A special type of such processes is a *Markov decision process* (MDP) which was first introduced by Bellman (1957). The term 'Markov' is used since this type of process features the Markov property, i.e. only the present state has an impact on the future behavior of the process; if the present state is known, the entire history of the process can be neglected (Puterman, 1994, p. 2). Since the decision maker is able to influence a probabilistic system's behavior by undertaking actions, her or his goal is to determine a sequence of decisions that causes the system to perform optimally with regard to a predefined target criterion (Puterman, 1994, p. 17).

A comprehensive overview of MDPs is provided in White (1993), Puterman (1994), Sennott (1999), or Waldmann & Stocker (2012). An overview of real world applications of MDPs is given, for instance, in White (1985), White (1988), and Feinberg & Shwartz (2002).

Various types of MDPs can be used depending on the specific application. In Section 3.1.1, we introduce a framework for discrete-time models with finite planning horizon, which is adequate for modeling (cargo) revenue management problems. Note that this decision model could be embedded into the general framework set out by Hinderer (1970) and Schäl (1975). As an enhancement of finite-horizon MDPs, Section 3.1.2 outlines MDPs explicitly considering a random environment. In revenue management, such a random environment could be uncertain demand for booking classes.

3.1.1 Finite-Horizon Markov Decision Processes

Consider a decision maker who seeks to control a probabilistic system by undertaking actions. The system evolves through time, where the entire time horizon T is finite. Note that we consider T as the beginning of the planning horizon and 0 as its end. Further, the horizon is divided into discrete *decision periods* with *decision epochs* $t = T, ..., 1$ representing the beginning of each period (despite slight abuse of terminology, we will hereafter refer to the point of time where the action is taken also as decision period or just time). Note that in $t = 0$ no action is taken. At each time t, a system state s is observed, and the decision maker selects an admissible action $a \in A(s)$. An action results immediately in a one-stage reward $r_t(s, a)$ which also depends on the current state s. Further, the system occupies a state s' at time $t - 1$ with transition probability $p_t(s, a, s')$. When the end of the planning horizon is reached, the decision maker receives a terminal reward $V_0(s)$ depending on the system's terminal state.

In summary, a finite-horizon MDP with discrete decision periods is a tuple (T, S, A, p_t, r_t, V_0) with

(i) a finite planning horizon $T \in \mathbb{N}_0$;

(ii) a finite state space S;

(iii) a finite action space A, where $A(s)$ is the non-empty finite set of admissible actions in state $s \in S$, with $A = \bigcup_{s \in S} A(s)$; further, we define the set $J = \{(s, a) : s \in S, a \in A(s)\} \subseteq S \times A$;

(iv) transition law $p_t : J \times S \to [0, 1]$, which specifies the probability $p_t(s, a, s')$ for a transition from state $s \in S$ to state $s' \in S$ at time $t = T, ..., 1$ if action $a \in A(s)$ is chosen; note that for $s \in S$, $a \in A(s)$ and $t = T, ..., 1$, $p_t(s, a, s')$ is a discrete density function on S;

(v) a one-stage reward function $r_t : J \to \mathbb{R}$ which represents a reward $r_t(s, a)$ if at time $t = T, ..., 1$ and state $s \in S$ action $a \in A(s)$ is chosen;

(vi) a terminal reward function $V_0 : S \rightarrow \mathbb{R}$ which corresponds to the reward $V_0(s)$ that is earned if at time $t = 0$ the system is in state $s \in S$.

Note that the state space and the action space may also depend on t. For instance, a state space might be time-dependent if the decision process starts in a particular initial state, and if in each decision period the state space can only increase by one unit.

The decision maker's objective is to choose a sequence of actions over the entire planning horizon so that the system performs optimally with respect to a particular target criterion. The action the decision maker should choose is specified by a *decision rule*. Formally, a decision rule is a function $f : S \rightarrow A$, which specifies the action $f(s) \in A(s)$ to be taken in state $s \in S$. Let F denote the set of decision rules. From the formulation given above, it is obvious that this kind of decision rule requires only information about the current state rather than about the entire history of the process, and the action to be taken is unambiguous. Note that decision rules can also be randomized and/or history dependent, which, however, does not lead to any improvement in the context of processes featuring the Markov property.

A *policy* $\pi = (f_T, ..., f_1)$ is a sequence of decision rules $f_t \in F$ for each time $t = T, ..., 1$ specifying actions $a = f_t(s)$ to be taken at time t and in state s. We let F^T denote the set of all policies. Further, if a policy comprises only deterministic (Markovian) decision rules, it is called a deterministic (Markovian) policy (hereafter abbreviated to 'policy').

Since the reward of the system in each state is uncertain, sequences of random variables have to be compared in order to evaluate the performance of different policies. Below, we introduce an optimality criterion which allows us to compare policies based on the expected value of the sum of one-stage rewards (cf. Waldmann & Stocker, 2012, pp. 149-150).

The Total Reward Criterion

We assume that a decision maker seeks to *maximize* the total reward over the entire planning horizon. Since the system evolves stochastically, the total reward itself is random. Therefore, we consider $s_T, s_{T-1}, ..., s_0$ as realizations of the random variables $\tilde{S}_T, \tilde{S}_{T-1}, ..., \tilde{S}_0$ which describe the state process. The total reward under policy $\pi \in F^T$ is also random and can be computed as

$$R_\pi := \sum_{t=1}^{T} r_t(\tilde{S}_t, f_t(\tilde{S}_t)) + V_0(\tilde{S}_0).$$

In order to find an optimal policy, expected values of R_π, i.e. $\mathbb{E}_\pi[R_\pi]$, may be compared for all different policies $\pi \in F^T$. Since R_π is a function of $\tilde{S}_T, ..., \tilde{S}_0$, we can define a probability measure P_π on $(\tilde{S}^{T+1})$ with

$$P_\pi(\tilde{S}_T = s_T, ..., \tilde{S}_0 = s_0)$$
$$= P(\tilde{S}_T = s_T) \cdot p_T(s_T, f_T(s_T), s_{T-1}) \cdot ... \cdot p_1(s_1, f_1(s_1), s_0).$$

Accordingly, $\mathbb{E}_\pi$ is the expectation of R_π with respect to P_π.

Now consider a decision maker who seeks to maximize the total reward of a system that is in a particular initial state $\hat{s} \in S$. Then, if policy $\pi \in F^T$ is followed starting from state $\hat{s} \in S$, $\mathbb{E}_\pi[R_\pi]$ is replaced by the conditional expected total reward $\mathbb{E}_\pi\left[R_\pi | \tilde{S}_T = \hat{s}\right] =: V_{T,\pi}(\hat{s})$.

Now the target is to find a policy π^* that maximizes the expected total reward starting in state $\hat{s}$. That is

$$V_{T,\pi^*}(\hat{s}) = \sup_{\pi \in F^T} V_{T,\pi}(\hat{s}) =: V_T(\hat{s}). \tag{3.1}$$

If a policy π^* fulfills the property in (3.1), it is called *optimal*. Further, we call the expected total reward at time t and state $s \in S$ the *value function* of the MDP which is defined as

$$V_t(s) := \sup_{\pi \in F^T} V_{t,\pi}(s) \quad \forall s \in S, t = T, ..., 1.$$

Note that the existence of an optimal policy is ensured because we consider an MDP with a finite state space and a finite set of admissible actions (Puterman, 1994, p. 90).

The maximum expected reward and optimal policies at each time t and state s can be determined by means of an *optimality equation*. A proof of the following theorem can be found in Puterman (1994, p. 92).

Theorem 3.1. *V_T is the unique solution to the optimality equation*

$$V_t(s) = \max_{a \in A(s)} \left\{ r_t(s,a) + \sum_{s' \in S} p_t(s,a,s')V_{t-1}(s') \right\} \quad \forall s \in S, \qquad (3.2)$$

which can be obtained for $t = T, ..., 1$ recursively when the terminal value is V_0. Furthermore, each policy $\pi = (f_T, f_{T-1}, ..., f_1)$ formed by actions $a = f_t(s) \in F$ maximizing the right hand side of (3.2) is optimal.

The optimality equation finds for each time t and state s the action that maximizes the right hand side. Since the set of admissible actions is assumed to be finite, we can determine the maximum rather than the supremum. Further, note that there may be several optimal policies.

We now turn to a technique that determines an optimal solution of the optimality equation efficiently.

Backward Induction

An intuitive way to find an optimal policy is to enumerate and compare all policies $\pi \in F^T$, which would be very time-consuming. A more efficient solution technique for discrete-time finite-horizon MDPs is *backward induction*. The algorithm, which we present below, starts with the terminal reward function and determines backwards for $t = 1, ..., T$ an action that maximizes the right hand side of the optimality equation (cf. Puterman, 1994, p. 92).

Step 1 Set $t = 0$ and $V'(s) = V_0(s)$ for all $s \in S$.

Step 2 Set $t = t + 1$, $V(s) = V'(s)$, and determine $V'(s)$ for every $s \in S$ by solving

$$V'(s) = \max_{a \in A(s)} \left\{ r_t(s, a) + \sum_{s' \in S} p_t(s, a, s') V(s') \right\}. \quad (3.3)$$

Set $f_t^*(s)$ as an action maximizing the right hand side of (3.3).

Step 3 If $t = T$, set $V_T(s) = V'(s)$ for all $s \in S$, and then stop. Otherwise return to step 2.

This algorithm determines the maximum expected reward and optimal actions for all $s \in S$ at each time $t = T, ..., 1$. Optimal policies are obtained by building a sequence of decision rules $f_t^*(s)$. Note that the algorithm given above stores only one optimal action per system state at a particular time. Thus, it does not provide multiple policies generating the same maximum expected reward.

The optimal policy that is determined through this procedure will give decision support to a decision maker. Depending on the specific decision problem, optimal actions may follow a particular pattern. Below, we discuss policies that feature such specific structures.

Structured Policies

The previous results show that only optimal decision rules $f_t^*(s)$ need to be considered when controlling a system. We are now interested in optimal policies that do not have to be determined for all possible values of $s \in S$ and $t = T, ..., 1$ since they feature a simply structured form. A class of policies fulfilling this condition is what we call *structured policies*.

A well-known example of a structured policy is the *(s,S) policy* in dynamic inventory problems (cf. Axsäter, 2006, pp. 49-50). Its decision rule is: If inventory is above the level s, do not order; and if inventory is below the level s, order a quantity so that the inventory level becomes S. In this example, only two values are necessary in order to determine actions.

33

A decision problem featuring an optimal structured policy is generally desirable. According to Glasserman & Yao (1994, p. 449), identifying optimal controls for MDPs is even computationally infeasible in general if no particular structure can be determined. Furthermore, Powell (2007, p. 64) describes the identification of structured policies as "[o]ne of the most dramatic success stories from the study of Markov decision processes". In summary, optimal structured policies are very important since they yield (Puterman, 1994, p. 103)

(i) a decreased storage requirement,

(ii) a reduction of computational effort since specialized algorithms can be applied to determine optimal policies,

(iii) a high acceptance by decision makers because of the policy's comprehensibility, and

(iv) an ease of implementation due to less complex decision rules.

Monotone policies are a special kind of structured policies. They comprise decision rules that have a monotone relation to the current state. That is, for example, an optimal action changes from a to $a + 1$ if the state increases. In our work, we focus on a special type of monotone policies which is defined below.

Definition 3.1. Suppose in each state $s \in S$ the set of admissible actions is $A(s) = \{a_1, a_2\}$. A Markov policy is called *control limit policy* if one action is optimal when the current state is below a particular threshold, and the other action is optimal when the current state is equal to or greater than this threshold. We call such a threshold *control limit*.

Accordingly, a control limit policy comprises a sequence of decision rules $f_T, f_{T-1}, ..., f_1$ with

$$f_t(s) = \begin{cases} a_1 & s < s_t^* \\ a_2 & s \geq s_t^*, \end{cases}$$

and s_t^* as the control limit. The term 'control limit rule' was first introduced by Ignall & Kolesar (1974), whereas Yadin & Naor (1963) reported the first control limit policy already earlier. Further, this special form of policy plays an important role in revenue management and is quite easy to obtain in passenger capacity control models (see for instance Lautenbacher & Stidham, 1999).

The concept of control limit policies does only apply to systems with a one-dimensional system state. In Section 3.2, we provide the theoretical concepts that are necessary to prove the optimality of monotone policies if the system state is *two-dimensional*.

3.1.2 Finite-Horizon Markov Decision Processes in a Random Environment

An MDP in a random environment is an enhancement of a standard MDP. It is assumed that the sequential decision process is exposed to a randomly evolving environment. A general overview of MDPs in a random environment is provided in Waldmann (1981). Applications of this type of decision process can be found, for instance, in Waldmann (1983), Waldmann (1984), Helm & Waldmann (1984), Waldmann (1998), and Hinderer & Waldmann (2001).

We consider a special type of MDPs in a random environment, where the environment is represented by a *Markov chain*. Such an MDP's peculiarity is that an exogenous process is observed, which can be described by a Markov chain with state space E and transition probability $\tilde{p}_t(\epsilon, \epsilon')$ with $\epsilon, \epsilon' \in E$. We assume that the external process may affect the behavior of the system; however, the decision maker is not able to influence the external process by undertaking actions. The MDP has a two-dimensional state space which comprises a system state on the one hand and an environmental state on the other hand. Without loss of generality, we assume that the environment has an impact on one-stage rewards and on transition probabilities.

The capacity control process in cargo revenue management can be modeled as an MDP with an external Markov chain: The remaining space represents the system state, and the requested shipment class (which is a Markovian demand) is an exogenous stochastic process which is not influenced by the accept/reject decision. Further, if a request is accepted, its size determines the gained revenue. The transition probability of the Markov chain is the probability of a request for a particular shipment class in the next period.

The general decision problem is as follows: A decision maker observes a system state s and an environmental state ϵ at a particular time t. Based on this information, action a from the set of admissible actions $A(s, \epsilon)$ is chosen. This results in a reward $r_t(s, \epsilon, a)$ which depends on both the current system and environmental state. Further, the system takes a value s' at $t - 1$ with probability $p_t(s, \epsilon, a, s')$ if the current state is (s, ϵ) and action a is taken. The environmental process evolves independently of the system and is at time $t - 1$ in state ϵ' with transition probability $\tilde{p}_t(\epsilon, \epsilon')$.

In our setting, a finite-horizon MDP in a random environment is a tuple $(T, S, E, A, p_t, \tilde{p}_t, r_t, V_0)$ with

(i) a finite planning horizon $T \in \mathbb{N}_0$;

(ii) an extended finite state space $S \times E$;

(iii) a finite action space A; $A(s, \epsilon)$ is the non-empty finite set of admissible actions in state $s \in S$ and $\epsilon \in E$ with $A = \bigcup_{s \in S, \epsilon \in E} A(s, \epsilon)$; $\tilde{J} = \{(s, \epsilon, a) : s \in S, \epsilon \in E, a \in A(s, \epsilon)\} \subseteq S \times E \times A$;

(iv) a transition law $p_t : \tilde{J} \times S \to [0, 1]$, which specifies the probability $p_t(s, \epsilon, a, s')$ for a transition from system state $s \in S$ and environmental state $\epsilon \in E$ to state $s' \in S$ at time $t = T, ..., 1$ if action $a \in A(s, \epsilon)$ is chosen; for $s \in S$, $\epsilon \in E$, $a \in A(s, \epsilon)$ and $t = T, ..., 1$, $p_t(s, \epsilon, a, s')$ is a discrete density function on S;

(v) a transition law $\tilde{p}_t : E \times E \to [0, 1]$, which represents the probability $\tilde{p}_t(\epsilon, \epsilon')$ for a transition from environmental state $\epsilon \in E$ to $\epsilon' \in E$; for a fixed $\epsilon \in E$, $\tilde{p}_t(\epsilon, \epsilon')$ is a discrete density function on E;

(vi) a one-stage reward function $r_t : \tilde{J} \to \mathbb{R}$, which represents the reward $r_t(s, \epsilon, a)$ if at time $t = T, ..., 1$, in system state $s \in S$ and in environmental state $\epsilon \in E$ action $a \in A(s, \epsilon)$ is chosen;

(vii) a terminal reward function $V_0 : S \times E \to \mathbb{R}$ which corresponds to the reward $V_0(s, \epsilon)$ that is earned if at time $t = 0$ the system is in state s and ϵ.

As in the model without an external process, the maximum total expected reward, if the system is in state (s, ϵ) and t decision periods are remaining, is the unique solution to the optimality equation

$$V_t(s, \epsilon) = \max_{a \in A(s, \epsilon)} \left\{ r_t(s, \epsilon, a) + \sum_{s' \in S} \sum_{\epsilon' \in E} p_t(s, \epsilon, a, s') \tilde{p}_t(\epsilon, \epsilon') V_{t-1}(s', \epsilon') \right\}.$$

$$(3.4)$$

We now outline a very popular application of MDPs exposed to an external Markov chain, which can be found in the field of revenue management. The optimality equation, in its standard form as stated in (3.4), is given in Talluri & van Ryzin (2004, p. 654). In their model, the requested booking class (here state ϵ) and the number of remaining seats (here state s) are observed at the same time, and a decision is made based on this information. Moreover, the authors propose a different form of the optimality equation that determines the maximum expected reward before the environmental state is observed. Talluri & van Ryzin call this alternative formulation the *observable-disturbance form*, which we outline next.

In a revenue management context, the probability that a request for a particular booking class arrives at time t is assumed to be independent of the requested booking class at time $t + 1$. Therefore, we define $\hat{p}_{t-1}(\epsilon') := \tilde{p}_t(\epsilon, \epsilon')$ for all $\epsilon \in E$ and $t = T, ..., 1$. We further define the operator

$$\hat{H}_t u(s) := \sum_{e \in E} \hat{p}_t(\epsilon) u(s, \epsilon)$$

for an arbitrary real-valued function u on $S \times E$. Then, we can rewrite the optimality equation (3.4) as

$$V_t(s, \epsilon) = \max_{a \in A(s,\epsilon)} \left\{ r_t(s, \epsilon, a) + \sum_{s' \in S} p_t(s, \epsilon, a, s') \hat{H}_{t-1} V_{t-1}(s') \right\}. \quad (3.5)$$

Rewriting this in observable-disturbance form, which is simply taking expectations on both sides of the optimality equation, yields

$$\hat{H}_t V_t(s) = \sum_{e \in E} \hat{p}_t(\epsilon) \max_{a \in A(s,\epsilon)} \left\{ r_t(s, \epsilon, a) + \sum_{s' \in S} p_t(s, \epsilon, a, s') \hat{H}_{t-1} V_{t-1}(s') \right\}.$$
$$(3.6)$$

According to Talluri & van Ryzin (2004), the underlying decision process of this optimality equation can be described as follows: First, a state s is observed but ϵ is unknown. At this point, one determines the maximum expected reward. Afterwards, a booking class ϵ is observed, the optimal decision is made, and the system moves to state s'.

The form (3.6) is usually presented for revenue management models in literature. The benefit of the observable-disturbance form is that it decreases the MDP's state space since the number of booking classes does not have to be considered. Note, however, that this does not decrease the number of optimal actions because they depend on time, system state, and environmental state. Note further that (3.5) and (3.6) determine identical optimal actions since the maximum functions in both optimality equations are identical.

We now turn to the concepts that are necessary to show that a two-dimensional decision problem features an optimal monotone policy.

3.2 Optimal Monotone Control in Two-Dimensional Problems

The importance of structured policies was already highlighted in Section 3.1.1. In case of a one-dimensional state space, well-known concepts like concavity or convexity ensure the optimality of monotone policies (see for example Helm & Waldmann, 1984). On the other hand, the sufficient conditions for the existence of *two-dimensional* optimal monotone policies are more complex.

Optimal monotone control in two-dimensional problems has been studied in numerous fields of application. It first appeared in the context of queuing systems, see e.g. Hajek (1984), Ghoneim & Stidham (1985), Weber & Stidham (1987), Veatch & Wein (1992), and Stidham & Weber (1993). Two-dimensional monotone control has also been researched in production and manufacturing, for instance by Veatch & Wein (1994), Ha (1997a), Ha (1997b), Ha (2000), Carr & Duenyas (2000), and Benjaafar et al. (2010). Further studies have been conducted in health care management, e.g. by Green et al. (2006), and in revenue management, see for instance You (1999), Savin et al. (2005), Morton (2006), and Chen et al. (2010).

Section 3.2.1 provides an overview of the conditions that yield optimal monotone policies in two-dimensional problems. Furthermore, we show in Section 3.2.2 that two particular problems, which are relevant in cargo capacity control, feature some of these properties which ensure the existence of optimal monotone control policies.

3.2.1 Two-Dimensional Structural Concepts

We already introduced a control limit policy in case of a one-dimensional system state. Now consider a state space comprising two dimensions (say $S_1 \times S_2$). Then a control limit is not a particular state s^* any more but rather a function of the other dimension, which we call a *switching curve*.

Definition 3.2. (cf. Lewis, 2001). Suppose in each state $(s_1, s_2) \in S_1 \times S_2$ the set of admissible actions is $A(s) = \{a_1, a_2\}$. A deterministic Markov policy is

39

called *switching curve policy* if some curve (i.e. a function) separates $S_1 \times S_2$ into two adjacent regions. Then one action is optimal for states below the curve, and the other action is optimal for states above the curve. If the curve is monotone, a policy is called *monotone switching curve policy*.

An example of a monotone switching curve policy is shown in Figure 3.1.

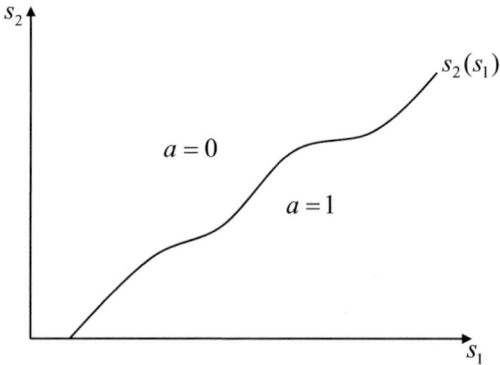

Figure 3.1: A switching curve

We now turn to the necessary and sufficient conditions for the optimality of monotone switching curve policies. These conditions are given by the concept of multimodularity, which comprises two individual structural properties. All properties that may be related to multimodularity are outlined below.

Definition 3.3. (Zhuang & Li, 2010). Let $l : \mathbb{Z}^2 \to \mathbb{R}$ be a real-valued function and $e_1 := (1, 0)$ as well as $e_2 := (0, 1)$. Let further $x \in \mathbb{Z}^2$ and $j, k \in \{1, 2\}, j \neq k$.

(i) $l(x)$ is *supermodular* (*submodular*) in j and k if

$$l(x) - l(x - e_j) \leq (\geq) l(x + e_k) - l(x - e_j + e_k).$$

(ii) $l(x)$ is *superconcave* (*subconvex*) in j and k if both

$$l(x) - l(x - e_j) \leq (\geq)l(x - e_j - e_k) - l(x - 2e_j - e_k) \text{ and}$$
$$l(x) - l(x - e_k) \leq (\geq)l(x - e_j - e_k) - l(x - e_j - 2e_k).$$

(iii) $l(x)$ is *subconcave* (*superconvex*) in j and k if both

$$l(x + e_j) - l(x) \leq (\geq)l(x + e_k) - l(x - e_j + e_k) \text{ and}$$
$$l(x + e_k) - l(x) \leq (\geq)l(x + e_j) - l(x + e_j - e_k).$$

(iv) $l(x)$ is *componentwise concave* (*convex*) in j if

$$l(x) - l(x - e_j) \leq (\geq)l(x - e_j) - l(x - 2e_j).$$

Before we outline the relationship between multimodularity and these concepts in the two-dimensional case, we derive multimodularity for n dimensions by means of the following definitions. Note that we assume the decision maker seeks to maximize total expected reward. Thus, we consider multimodularity in the context of concavity.

Definition 3.4. (Altman et al., 2003). A matrix D of size $(n + 1) \times n$ and of rank n is called *multimodular* if the rows of the matrix define $n + 1$ vectors $(g_0, g_1, ..., g_n)$ satisfying $g_0 + g_1 + ... + g_n = 0$.

Definition 3.5. (Altman et al., 2003, Definition 17). The *mesh* M_D associated with the multimodular matrix D is the set of all points $\{\sum_{i=0}^{n} \theta_i g_i, \theta_i \in \mathbb{Z}\}$.

Definition 3.6. (cf. Altman et al., 2003, Definition 20). A function $l : M_D \to \mathbb{R}$ is *D-multimodular* in the context of concavity if and only if for all $x \in M_D$ and $0 \leq j, k \leq n$,

$$l(x + g_j) + l(x + g_k) \leq l(x) + l(x + g_j + g_k). \tag{3.7}$$

This definition implies that the vectors g determine how a state x may change. Thus, each row vector in D represents a particular transition. Further, note that D-multimodularity can be defined in the context of convexity which would require to reverse the inequality in (3.7).

From now on, we limit this general definition of D-multimodularity to two dimensions and to row vectors with entries -1, 0, or 1 (thus, M_D is $\mathbb{Z}^2$). We consider this specified definition since we require multimodularity of MDPs having only a two-dimensional system state and with transitions that are bounded by the unity vector. That means, we only need to consider the following two multimodular matrices (cf. Zhuang & Li, 2012).

$$D^s = \begin{pmatrix} 1 & 0 \\ -1 & 1 \\ 0 & -1 \end{pmatrix}, \; D^c = \begin{pmatrix} 1 & 0 \\ -1 & -1 \\ 0 & 1 \end{pmatrix}$$

Note that we might as well consider $-D^s$ and $-D^c$, which would yield the same result that is derived next.

The difference between these multimodular bases allows us to characterize two-dimensional decision problems (cf. Zhuang & Li, 2012). Each row vector in D^s and D^c represents a specific transition. In particular, the second row vector indicates the most important property of the base: $(-1, 1)$ in D^s corresponds to the event of transferring resources from one dimension to the other. For instance, in case of two queues, a waiting customer can be transferred from one queue to the other. This possible transition indicates *substitutability* of the two dimensions of the state space. On the other hand, $(-1, -1)$ in D^c corresponds to the event of decreasing both dimensions of the state space to the same extent and at the same time. In case of two queues, this would be to accept one customers from both queues at the same time. This transition indicates *complementarity* of resources.

This insight allows us to characterize two-dimensional MDPs according to substitutability and complementarity of system states. Below, we categorize multimodularity according to substitutability and complementarity of resources.

Hereafter, we will use this categorization rather than referring to multimodularity with respect to a particular base D.

Multimodularity in the Context of Substitutability

In case of substitutable resources, only D^s needs to be considered as a multimodular base. Then, it is easy to show that (3.7) reduces to three different inequalities that are equal to the inequalities in the definition of submodularity and subconcavity. This result is outlined in the following lemma (cf. Zhuang & Li, 2010).

Proposition 3.1. *A real-valued function $l : \mathbb{Z}^2 \to \mathbb{R}$ is multimodular in the context of substitutability if and only if l is submodular and subconcave. Furthermore, any multimodular function is componentwise concave.*

This proposition applies to decision problems maximizing the objective value (i.e. in the context of concavity). A parallel definition of multimodularity can be given for systems that minimize the objective value. As an example, consider a server that admits only one request from two different queues while seeking to minimize cost. In this case, the necessary and sufficient conditions for multimodularity are *supermodularity* and *superconvexity* since (3.7) is reversed.

Multimodularity in the Context of Complementarity

In case of complementary resources, D^c is the only multimodular base that needs to be considered. Then, it is easy to show that (3.7) reduces to supermodularity and superconcavity as outlined below.

Proposition 3.2. *A real-valued function $l : \mathbb{Z}^2 \to \mathbb{R}$ is multimodular in the context of complementarity if and only if l is supermodular and superconcave. Furthermore, any multimodular function is componentwise concave.*

Again, an analogue proposition exists in the context of convexity (minimization of objective value). Then, the necessary and sufficient conditions for multimodularity are *submodularity* and *subconvexity*.

In summary, multimodularity ensures that the differences in value over two states are horizontally, vertically, and diagonally monotone over state variables (Zhuang & Li, 2010). An overview of the introduced concepts is provided in Table 3.1.

Objective	Resources' relationship	Structural properties	Example
Maximization	Substitutability	Submodularity & subconcavity	Green et al. (2006)
Minimization	Substitutability	Supermodularity & superconvexity	Hajek (1984)
Maximization	Complementarity	Supermodularity & superconcavity	Morton (2006)
Minimization	Complementarity	Submodularity & subconvexity	Benjaafar et al. (2010)

Table 3.1: Overview of multimodularity in different contexts

3.2.2 Two-Dimensional Structural Properties of Particular Problems

In this section, we prove that multimodularity is preserved under two particular operators that are relevant in the decision models we will analyze later. The following lemma will help us to conduct the proofs efficiently.

Lemma 3.1. (Zhuang & Li, 2010) *Let $\{\nu_j, \eta_j, \tilde{\nu}_j, \tilde{\eta}_j : j = 1, ..., n\}$ be four arbitrary real sequences. Assume that for any j and k, there exist $z_1, z_2 \in \{1, ..., n\}$ so that*

$$\nu_j - \eta_{z_1} \le \tilde{\nu}_{z_2} - \tilde{\eta}_k. \tag{3.8}$$

Then the following inequality holds:

$$\max\{\nu_1, ..., \nu_n\} - \max\{\eta_1, ..., \eta_n\} \leq \max\{\tilde{\nu}_1, ..., \tilde{\nu}_n\} - \max\{\tilde{\eta}_1, ..., \tilde{\eta}_n\}.$$

Proof. We denote $\nu_{max}, \eta_{max}, \tilde{\nu}_{max}, \tilde{\eta}_{max}$ as the maximum element of each sequence. According to the assumption, there exist $z_1, z_2 \in \{1, ..., n\}$ so that

$$\nu_{max} - \eta_{z_1} \leq \tilde{\nu}_{z_2} - \tilde{\eta}_{max}.$$

Further, we have for every $z_1 \in \{1, ..., n\}$ that $\nu_{max} - \eta_{max} \leq \nu_{max} - \eta_{z_1}$ and for every $z_2 \in \{1, ..., n\}$ that $\tilde{\nu}_{z_2} - \tilde{\eta}_{max} \leq \tilde{\nu}_{max} - \tilde{\eta}_{max}$. It follows that

$$\nu_{max} - \eta_{max} \leq \tilde{\nu}_{max} - \tilde{\eta}_{max}.$$

$\square$

Zhuang & Li (2010) describe this lemma as an alternative to the theory of ordered optimal solutions developed by Topkis (1978) and Glasserman & Yao (1994), which can be applied to show the existence of optimal monotone policies.

We now show that multimodularity is preserved under a particular operator.

Proposition 3.3. *If $l(\boldsymbol{x}) : \mathbb{Z}^2 \to \mathbb{R}$ is multimodular, and if x_1 and x_2 are complementary resources, the operator $U\tilde{l}(\boldsymbol{x}, \iota) : \mathbb{Z}^2 \to \mathbb{R}$ is also multimodular where*

$$U\tilde{l}(\boldsymbol{x}, \iota) = \max_{a \in \{0,1\}} \{ar_\iota + l(\boldsymbol{x} - \boldsymbol{a})\}$$

for $\boldsymbol{x} = (x_1, x_2)$, $r_\iota \in \mathbb{R}_0^+$, $\iota \in \mathbb{N}_0$, and $\boldsymbol{a} = (a, a)$.

Proof. Since we assume that $l(\boldsymbol{x})$ is multimodular and resources are complements, $l(\boldsymbol{x})$ is supermodular and superconcave. We first show that $U\tilde{l}(\boldsymbol{x}, \iota)$ is supermodular. Thus, we need to proof that for distinct $j, k \in \{1, 2\}$ and some $\iota \in \mathbb{N}_0$,

$$U\tilde{l}(\boldsymbol{x}, \iota) - U\tilde{l}(\boldsymbol{x} - \boldsymbol{e}_j, \iota) \leq U\tilde{l}(\boldsymbol{x} + \boldsymbol{e}_k, \iota) - U\tilde{l}(\boldsymbol{x} - \boldsymbol{e}_j + \boldsymbol{e}_k, \iota). \qquad (3.9)$$

(3.9) is equivalent to

$$\max_{a_1 \in \{0,1\}} \{a_1 r_\iota + l(\boldsymbol{x} - \boldsymbol{a_1})\} - \max_{a_2 \in \{0,1\}} \{a_2 r_\iota + l(\boldsymbol{x} - \boldsymbol{e}_j - \boldsymbol{a_2})\}$$
$$\leq \max_{a_3 \in \{0,1\}} \{a_3 r_\iota + l(\boldsymbol{x} + \boldsymbol{e}_k - \boldsymbol{a_3})\}$$
$$- \max_{a_4 \in \{0,1\}} \{a_4 r_\iota + l(\boldsymbol{x} - \boldsymbol{e}_j + \boldsymbol{e}_k - \boldsymbol{a_4})\}.$$

In order to prove supermodularity, we enumerate the combinations of optimal values for $U\tilde{l}(\boldsymbol{x}, \iota)$ and $U\tilde{l}(\boldsymbol{x} - \boldsymbol{e}_j + \boldsymbol{e}_k, \iota)$ and find feasible values for $U\tilde{l}(\boldsymbol{x} - \boldsymbol{e}_j, \iota)$ and $U\tilde{l}(\boldsymbol{x} + \boldsymbol{e}_k, \iota)$ so that (3.8) holds. For $a_1 = a_4$, the proof simply follows from supermodularity when setting $a_1 = a_2 = a_3 = a_4$. We further have to consider the cases $a_1 < a_4$ and $a_1 > a_4$.

(i) If $a_1 = 0$ and $a_4 = 1$, set $a_2 = 0$ and $a_3 = 1$, which yields

$$a_1 r_\iota + l(\boldsymbol{x} - \boldsymbol{a_1}) - a_2 r_\iota - l(\boldsymbol{x} - \boldsymbol{e}_j - \boldsymbol{a_2})$$
$$= l(\boldsymbol{x}) - l(\boldsymbol{x} - \boldsymbol{e}_j)$$
$$= l(\boldsymbol{x} + \boldsymbol{e}_j + \boldsymbol{e}_k - \boldsymbol{a_3}) - l(\boldsymbol{x} + \boldsymbol{e}_k - \boldsymbol{a_4})$$
$$\leq l(\boldsymbol{x} + \boldsymbol{e}_k - \boldsymbol{a_3}) - l(\boldsymbol{x} - \boldsymbol{e}_j + \boldsymbol{e}_k - \boldsymbol{a_4})$$
$$= l(\boldsymbol{x} + \boldsymbol{e}_k - \boldsymbol{a_3}) + a_3 r_\iota - l(\boldsymbol{x} - \boldsymbol{e}_j + \boldsymbol{e}_k - \boldsymbol{a_4}) - a_4 r_\iota,$$

where the inequality follows from componentwise concavity.

(ii) If $a_1 = 1$ and $a_4 = 0$, set $a_2 = 0$ and $a_3 = 1$, which yields

$$a_1 r_\iota + l(\boldsymbol{x} - \boldsymbol{a_1}) - a_2 r_\iota - l(\boldsymbol{x} - \boldsymbol{e}_j - \boldsymbol{a_2})$$
$$= l(\boldsymbol{x} - \boldsymbol{e}_j - \boldsymbol{e}_k) + r_\iota - l(\boldsymbol{x} - \boldsymbol{e}_j)$$
$$\leq l(\boldsymbol{x}) + r_\iota - l(\boldsymbol{x} + \boldsymbol{e}_k)$$
$$= l(\boldsymbol{x} + \boldsymbol{e}_j + \boldsymbol{e}_k - \boldsymbol{a_3}) + r_\iota - l(\boldsymbol{x} + \boldsymbol{e}_k - \boldsymbol{a_4})$$
$$\leq l(\boldsymbol{x} + \boldsymbol{e}_k - \boldsymbol{a_3}) + r_\iota - l(\boldsymbol{x} - \boldsymbol{e}_j + \boldsymbol{e}_k - \boldsymbol{a_4})$$
$$= l(\boldsymbol{x} + \boldsymbol{e}_k - \boldsymbol{a_3}) + a_3 r_\iota - l(\boldsymbol{x} - \boldsymbol{e}_j + \boldsymbol{e}_k - \boldsymbol{a_4}) - a_4 r_\iota,$$

where the first inequality follows from superconcavity. Note that we multiplied the inequality in the definition of superconcavity by -1. The second inequality follows from componentwise concavity. According to Lemma 3.1, $U\tilde{l}(\boldsymbol{x}, \iota)$ is supermodular in x_1 and x_2 for $\iota \in \mathbb{N}_0$.

We now prove that $U\tilde{l}(\boldsymbol{x}, \iota)$ is superconcave, i.e. for distinct $j, k \in \{1, 2\}$ and $\iota \in \mathbb{N}_0$,

$$U\tilde{l}(\boldsymbol{x}, \iota) - U\tilde{l}(\boldsymbol{x} - \boldsymbol{e}_j, \iota) \leq U\tilde{l}(\boldsymbol{x} - \boldsymbol{e}_j - \boldsymbol{e}_k, \iota) - U\tilde{l}(\boldsymbol{x} - 2\boldsymbol{e}_j - \boldsymbol{e}_k, \iota)$$
$$(3.10)$$
$$U\tilde{l}(\boldsymbol{x}, \iota) - U\tilde{l}(\boldsymbol{x} - \boldsymbol{e}_k, \iota) \leq U\tilde{l}(\boldsymbol{x} - \boldsymbol{e}_j - \boldsymbol{e}_k, \iota) - U\tilde{l}(\boldsymbol{x} - \boldsymbol{e}_j - 2\boldsymbol{e}_k, \iota).$$
$$(3.11)$$

(3.10) is equivalent to

$$\max_{a_1 \in \{0,1\}} \{a_1 r_\iota + l(\boldsymbol{x} - \boldsymbol{a_1})\} - \max_{a_2 \in \{0,1\}} \{a_2 r_\iota + l(\boldsymbol{x} - \boldsymbol{e}_j - \boldsymbol{a_2})\}$$
$$\leq \max_{a_3 \in \{0,1\}} \{a_3 r_\iota + l(\boldsymbol{x} - \boldsymbol{e}_j - \boldsymbol{e}_k - \boldsymbol{a_3})\}$$
$$- \max_{a_4 \in \{0,1\}} \{a_4 r_\iota + l(\boldsymbol{x} - 2\boldsymbol{e}_j - \boldsymbol{e}_k - \boldsymbol{a_4})\}.$$

We enumerate the combinations of optimal values for $U\tilde{l}(\boldsymbol{x}, \iota)$ and $U\tilde{l}(\boldsymbol{x} - 2\boldsymbol{e}_j - \boldsymbol{e}_k, \iota)$ and find feasible values for $U\tilde{l}(\boldsymbol{x} - \boldsymbol{e}_j, \iota)$ and $U\tilde{l}(\boldsymbol{x} - \boldsymbol{e}_j - \boldsymbol{e}_k, \iota)$ so that

(3.8) holds. In case of $a_1 = a_4$, the proof follows from superconcavity with $a_1 = a_2 = a_3 = a_4$. Consider the remaining two cases:

(i) If $a_1 = 0$ and $a_4 = 1$, set $a_2 = 0$ and $a_3 = 1$, which yields

$$
\begin{aligned}
&a_1 r_\iota + l(\boldsymbol{x} - \boldsymbol{a_1}) - a_2 r_\iota - l(\boldsymbol{x} - \boldsymbol{e}_j - \boldsymbol{a_2}) \\
=&l(\boldsymbol{x}) - l(\boldsymbol{x} - \boldsymbol{e}_j) \\
\leq&l(\boldsymbol{x} - \boldsymbol{e}_j - \boldsymbol{e}_k) - l(\boldsymbol{x} - 2\boldsymbol{e}_j - \boldsymbol{e}_k) \\
\leq&l(\boldsymbol{x} - 2\boldsymbol{e}_j - 2\boldsymbol{e}_k) - l(\boldsymbol{x} - 3\boldsymbol{e}_j - 2\boldsymbol{e}_k) \\
=&l(\boldsymbol{x} - \boldsymbol{e}_j - \boldsymbol{e}_k - \boldsymbol{a_3}) - l(\boldsymbol{x} - 2\boldsymbol{e}_j - \boldsymbol{e}_k - \boldsymbol{a_4}) \\
=&l(\boldsymbol{x} - \boldsymbol{e}_j - \boldsymbol{e}_k - \boldsymbol{a_3}) + a_3 r_\iota - l(\boldsymbol{x} - 2\boldsymbol{e}_j - \boldsymbol{e}_k - \boldsymbol{a_4}) - a_4 r_\iota,
\end{aligned}
$$

where both inequalities follow from superconcavity.

(ii) If $a_1 = 1$ and $a_4 = 0$, set $a_3 = 0$ and $a_2 = 1$. Then, we have

$$
\begin{aligned}
&a_1 r_\iota + l(\boldsymbol{x} - \boldsymbol{a_1}) - a_2 r_\iota - l(\boldsymbol{x} - \boldsymbol{e}_j - \boldsymbol{a_2}) \\
=&l(\boldsymbol{x} - \boldsymbol{e}_j - \boldsymbol{e}_k) - l(\boldsymbol{x} - 2\boldsymbol{e}_j - \boldsymbol{e}_k) \\
=&a_3 r_\iota + l(\boldsymbol{x} - \boldsymbol{e}_j - \boldsymbol{e}_k - \boldsymbol{a_3}) - a_4 r_\iota - l(\boldsymbol{x} - 2\boldsymbol{e}_j - \boldsymbol{e}_k - \boldsymbol{a_4}).
\end{aligned}
$$

The proof of the second case of superconcavity, (3.11), can be done analogously. Thus, according to Lemma 3.1, $U\tilde{l}(\boldsymbol{x}, \iota)$ is superconcave in x_1 and x_2 for $\iota \in \mathbb{N}_0$. In combination with supermodularity $U\tilde{l}(\boldsymbol{x}, \iota)$ is multimodular in x_1 and x_2. $\quad\square$

Now we prove that the following operator preserves multimodularity.

Proposition 3.4. *If $l(\boldsymbol{x}) : \mathbb{Z}^2 \to \mathbb{R}$ is multimodular, and if x_1 and x_2 are complementary resources, the operator $U_j \tilde{l}(\boldsymbol{x}, \iota) : \mathbb{Z}^2 \to \mathbb{R}$ is also multimodular where*

$$
U_j \tilde{l}(\boldsymbol{x}, \iota) = \max_{a \in \{0, \dots, n_\iota\}} \{a r_\iota + l(\boldsymbol{x} - a \boldsymbol{e}_j)\}, \quad j \in \{1, 2\}
$$

for $\boldsymbol{x} = (x_1, x_2)$, $r_\iota \in \mathbb{R}_0^+$, $\iota \in \mathbb{N}_0$, and $n_\iota \in \mathbb{N}$.

Proof. Since $l(\boldsymbol{x})$ is multimodular and resources are complements, $l(\boldsymbol{x})$ is super-modular and superconcave. We start showing that supermodularity is preserved under the operator U_j. Thus, we need to prove that for distinct $j, k \in \{1, 2\}$ and $\iota \in \mathbb{N}_0$

$$U_j \tilde{l}(\boldsymbol{x}, \iota) - U_j \tilde{l}(\boldsymbol{x} - \boldsymbol{e}_j, \iota) \leq U_j \tilde{l}(\boldsymbol{x} + \boldsymbol{e}_k, \iota) - U_j \tilde{l}(\boldsymbol{x} - \boldsymbol{e}_j + \boldsymbol{e}_k, \iota), \quad (3.12)$$

which is equivalent to

$$\max_{a_1 \in \{0, \ldots, n_\iota\}} \{a_1 r_\iota + l(\boldsymbol{x} - a_1 \boldsymbol{e}_j)\} - \max_{a_2 \in \{0, \ldots, n_\iota\}} \{a_2 r_\iota + l(\boldsymbol{x} - \boldsymbol{e}_j - a_2 \boldsymbol{e}_j)\}$$
$$\leq \max_{a_3 \in \{0, \ldots, n_\iota\}} \{a_3 r_\iota + l(\boldsymbol{x} + \boldsymbol{e}_k - a_3 \boldsymbol{e}_j)\}$$
$$- \max_{a_4 \in \{0, \ldots, n_\iota\}} \{a_4 r_\iota + l(\boldsymbol{x} - \boldsymbol{e}_j + \boldsymbol{e}_k - a_4 \boldsymbol{e}_j)\}.$$

Note that we also have to prove $U_k \tilde{l}(\boldsymbol{x}, \iota) - U_k \tilde{l}(\boldsymbol{x} - \boldsymbol{e}_j, \iota) \leq U_k \tilde{l}(\boldsymbol{x} + \boldsymbol{e}_k, \iota) - U_k \tilde{l}(\boldsymbol{x} - \boldsymbol{e}_j + \boldsymbol{e}_k, \iota)$; however, this inequality can be rearranged to (3.12) with transformed $\boldsymbol{x}$. Thus, the proof works analogously and is omitted. Below, we enumerate the combinations of optimal values for $U_j \tilde{l}(\boldsymbol{x}, \iota)$ and $U_j \tilde{l}(\boldsymbol{x} - \boldsymbol{e}_j + \boldsymbol{e}_k, \iota)$ and find feasible values for $U_j \tilde{l}(\boldsymbol{x} - \boldsymbol{e}_j, \iota)$ and $U_j \tilde{l}(\boldsymbol{x} + \boldsymbol{e}_k, \iota)$ so that (3.8) holds. The proof for $a_1 = a_4$ follows simply from supermodularity when setting $a_1 = a_2 = a_3 = a_4$. Further, the following two cases have to be considered.

(i) If $n_\iota \geq a_1 > a_4$, set $a_2 = a_1 - 1$ and $a_3 = a_4 + 1$, which yields

$$a_1 r_\iota + l(\boldsymbol{x} - a_1 \boldsymbol{e}_j) - a_2 r_\iota - l(\boldsymbol{x} - \boldsymbol{e}_j - a_2 \boldsymbol{e}_j)$$
$$= l(\boldsymbol{x} - a_1 \boldsymbol{e}_j) - l(\boldsymbol{x} - a_1 \boldsymbol{e}_j) + r_\iota$$
$$= r_\iota$$
$$= l(\boldsymbol{x} + \boldsymbol{e}_k - a_3 \boldsymbol{e}_j) - l(\boldsymbol{x} + \boldsymbol{e}_k - a_3 \boldsymbol{e}_j) + r_\iota$$
$$= l(\boldsymbol{x} + \boldsymbol{e}_k - a_3 \boldsymbol{e}_j) + a_3 r_\iota - l(\boldsymbol{x} - \boldsymbol{e}_j + \boldsymbol{e}_k - a_4 \boldsymbol{e}_j) - a_4 r_\iota.$$

(ii) If $a_1 < a_4 \leq n_\iota$, set $a_2 = a_1$ and $a_3 = a_4$, which yields

$$a_1 r_\iota + l(\boldsymbol{x} - a_1 \boldsymbol{e}_j) - a_2 r_\iota - l(\boldsymbol{x} - \boldsymbol{e}_j - a_2 \boldsymbol{e}_j)$$
$$= l(\boldsymbol{x} - a_1 \boldsymbol{e}_j) - l(\boldsymbol{x} - \boldsymbol{e}_j - a_1 \boldsymbol{e}_j)$$
$$\leq l(\boldsymbol{x} + \boldsymbol{e}_k - a_1 \boldsymbol{e}_j) - l(\boldsymbol{x} - \boldsymbol{e}_j + \boldsymbol{e}_k - a_1 \boldsymbol{e}_j)$$
$$\leq l(\boldsymbol{x} - \boldsymbol{e}_j + \boldsymbol{e}_k - a_1 \boldsymbol{e}_j) - l(\boldsymbol{x} - 2\boldsymbol{e}_j + \boldsymbol{e}_k - a_1 \boldsymbol{e}_j)$$
$$\vdots$$
$$\leq l(\boldsymbol{x} + \boldsymbol{e}_k - (a_4 - a_1)\boldsymbol{e}_j - a_1 \boldsymbol{e}_j)$$
$$- l(\boldsymbol{x} - \boldsymbol{e}_j + \boldsymbol{e}_k - (a_4 - a_1)\boldsymbol{e}_j - a_1 \boldsymbol{e}_j)$$
$$= l(\boldsymbol{x} + \boldsymbol{e}_k - a_3 \boldsymbol{e}_j) + a_3 r_\iota - l(\boldsymbol{x} - \boldsymbol{e}_j + \boldsymbol{e}_k - a_4 \boldsymbol{e}_j) - a_4 r_\iota,$$

where the first inequality follows from supermodularity. All other inequalities follow from componentwise concavity (which is applied $(a_4 - a_1)$ times). According to Lemma 3.1, $U_j \tilde{l}(\boldsymbol{x}, \iota)$ is supermodular in x_1 and x_2 for $j \in \{1, 2\}$ and $\iota \in \mathbb{N}_0$.

We next prove that superconcavity is preserved under $U_j \tilde{l}(\boldsymbol{x}, \iota)$, i.e. for distinct $j, k \in \{1, 2\}$ and some $\iota \in \mathbb{N}_0$,

$$U_j \tilde{l}(\boldsymbol{x}, \iota) - U_j \tilde{l}(\boldsymbol{x} - \boldsymbol{e}_j, \iota) \leq U_j \tilde{l}(\boldsymbol{x} - \boldsymbol{e}_j - \boldsymbol{e}_k, \iota) - U_j \tilde{l}(\boldsymbol{x} - 2\boldsymbol{e}_j - \boldsymbol{e}_k, \iota)$$
$$(3.13)$$
$$U_j \tilde{l}(\boldsymbol{x}, \iota) - U_j \tilde{l}(\boldsymbol{x} - \boldsymbol{e}_k, \iota) \leq U_j \tilde{l}(\boldsymbol{x} - \boldsymbol{e}_j - \boldsymbol{e}_k, \iota) - U_j \tilde{l}(\boldsymbol{x} - \boldsymbol{e}_j - 2\boldsymbol{e}_k, \iota).$$
$$(3.14)$$

Note that we might as well prove superconcavity when using U_k instead of U_j in the above inequalities, which would give the same result that is derived below. (3.13) is equivalent to

$$\max_{a_1 \in \{0,\ldots,n_\iota\}} \{a_1 r_\iota + l(\boldsymbol{x} - a_1 \boldsymbol{e}_j)\} - \max_{a_2 \in \{0,\ldots,n_\iota\}} \{a_2 r_\iota + l(\boldsymbol{x} - \boldsymbol{e}_j - a_2 \boldsymbol{e}_j)\}$$

$$\leq \max_{a_3 \in \{0,\ldots,n_\iota\}} \{a_3 r_\iota + l(\boldsymbol{x} - \boldsymbol{e}_j - \boldsymbol{e}_k - a_3 \boldsymbol{e}_j)\}$$

$$- \max_{a_4 \in \{0,\ldots,n\}} \{a_4 r_\iota + l(\boldsymbol{x} - 2\boldsymbol{e}_j - \boldsymbol{e}_k - a_4 \boldsymbol{e}_j)\}.$$

We enumerate the combinations of optimal values for $U_j \tilde{l}(\boldsymbol{x}, \iota)$ and $U_j \tilde{l}(\boldsymbol{x} - 2\boldsymbol{e}_j - \boldsymbol{e}_k, \iota)$ and find feasible values for $U_j \tilde{l}(\boldsymbol{x} - \boldsymbol{e}_j, \iota)$ and $U_j \tilde{l}(\boldsymbol{x} - \boldsymbol{e}_j - \boldsymbol{e}_k, \iota)$ so that (3.8) holds. For $a_1 = a_4$, the proof follows from superconcavity when setting $a_1 = a_2 = a_3 = a_4$. Now consider the remaining cases:

(i) If $n_\iota \geq a_1 > a_4$, set $a_2 = a_1 - 1$ and $a_3 = a_4 + 1$, which yields

$$a_1 r_\iota + l(\boldsymbol{x} - a_1 \boldsymbol{e}_j) - a_2 r_\iota - l(\boldsymbol{x} - \boldsymbol{e}_j - a_2 \boldsymbol{e}_j)$$

$$= l(\boldsymbol{x} - a_1 \boldsymbol{e}_j) - l(\boldsymbol{x} - a_1 \boldsymbol{e}_j) + r_\iota$$

$$= r_\iota$$

$$= l(\boldsymbol{x} - 2\boldsymbol{e}_j - \boldsymbol{e}_k - a_4 \boldsymbol{e}_j) - l(\boldsymbol{x} - 2\boldsymbol{e}_j - \boldsymbol{e}_k - a_4 \boldsymbol{e}_j) + r_\iota$$

$$= l(\boldsymbol{x} - \boldsymbol{e}_j - \boldsymbol{e}_k - a_3 \boldsymbol{e}_j) + a_3 r_\iota - l(\boldsymbol{x} - 2\boldsymbol{e}_j - \boldsymbol{e}_k - a_4 \boldsymbol{e}_j) - a_4 r_\iota.$$

(ii) If $a_1 < a_4 \leq n_\iota$, set $a_2 = a_1$ and $a_3 = a_4$, which yields

$$a_1 r_\iota + l(\boldsymbol{x} - a_1 \boldsymbol{e}_j) - a_2 r_\iota - l(\boldsymbol{x} - \boldsymbol{e}_j - a_2 \boldsymbol{e}_j)$$

$$= l(\boldsymbol{x} - a_1 \boldsymbol{e}_j) - l(\boldsymbol{x} - \boldsymbol{e}_j - a_1 \boldsymbol{e}_j)$$

$$\leq l(\boldsymbol{x} - \boldsymbol{e}_j - \boldsymbol{e}_k - a_1 \boldsymbol{e}_j) - l(\boldsymbol{x} - 2\boldsymbol{e}_j - \boldsymbol{e}_k - a_1 \boldsymbol{e}_j)$$

$$\leq l(\boldsymbol{x} - 2\boldsymbol{e}_j - \boldsymbol{e}_k - a_1 \boldsymbol{e}_j) - l(\boldsymbol{x} - 3\boldsymbol{e}_j - \boldsymbol{e}_k - a_1 \boldsymbol{e}_j)$$

$$\vdots$$

$$\leq l(\boldsymbol{x} - \boldsymbol{e}_j - \boldsymbol{e}_k - (a_4 - a_1)\boldsymbol{e}_j - a_1 \boldsymbol{e}_j)$$

$$- l(\boldsymbol{x} - 2\boldsymbol{e}_j - \boldsymbol{e}_k - (a_4 - a_1)\boldsymbol{e}_j - a_1 \boldsymbol{e}_j)$$

$$= l(\boldsymbol{x} - \boldsymbol{e}_j - \boldsymbol{e}_k - a_3 \boldsymbol{e}_j) + a_3 r_\iota - l(\boldsymbol{x} - 2\boldsymbol{e}_j - \boldsymbol{e}_k - a_4 \boldsymbol{e}_j) - a_4 r_\iota,$$

where the first inequality follows from superconcavity. All other inequalities follow from componentwise concavity (which is applied $(a_4 - a_1)$ times).

Unlike in the case of $U\tilde{l}(x, \iota)$, here the second part of superconcavity cannot be simply proven analogously. (3.14) is equivalent to

$$\max_{a_1 \in \{0,\ldots,n_\iota\}} \{a_1 r_\iota + l(x - a_1 e_j)\} - \max_{a_2 \in \{0,\ldots,n_\iota\}} \{a_2 r_\iota + l(x - e_k - a_2 e_j)\}$$
$$\leq \max_{a_3 \in \{0,\ldots,n_\iota\}} \{a_3 r_\iota + l(x - e_j - e_k - a_3 e_j)\}$$
$$- \max_{a_4 \in \{0,\ldots,n_\iota\}} \{a_4 r_\iota + l(x - e_j - 2e_k - a_4 e_j)\}.$$

We enumerate the combinations of optimal values for $U_j \tilde{l}(x, \iota)$ and $U_j \tilde{l}(x - e_j - 2e_k, \iota)$ and find feasible values for $U_j \tilde{l}(x - e_k, \iota)$ and $U_j \tilde{l}(x - e_j - e_k, \iota)$ so that (3.8) holds. The proof for $a_1 = a_4$ follows from superconcavity when setting $a_1 = a_2 = a_3 = a_4$. The following two cases need to be considered:

(i) If $n_\iota \geq a_1 > a_4$, set $a_2 = a_1$ and $a_3 = a_4$, which yields

$$a_1 r_\iota + l(x - a_1 e_j) - a_2 r_\iota - l(x - e_k - a_2 e_j)$$
$$= l(x - a_1 e_j) - l(x - e_k - a_1 e_j)$$
$$\leq l(x + e_j - a_1 e_j) - l(x + e_j - e_k - a_1 e_j)$$
$$\vdots$$
$$\leq l(x + (a_1 - a_4)e_j - a_1 e_j) - l(x + (a_1 - a_4)e_j - e_k - a_1 e_j)$$
$$= l(x - a_4 e_j) - l(x - e_k - a_4 e_j)$$
$$\leq l(x - e_j - e_k - a_4 e_j) - l(x - e_j - 2e_k - a_4 e_j)$$
$$= l(x - e_j - e_k - a_3 e_j) + a_3 r_\iota - l(x - e_j - 2e_k - a_4 e_j) - a_4 r_\iota.$$

Note that the first two inequalities follow from supermodularity, which is applied $(a_1 - a_4)$ times. The last inequality follows from superconcavity.

(ii) If $a_1 < a_4 \leq n_\iota$, set $a_2 = a_1 + 1$ and $a_3 = a_4 - 1$, which yields

$$a_1 r_\iota + l(\boldsymbol{x} - a_1 \boldsymbol{e}_j) - a_2 r_\iota - l(\boldsymbol{x} - \boldsymbol{e}_k - a_2 \boldsymbol{e}_j)$$
$$= l(\boldsymbol{x} - a_1 \boldsymbol{e}_j) - l(\boldsymbol{x} - \boldsymbol{e}_j - \boldsymbol{e}_k - a_1 \boldsymbol{e}_j) - r_\iota$$
$$\leq l(\boldsymbol{x} - \boldsymbol{e}_j - a_1 \boldsymbol{e}_j) - l(\boldsymbol{x} - 2\boldsymbol{e}_j - \boldsymbol{e}_k - a_1 \boldsymbol{e}_j) - r_\iota$$
$$\vdots$$
$$\leq l(\boldsymbol{x} - (a_4 - a_1)\boldsymbol{e}_j - a_1 \boldsymbol{e}_j)$$
$$\quad - l(\boldsymbol{x} - \boldsymbol{e}_j - \boldsymbol{e}_k - (a_4 - a_1)\boldsymbol{e}_j - a_1 \boldsymbol{e}_j) - r_\iota$$
$$= l(\boldsymbol{x} - a_4 \boldsymbol{e}_j) - l(\boldsymbol{x} - \boldsymbol{e}_j - \boldsymbol{e}_k - a_4 \boldsymbol{e}_j) - r_\iota$$
$$\leq l(\boldsymbol{x} - \boldsymbol{e}_k - a_4 \boldsymbol{e}_j) - l(\boldsymbol{x} - \boldsymbol{e}_j - 2\boldsymbol{e}_k - a_4 \boldsymbol{e}_j) - r_\iota$$
$$= l(\boldsymbol{x} - \boldsymbol{e}_j - \boldsymbol{e}_k - a_3 \boldsymbol{e}_j) + a_3 r_\iota - l(\boldsymbol{x} - \boldsymbol{e}_j - 2\boldsymbol{e}_k - a_4 \boldsymbol{e}_j) - a_4 r_\iota.$$

The first inequalities follow from superconcavity (which is applied $(a_4 - a_1)$ times). Here we rearranged the inequality in the original definition. The last inequality also follows from superconcavity using the same rearranged definition.

According to Lemma 3.1, $U_j \tilde{l}(\boldsymbol{x}, \iota)$ is superconcave in x_1 and x_2. In combination with supermodularity, it follows that $U_j \tilde{l}(\boldsymbol{x}, \iota)$ is multimodular in x_1 and x_2 for $j \in \{1, 2\}$ and $\iota \in \mathbb{N}_0$. □

We now turn to a technique that approximates the value function in order to reduce the model's complexity. This makes the decision model tractable in case of large-scale problem instances.

3.3 The Linear Programming Approach to Approximate Dynamic Programming

In order to solve multi-dimensional problems prevailing in cargo capacity control, we apply approximate dynamic programming. General introductions and overviews of approximate dynamic programming are given by Bertsekas & Tsitsiklis (1996), Bertsekas (2005), and Powell (2007). These authors focus on adaptively approximating the value function by means of simulations. We propose solution approaches that do not require simulation but solve an optimization problem directly. This is related to the linear programming approach for dynamic programs (cf. Puterman, 1994, pp. 223-231). Schweitzer & Seidmann (1985) first considered the idea to approximate the value function in the linear programming formulation by a linear combination of other functions. De Farias & Van Roy (2003) discuss the quality of the performance of such approximations.

The linear programming approach to approximate dynamic programming has been applied in various fields of research. In passenger revenue management, Adelman (2007) was the first to approximate the value function. He proposes an affine approximation to compute time-dependent bid prices. Topaloglu & Tong (2011) further analyze the model of Adelman (2007) to make the solution feasible even for large networks. When considering customer choice behavior in network revenue management, value function approximations are used in Zhang & Adelman (2009) as well as in Meissner & Strauss (2012). Kunnumkal & Talluri (2011) establish a connection between piecewise linear approximations and Lagrangian approximations, as discussed in Topaloglu (2009).

Other fields where the linear programming approach to approximate dynamic programming is applied are, among others, inventory routing (e.g. Adelman, 2003), health care management (e.g. Patrick et al., 2008), and cargo capacity control (e.g. Levina et al., 2011).

In this section, we first introduce the linear programming approach for dynamic programs. Building on that, the value function approximation is discussed.

Linear Programming Approach for Dynamic Programs

In Section 3.1.1, we introduced backward induction as a technique for determining a solution of a finite-horizon MDP. A further way is to compute the value function by a linear program (LP). The underlying idea of this approach is as follows: If $\hat{V}_\tau(s)$ is a feasible solution to (3.2) for some $s \in S$ and some $\tau = T, ..., 1$, and if

$$\hat{V}_\tau(s) \geq \max_{a \in A(s)} \left\{ r_\tau(s, a) + \sum_{s' \in S} p_\tau(s, a, s') \hat{V}_{\tau-1}(s') \right\}, \qquad (3.15)$$

then $\hat{V}_\tau(s)$ is an upper bound on the optimal value function $V_\tau(s)$ (Puterman, 1994, p. 223). Thus, the optimal value satisfying $V_\tau(s) = \max_{a \in A(s)} \{ r_\tau(s, a) + \sum_{s' \in S} p_\tau(s, a, s') V_{\tau-1}(s') \}$ is the smallest value $\hat{V}_\tau(s)$ that satisfies (3.15). Due to this result, one can formulate the following LP that determines the optimal value functions $V_\tau(s)$ at time τ for all $s \in S$ (cf. Puterman, 1994, p. 223):

(**P0**) $\quad \min_{\hat{V}_\tau, ..., \hat{V}_1} \sum_{s \in S} \hat{V}_\tau(s) \qquad (3.16)$

s.t. $\quad \hat{V}_t(s)$

$$\geq r_t(s, a) + \sum_{s' \in S} p_t(s, a, s') \hat{V}_{t-1}(s') \quad \forall s \in S, a \in A(s), t = \tau, ..., 1$$

$$(3.17)$$

$$\hat{V}_t(s) \in \mathbb{R} \quad \forall s \in S, t = \tau, ..., 1. \qquad (3.18)$$

Note that $\hat{V}_0(s) = V_0(s)$ is given for all $s \in S$ and does not have to be determined in the LP. Note further that for some $s \in S$ and $t = T, ..., 1$, $V_\tau(s) = \max_{a \in A(s)} \{ r_\tau(s, a) + \sum_{s' \in S} p_\tau(s, a, s') V_{\tau-1}(s') \}$ implies $V_\tau(s) \geq r_\tau(s, a) + \sum_{s' \in S} p_\tau(s, a, s') V_{\tau-1}(s')$ for all $a \in A(s)$. It follows that $V_t(s)$ is a feasible solution of (**P0**).

Below, we provide a proof for the fact that any feasible solution to (**P0**) provides indeed an upper bound on the optimal objective value in (3.2)(based on Adelman, 2007).

Proposition 3.5. *Suppose $V_t(s)$ solves the optimality equation in (3.2) for some $t = T, ..., 1$ and $s \in S$. If $\hat{V}_t(s)$ is a feasible solution to (P0), it follows that $\hat{V}_t(s) \geq V_t(s)$.*

Proof. The proof follows by induction. For $\tau = 1$, (3.17) reads for all $s \in S, a \in A(s)$

$$\hat{V}_1(s) \geq r_1(s, a) + \sum_{s' \in S} p_1(s, a, s')\hat{V}_0(s').$$

This implies that for all $s \in S$, we have

$$\hat{V}_1(s) \geq \max_{a \in A(s)} \left\{ r_1(s, a) + \sum_{s' \in S} p_1(s, a, s')\hat{V}_0(s') \right\} = V_1(s).$$

This is true since $V_0 \equiv \hat{V}_0$. Now assume the assertion holds for all $\tau = 1, ..., t$ and consider (3.17) for $\tau = t + 1$. Then, we have

$$\hat{V}_{t+1}(s) \geq r_{t+1}(s, a) + \sum_{s' \in S} p_{t+1}(s, a, s')\hat{V}_t(s') \quad \forall s \in S, a \in A(s)$$

$$\geq r_{t+1}(s, a) + \sum_{s' \in S} p_{t+1}(s, a, s')V_t(s') \quad \forall s \in S, a \in A(s)$$

$$\geq \max_{a \in A(s)} \left\{ r_{t+1}(s, a) + \sum_{s' \in S} p_{t+1}(s, a, s')V_t(s') \right\} \quad \forall s \in S$$

$$= V_{t+1}(s) \quad \forall s \in S.$$

The inequality in the second line follows from the induction assumption. The next inequality uses the fact that if the inequality in the second line holds for all $a \in A(s)$, it holds in particular for the $a \in A(s)$ that maximizes the right hand side of the inequality. □

Linear programming is traditionally not considered as a solution technique for finite-horizon MDPs because the problem features an excessive number of constraints and variables making it very expensive to solve. We now introduce a technique that makes the LP tractable.

Value Function Approximation

The optimization problem (3.16)-(3.18) gives a solution to the optimality equation (3.2), however, the problem becomes computationally intractable for large-scale problems due to the *curse of dimensionality* (this term was introduced by Bellman, 1957). In order to reduce the problem's dimensionality, Schweitzer & Seidmann (1985) were the first to propose an approximation of the value function by a linear combination of multiple basis functions. For the MDP introduced in this chapter, the value function can be approximated by n basis functions in the following way

$$V_t(s) \approx \sum_{i=1}^{n} \alpha_{t,i} h_i(s) \quad \forall s \in S, t = T, ..., 0, \tag{3.19}$$

with *basis functions* $h_i(s)$ and *approximation parameters* $\alpha_{t,i}$ which weight the i-th basis function at time t. Note that n is chosen so that $n < S^{max}$ with S^{max} as the number of possible states. If n was equal to S^{max}, the approximation would be as complex as the original value function.

Plugging approximation (3.19) into (**P0**) yields

$$(\mathbf{P}) \quad \min_{\alpha} \sum_{s \in S} \sum_{i=1}^{n} \alpha_{\tau,i} h_i(s) \tag{3.20}$$

$$\text{s.t.} \quad \sum_{i=1}^{n} \alpha_{t,i} h_i(s) \geq r_t(s, a) + \sum_{s' \in S} p_t(s, a, s') \sum_{i=1}^{n} \alpha_{t-1,i} h_i(s')$$

$$\forall s \in S, a \in A(s), t = \tau, ..., 1 \tag{3.21}$$

$$\alpha_{t,i} \in \mathbb{R} \quad \forall t = \tau, ..., 1, i = 1, ..., n, \tag{3.22}$$

with given $\alpha_{0,i}$, for all $i = 1, ..., n$ approximating the terminal reward function.

Note that (**P**) is feasible if one of the basis functions is a constant function (Schweitzer & Seidmann, 1985). For example, if $h_1(s) = 1$ for all $s \in S$, a feasible solution is

$$\alpha_{1,1} = \max_{s \in S, a \in A(s)} \left\{ r_1(s,a) + \sum_{s' \in S} p_1(s,a,s') \sum_{i=1}^{n} \alpha_{0,i} h_i(s') \right\},$$

$$\alpha_{t,1} = \max_{s \in S, a \in A(s)} \left\{ r_t(s,a) + \sum_{s' \in S} p_t(s,a,s') \alpha_{t-1,1} \right\} \quad \forall t = \tau, ..., 2,$$

$$\alpha_{t,i} = 0 \quad \forall i \neq 1, t = \tau, ..., 1.$$

Further, the objective function in (3.20) is bounded below: In Proposition 3.5, we showed that any feasible solution to (**P0**) is an upper bound on the optimal objective value in (3.2). Since (**P**) provides a feasible solution to (**P0**), it follows that any feasible solution to (**P**) provides an upper bound on the optimal objective.

Feasibility in combination with boundedness yields that (**P**) and its dual (which is outlined below) have finite optima. Further, note that we reduced (**P0**), which features $S^{max} \times \tau$ decision variables, to a problem with $n \times \tau$ decision variables. Depending on the size of n, this makes the problem tractable.

The dual formulation is usually computationally preferable since it has fewer constraints than the primal formulation (Schweitzer & Seidmann, 1985). The dual of (**P**) is

$$(\mathbf{D}) \quad \max_{X} \sum_{1 \leq t \leq \tau, s \in S, a \in A(s)} X_{t,s,a} r_t(s,a) \tag{3.23}$$

$$\text{s.t.} \quad \sum_{s \in S, a \in A(s)} X_{t,s,a} h_i(s)$$

$$= \begin{cases} \sum_{s \in S} h_i(s) & t = \tau, i = 1, ..., n \\ \sum_{s \in S, a \in A(s)} X_{t+1,s,a} \sum_{s' \in S} p_{t+1}(s,a,s') h_i(s') & 1 \leq t < \tau, i = 1, ..., n \end{cases}$$

$$\tag{3.24}$$

$$X_{t,s,a} \geq 0 \quad t = \tau, ..., 1, s \in S, a \in A(s). \tag{3.25}$$

An important relation between primal and dual optimal solutions is given by the *complementary slackness conditions*, which we will use later to prove structural properties. These conditions are outlined next for the above introduced primal and dual formulation (for a proof, see Bertsimas & Tsitsiklis, 1997, pp. 151-152).

Theorem 3.2. *Let α and X be feasible solutions to the primal and the dual problem, respectively. α and X are optimal solutions for the two respective problems if and only if*

(i) $X_{t,s,a} \left[\sum_{i=1}^{n} \alpha_{t,i} h_i(s) - r_t(s,a) - \sum_{s' \in S} p_t(s,a,s') \sum_{i=1}^{n} \alpha_{t-1,i} h_i(s') \right] = 0$

$\forall 1 \leq t \leq \tau, s \in S, a \in A(s),$

(ii) $\alpha_{t,i} \left[\sum_{s \in S} h_i(s) - \sum_{s \in S, a \in A(s)} X_{t,s,a} h_i(s) \right] = 0 \quad \forall t = \tau, i = 1, ..., n,$

(iii) $\alpha_{t,i} \left[\sum_{s \in S, a \in A(s)} X_{t+1,s,a} \sum_{s' \in S} p_{t+1}(s,a,s') h_i(s') \right.$

$\left. - \sum_{s \in S, a \in A(s)} X_{t,s,a} h_i(s) \right] = 0 \quad \forall 1 \leq t < \tau, i = 1, ..., n.$

The first condition ensures that the dual variable $X_{t,s,a}$ is zero unless the corresponding constraint of the primal problem is active. We say that a constraint is active if its left hand side equals its right hand side. Bertsimas & Tsitsiklis (1997) give an intuitive explanation of such a condition: If a constraint is not active at an optimal solution, it can be removed from the problem without affecting the objective value. Thus, there is no point in associating a non-negative shadow price with such a constraint, and hence the dual variable $X_{t,s,a}$ will be zero. Note that the second and the third condition are automatically satisfied by every feasible solution to (**D**).

In summary, the linear programming approach to approximate dynamic programming gives an upper bound on the maximum expected reward on the one hand and parameters approximating the value function on the other hand. These parameters can be used to create heuristic decision rules; for instance, a heuristic decision rule is obtained by substituting the value function for the approximation in the original decision rule. We will follow this approach in the next chapters.

CHAPTER 4

Single-Leg Cargo Capacity Control

In this chapter, we propose and analyze single-leg capacity control models by means of the methodology that was introduced in the previous chapter. A basic capacity control model for carriers operating flights on single legs is outlined in Section 4.1. The shortcoming of this model is the fact that its optimal policy does not feature a monotone structure and is therefore not comprehensible. A further consequence of the lack of structure is that, for large problems, the model is computationally intractable. Therefore, we propose in Section 4.2 two particular capacity control models which feature an optimal simply structured control policy. These models make specific assumptions regarding the market demand and the options of dealing with requests. In Section 4.3, we suggest several heuristics that can be applied even if these specific assumption are not fulfilled. Our heuristics provide decision rules that are easy to obtain and can thus be used, even for large problems, to determine a solution to the basic model. In the same section, we provide two bounds on the maximum expected revenue. Section 4.4 demonstrates, by means of numerical experiments, how well the heuristics perform. Most of the ideas in this chapter are based on Hoffmann (2013b).

4.1 Basic Capacity Control Model

We consider a carrier that operates flights on single legs and does not offer connecting flights. Consequently, capacity on each leg is controlled independently of any other leg. An aircraft on a particular leg has a remaining weight capacity $c_w \in C_w = \{0, 1, ..., \mathfrak{C}_w\}$ and volume capacity $c_v \in C_v = \{0, 1, ..., \mathfrak{C}_v\}$. We let $\mathfrak{C}_w$ and $\mathfrak{C}_v$ denote the aircraft's deterministic total weight and volume capacity, respectively. Note that the term 'capacity' in this context means capacity available on the spot market (i.e. total capacity minus capacity sold through long-term contracts). Over a booking horizon of T time periods, the carrier may receive in each period a short-term booking request for a particular *shipment class* $i \in I = \{0, ..., m\}$. A shipment class is a combination of a shipment category, which has a specific weight and volume requirement, and a particular per unit contribution margin. Thus, each shipment class is characterized by its weight and volume requirement $w_i \in \mathbb{N}_0$ and $v_i \in \mathbb{N}_0$, respectively, and its per unit contribution margin $\varphi_i \geq 0$ (which we hereafter refer to as revenue despite abusing the terminology). Note that a difference in revenue may occur due to special treatment like express shipping, cooling, or special care for hazardous goods. Class $i = 0$ represents the event of no arriving request, where we define $w_0 = 0$, $v_0 = 0$, and $\varphi_0 = 0$. As is common in a revenue management context, we count time backwards with time period T denoting the beginning of the booking process and $t = 0$ representing the departure of the aircraft. At each time $t = T, ..., 0$, the probability of an arriving request for a shipment class i is denoted by $q_{t,i} \geq 0$. The probability that no request arrives is given by $q_{t,0} = 1 - \sum_{i=1}^{m} q_{t,i} \geq 0$. We further define $q_{0,0} = 1$ and $q_{0,i} = 0$ for $i = 1, ..., m$. This means, no request arrives at $t = 0$. We assume that the arrival process follows a Poisson process, which we approximate by a Bernoulli experiment at each discrete time t. Thus, the probability for an arriving request at time t is $\sum_{i=1}^{m} q_{t,i}$. Choosing T sufficiently large ensures that the probability of more than one arrival per time period can be neglected. We further assume that the demand for a particular shipment class is independent of, first, the demand for all other classes, and second, the availability of other classes. Another assumption is that neither cancellations nor no-shows occur. Hence, overbooking is not necessary. Further, customers are assumed to be myopic, and thus strategic behavior is not accounted for.

In each period, in which a request is observed, the decision maker has to decide if the incoming request is accepted or rejected. We assume that at the time the decision is made, the weight and volume requirement of the shipment class is known. Thus, acceptance of a request gives a revenue $\varphi_i \max\{w_i, v_i/\vartheta\}$, where ϑ denotes a constant representing the ratio of volume to weight of a standard shipment (usually 6000 cm^3/kg). The expression $\max\{w_i, v_i/\vartheta\}$ is referred to as chargeable weight and v_i/ϑ as dimensional weight. Rejected demand is lost.

The risk-neutral decision maker faces the problem of whether to generate revenue by accepting a request or saving capacity for later requests that might generate higher revenue. The objective is to identify an optimal control policy that maximizes the total expected revenue over the entire booking horizon. This can be reduced to solving the optimality equation of the following finite-horizon MDP $(T, S, E, A, p_t, r_t, V_0)$ with:

(i) *Planning horizon* $T \in \mathbb{N}_0$, indexed by t.

(ii) *State space* $S \times E = (C_w \times C_v) \times I$.
The state space comprises remaining weight and volume as system states and the requested shipment class as an environmental state.

(iii) *Action space* $A \in \{0, 1\}$ indicates whether a request is denied or accepted. The set of *admissible actions* is defined as
$$A(c_w, c_v, i) := \begin{cases} \{0, 1\} & c_w \geq w_i, c_v \geq v_i, i \in I \\ \{0\} & \text{otherwise.} \end{cases}$$

(iv) *Transition law* $p_t(c_w, c_v, i, a, c_w - aw_i, c_v - av_i, i') = q_{t-1, i'}$
for all $t = T, ..., 1$, $c_w \in C_w$, $c_v \in C_v$, $i, i' \in I$, and $a \in A(c_w, c_v, i)$. Note that the transition probability is independent of the current state and action. It only represents the probability of a booking request for class i' arriving at time $t - 1$.

63

(v) *One-stage reward function* $r_t(c_w, c_v, i, a) = a\varphi_i \max\{w_i, v_i/\vartheta\} =: a\rho_i$ for all $t = T, \dots, 1$, $c_w \in C_w$, $c_v \in C_v$, $i \in I$, and $a \in A(c_w, c_v, i)$.

(vi) *Terminal reward function* $V_0 \equiv 0$

We let the terminal reward be zero since we do not account for overbooking in this model.

The maximum expected revenue at time $t = T, \dots, 1$ given remaining capacity $c_w \in C_w, c_v \in C_v$ and a request for shipment class $i \in I$ is the unique solution to the optimality equation

$$V_t(c_w, c_v, i) = \max_{a \in A(c_w, c_v, i)} \left\{ a\rho_i + \sum_{i'=0}^{m} q_{t-1, i'} V_{t-1}(c_w - aw_i, c_v - av_i, i') \right\}.$$
(4.1)

For an arbitrary real-valued function u on $C_w \times C_v \times I$, we define the operator H as

$$H_t u(c_w, c_v) := \sum_{i=0}^{m} q_{t,i} u(c_w, c_v, i) \quad \forall t = T, \dots, 0.$$

Accordingly, we can rewrite (4.1) as:

$$V_t(c_w, c_v, i) = \max_{a \in A(c_w, c_v, i)} \{ a\rho_i + H_{t-1} V_{t-1}(c_w - aw_i, c_v - av_i) \}. \quad (4.2)$$

The observable-disturbance form (cf. Section 3.1.2) of (4.2) is

$$H_t V_t(c_w, c_v) = \sum_{i=0}^{m} q_{t,i} \max_{a \in A(c_w, c_v, i)} \{ a\rho_i + H_{t-1} V_{t-1}(c_w - aw_i, c_v - av_i) \}.$$
(4.3)

We will use the maximum expected revenue determined by the optimality equation in observable-disturbance form later in our numerical experiments. For the following analysis of the decision model, we consider the form given in (4.2).

If a request arrives and sufficient capacity is available (i.e. $c_w \geq w_i$ and $c_v \geq v_i$), we can write (4.2) as

$$V_t(c_w, c_v, i) = \max\{\rho_i + H_{t-1}V_{t-1}(c_w - w_i, c_v - v_i), H_{t-1}V_{t-1}(c_w, c_v)\}.$$

If a booking request for shipment class i is accepted at time t, the expected revenue is $\rho_i + H_{t-1}V_{t-1}(c_w - w_i, c_v - v_i)$. If the request is rejected, the expected revenue is $H_{t-1}V_{t-1}(c_w, c_v)$. Accordingly, the optimal decision rule in t given a request for shipment class $i \in I$ is

$$f_t^*(c_w, c_v, i) = \begin{cases} 1 & \rho_i \geq H_{t-1}V_{t-1}(c_w, c_v) - H_{t-1}V_{t-1}(c_w - w_i, c_v - v_i), \\ & c_w \geq w_i, c_v \geq v_i \\ 0 & \text{otherwise.} \end{cases}$$

$$(4.4)$$

That means, a request is accepted if sufficient capacity is remaining and if revenue ρ_i is greater than the opportunity cost of the amount of weight and volume that is required by the requested shipment class. For the ease of notation, we define opportunity cost $\delta_{t-1}(c_w, c_v, i) := H_{t-1}V_{t-1}(c_w, c_v) - H_{t-1}V_{t-1}(c_w - w_i, c_v - v_i)$.

In order to determine optimal actions at time t, all values $H_{t-1}V_{t-1}(c_w, c_v)$ for $c_w \in C_w$ and $c_v \in C_v$ need to be computed. This is the major drawback of this model because determining optimal actions for real world problems (e.g. a freighter having a capacity of 590 m^3 and 92,000 kg) is computationally intractable. One way to reduce computational load is to identify monotone policies (cf. Section 3.1.1). In passenger revenue management, a well-known approach is to explore whether opportunity cost is monotone in capacity or time. If this is proven to be true, the optimal control policy follows a control limit policy that indicates when to switch from accepting to rejecting a request. However, as is shown next, opportunity cost in the basic cargo capacity control model is neither monotone in capacity nor in time.

Non-Monotone Behavior

Proposition 4.1. *For $(c_w, c_v, i) \in C_w \times C_v \times I$ and $t = T-1, ..., 0$, $\delta_t(c_w, c_v, i)$ is not monotone in c_w and neither in c_v.*

The following counterexample for monotonicity of opportunity cost in weight shows that the proposition holds. An analog example for non-monotone behavior in volume can be easily constructed.

Example 4.1. Consider an aircraft with a remaining capacity of 5 weight and 6 volume units ($c_w = 5, c_v = 6$). In the last two decision periods, requests for two different shipment classes may arrive: Shipment class 1 requires 5 weight and 3 volume units ($w_1 = 5, v_1 = 3$) and gives a revenue $\varphi_1 = 1.0$, whereas shipment class 2 requires 6 weight and 3 volume units ($w_2 = 6, v_2 = 3$) and gives a revenue $\varphi_2 = 1.2$. The probability of a request for class 1 and 2 is $q_{t,1} = 0.1$ and $q_{t,2} = 0.9$, respectively, for $t \in \{1, 2\}$. For the sake of simplicity, we let $\vartheta = 1$. Now assume that in period 2 a request for shipment class 1 arrives (with $\rho_1 = 5$), and the decision maker has to decide whether to accept or to reject the request. For a remaining capacity of $c_w = 5$ and $c_v = 6$, the request should be *accepted* since $\rho_1 > \delta_1(5, 6, 1) = q_{1,1}\rho_1 = 0.5$. If the remaining capacity was $c_w = 8$ and $c_v = 6$, the request should be *rejected* since the opportunity cost for accepting it ($\delta_1(8, 6, 1) = q_{1,1}\rho_1 + q_{1,2}\rho_2 = 6.98$) is greater than the revenue that could be generated at $t = 2$. For a remaining capacity of $c_w = 11$ and $c_v = 6$, the request should be *accepted* because $\rho_1 > \delta_1(11, 6, 1) = 0$. This example demonstrates that as remaining weight increases, the optimal action changes from accepting to rejecting and back to accepting the request. The reasons is that opportunity cost first increases and then decreases. Figure 4.1 shows the non-monotone behavior of opportunity cost in weight for this example.

This phenomenon occurs because of two reasons: First, requests featuring different sizes compete for multiple and scarce resources. And second, requests have to be entirely accepted or denied. If resources are plentiful ($c_w = 11$), competition between different requests does not exist since accepting a class-1 request would leave sufficient capacity for accommodating a request for either

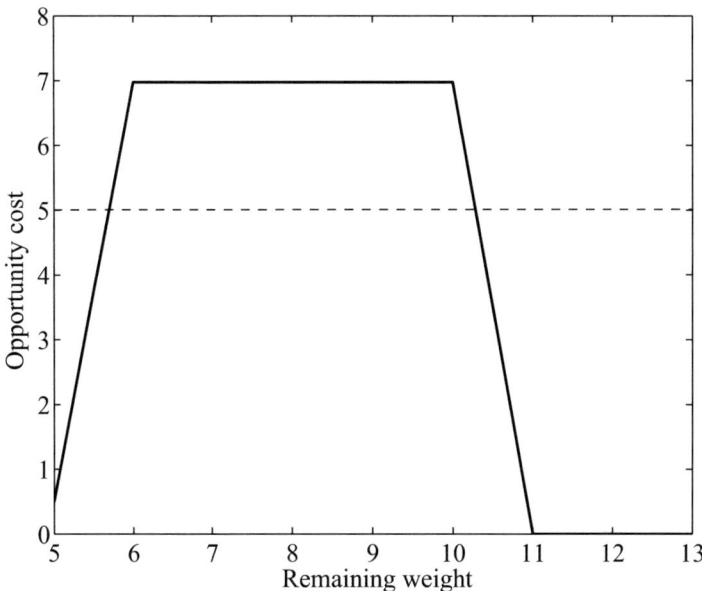

Figure 4.1: Non-monotone behavior of opportunity cost in weight

class 1 or class 2 in period 1. Thus, a class-1 request should be accepted. As less weight remains ($c_w = 8$), competition is created, and a class-1 request should be denied because accepting it would lower available capacity, so that a larger high-value request could not be accepted in period 1. As even less capacity is available ($c_w = 5$), competition vanishes. Rejecting a class-1 request is then pointless since it would not yield sufficient capacity for accepting a class-2 request during the remaining periods. Thus, the request should be accepted. Generally speaking, the higher the probability of a large high-value request arriving at the end of a booking period ($q_{1,2}$ in this example), the more likely is a situation with non-monotone opportunity cost.

Proposition 4.2. *For* $(c_w, c_v, i) \in C_w \times C_v \times I$, $\delta_t(c_w, c_v, i)$ *is not monotone in time t.*

The following example will demonstrate the proposition's validity.

Example 4.2. Consider an aircraft with a remaining capacity of 10 weight and 6 volume units ($c_w = 10, c_v = 6$). The same shipment classes as in the previous example may be requested, i.e. ($w_1 = 5, v_1 = 3$) with $\varphi_1 = 1.0$ and ($w_2 = 6, v_2 = 3$) with $\varphi_2 = 1.2$. We again assume that $\vartheta = 1$. The arrival probabilities are now given by $q_{t,1} = 0.3$ and $q_{t,2} = 0.7$ for all $t = T, ..., 1$. We consider an observed request for shipment class 1 with $\rho_1 = 5$. In $t = 1$, the request is *accepted* since $\rho_1 > \delta_0(10, 6, 1) = 0$. In $t = 2$, the request is *denied* because the revenue which would be generated through acceptance is lower than the opportunity cost associated with class 1, i.e. $\delta_1(10, 6, 1) = q_{1,2}\rho_2 = 5.04$. The decision changes again in $t = 3$, where the request is *accepted* since $\rho_1 > \delta_2(10, 6, 1)$ with $\delta_2(10, 6, 1) = q_{2,1}(q_{1,1}\rho_1 + q_{1,2}\rho_2) + q_{2,2}\rho_2 - q_{2,1}\rho_1 - q_{2,2}q_{1,1}\rho_1 = 4.452$. Accordingly, the opportunity cost is not monotone in time in this example, and thus a monotone policy based on time is not optimal. Figure 4.2 displays the opportunity cost's non-monotone behavior in time.

This example shows that a class-1 request should be accepted very close to departure (period 1) as this is the last opportunity to generate revenue. Further, the request should also be accepted earlier in the booking process (period 3)

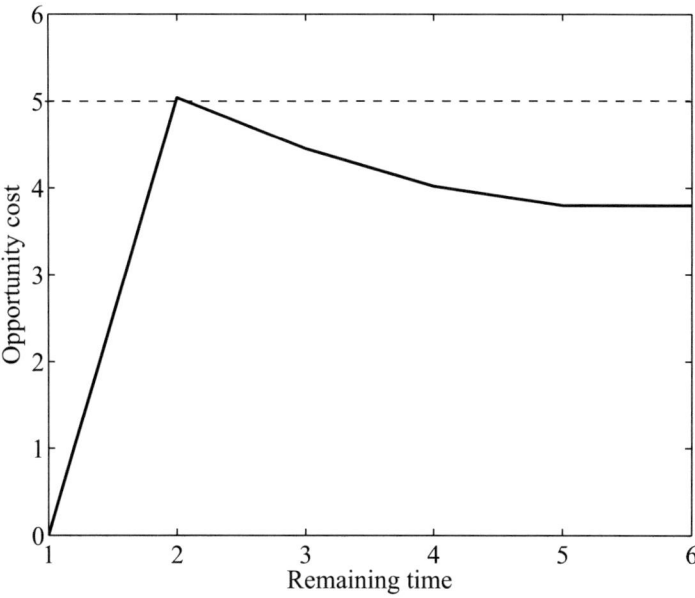

Figure 4.2: Non-monotone behavior of opportunity cost in time

when it is likely that another class-1 request might occur, and accepting two class-1 requests would generate a higher revenue than accepting a single class-2 request. However, as departure comes closer (period 2), an arrival of another class-1 request becomes less likely. Thus, the decision maker rejects the request in order to save capacity for a more likely arriving class-2 request. This suggests that a non-monotone behavior occurs if the probability and revenue of a class-1 request is neither too small nor too large. If the arrival probability was too large, it would still be profitable to accept a class-1 request closer to departure (period 2). If the probability was too small, it would be rejected in any period except just before departure. Transferring the results of Maddah et al. (2010) to our example, a non-monotone behavior in time is observed if the following relationship holds (assuming stationary request probabilities q_i):

$$\frac{1 + q_1}{1 + q_1 + q_1 q_2 - q_1^2} q_2 \rho_2 < \rho_1 < q_2 \rho_2.$$

The reason for the non-monotone behavior in time and remaining capacity is related to the difficulties caused by accepting several units at once. Numerous authors remark that, if requests comprising multiple units must be entirely accepted (usually referred to as batch arrivals), important monotonicity structures do not exist. This implies that a monotone policy may not be optimal. Models considering requests with multiple units can be found in Deb & Serfozo (1973), Weiss (1979), Lee & Hersh (1993), Kleywegt & Papastavrou (2001), Walczak (2001), Brumelle & Walczak (2003), and Walczak (2006). Papastavrou et al. (1996) provide some properties of the arrival probabilities of batches in the one-dimensional case so that opportunity cost is monotone in time and capacity.

We now turn to capacity control models that feature monotone opportunity costs. In the following section, we propose two models that are very similar to the basic control model but make some assumptions which yield an optimal monotone policy.

4.2 Capacity Control Models featuring Structured Control Policies

On the one hand, we highlighted in Section 3.1.1 the importance of structured decision rules. On the other hand, we have shown in the previous section that the optimal policy of the cargo capacity control problem is neither monotone in capacity nor in time. Therefore, our motivation in this section is to develop decision models that feature a simply structured optimal acceptance policy.

We first present a model which we hereafter refer to as *M1*. One underlying idea of this decision model is to consider cargo capacity as one-dimensional, i.e. decisions are made based on *either* available volume *or* weight. This approach is reasonable if the expected ratio of capacity to demand is much lower for one capacity dimension than for the other. For instance, if mainly flowers are carried on a leg, the aircraft is very likely to have sufficient weight capacity but too little volume capacity. Thus, the volume capacity-demand ratio is much lower than the weight capacity-demand ratio. In this situation, the remaining weight is not important for making acceptance decisions and thus can be neglected. Based on past and forecasted demand data on a leg, the decision maker can choose which cargo dimension to consider as the model's state space. Then, capacity requirement of all shipment classes is also considered as one-dimensional. A further characteristic of M1 is that it allows for requests to be partially accepted. This assumption may contradict some airlines' business practices. However, there are two reasons why such an approach might be still reasonable. First, a revenue manager generally has the option to sell only a part of the actual requested capacity. Second, freight forwarders often use only a part of the originally requested capacity without being penalized (Luo et al., 2009). By accepting only a part of a request, the gap between requested and eventually used capacity might be decreased, and thus more capacity would be available for other requests.

In M1, we again consider a carrier that operates flights on single legs. Now an aircraft on a particular leg has a remaining cargo capacity $c \in C = \{0, ..., \mathfrak{C}\}$, and we let $\mathfrak{C}$ denote the aircraft's total capacity. Further, each shipment class that may be requested is characterized by its capacity requirement $\gamma_i \in \mathbb{N}_0$ and its per unit revenue $\varphi_i \geq 0$. Similarly as in the basic model, we define $\gamma_0 = 0$ and $\varphi_0 = 0$. All other notations are equal to the notation of the basic model. Further, except allowing for partial acceptance, we make the same assumptions as in the basic model.

Again, our objective is to identify an optimal control policy that maximizes the expected revenue. This can be achieved by solving the optimality equations of an MDP $(T, S, E, A, p_t, r_t, V_0^{M1})$ with:

(i) *Planning horizon* $T \in \mathbb{N}_0$.

(ii) *State space* $S \times E = C \times I$.

(iii) *Action space* $A \subset \mathbb{N}_0$ with $a \in A$ as the number of accepted capacity units. The set of admissible actions is $A(c, i) := \{0, ..., \min\{\gamma_i, c\}\}$ for all $c \in C$ and $i \in I$.

  If the capacity requirement γ_i of the requested shipment class i is lower than the remaining capacity c, the entire request or any part of it can be accepted. However, if the inventory level is lower than the capacity requirement, the number of accepted capacity units must not exceed remaining capacity.

(iv) *Transition law* $p_t(c, i, a, c - a, i') = q_{t-1,i'}$
  for all $t = T, ..., 1$, $c \in C$, $i, i' \in I$, and $a \in A(c, i)$.

(v) *One-stage reward function* $r_t(c, i, a) = a\varphi_i$
  for all $t = T, ..., 1$, $c \in C$, $i \in I$, and $a \in A(c, i)$.

(vi) *Terminal reward function* $V_0^{M1} \equiv 0$.

The maximum expected revenue at time $t = T, ..., 1$ given remaining capacity $c \in C$ and a request for shipment class $i \in I$ is the unique solution to the optimality equation

$$V_t^{M1}(c, i) = \max_{a \in A(c,i)} \left\{ a\varphi_i + \sum_{i'=0}^{m} q_{t-1,i'} V_{t-1}^{M1}(c - a, i') \right\}. \qquad (4.5)$$

Using the operator $\hat{H}_t u(c) := \sum_{i=0}^{m} q_{t,i} u(c, i)$ for an arbitrary real-valued function u on $C \times I$, we can restate (4.5) as

$$V_t^{M1}(c, i) = \max_{a \in A(c,i)} \left\{ a\varphi_i + \hat{H}_{t-1} V_{t-1}^{M1}(c - a) \right\}.$$

Below, we explore the structural properties of M1. Before a statement on the characteristics of the optimal policy can be given, some necessary properties need to be provided.

Lemma 4.1. $V_t^{M1}(c, i)$ *is non-decreasing in c for all $i \in I$ and $t = T, ..., 0$.*

Proof. The proof follows by induction on t. Since $V_0^{M1} \equiv 0$, the assertion holds for $t = 0$. Now assume that $V_t^{M1}(c, i)$ is non-decreasing in c for $t \geq 0$ and for all $i \in I$. Further, let $a_i^* = f_{t+1}^*(c - 1, i)$ (with $c > 0$), i.e. a_i^* is the optimal action at $t + 1$ if $c - 1$ capacity units are remaining and class i is requested. Since $a_i^* \in A(c - 1, i)$, it follows that $a_i^* \in A(c, i)$. Now we prove the supposition for $t + 1$. For fixed $c > 0$ and $i \in I$, we have

$$
\begin{aligned}
&V_{t+1}^{M1}(c, i) - V_{t+1}^{M1}(c - 1, i) \\
&= \max_{a \in A(c,i)} \{a\varphi_i + \hat{H}_t V_t^{M1}(c - a)\} - \max_{a \in A(c-1,i)} \{a\varphi_i + \hat{H}_t V_t^{M1}(c - 1 - a)\} \\
&\geq \hat{H}_t V_t^{M1}(c - a_i^*) - \hat{H}_t V_t^{M1}(c - 1 - a_i^*) \\
&\geq 0.
\end{aligned}
$$

The last step follows from the induction assumption and from the fact that a convex combination of non-decreasing functions is non-decreasing as well. $\quad\square$

Lemma 4.2. *Let $h : \mathbb{N}_0 \to \mathbb{R}$ be defined by*

$$h(s) := \max_{a \in A(s)} \{r(a) + \tilde{h}(s - a)\}, \tag{4.6}$$

with

- $\tilde{h} : \mathbb{N}_0 \to \mathbb{R}$ *is concave*

- $r : \mathbb{N}_0 \to \mathbb{R}$ *is concave*

- $A(s) = \{a \in \mathbb{N}_0 \mid n_1(s) \le a \le n_2(s)\}, \quad s \in \mathbb{N}_0$

- n_1 *is non-decreasing and convex*

- n_2 *is non-decreasing and concave*

- $n_2(s+1) \le n_2(s) + 1, \quad s \in \mathbb{N}_0.$

Let further $f(s)$, $s \in \mathbb{N}_0$, be the action maximizing the right hand side of (4.6). Then, we have

(i) $f(s) \le f(s+1) \le f(s) + 1$ and

(ii) $h(s)$ is concave in s.

Proof. See Appendix A. □

Lemma 4.3. $V_t^{M1}(c, i)$ *is non-decreasing and concave in c for all $i \in I$ and $t = T, ..., 0$.*

Proof. The proof follows by induction on t. Since $V_0^{M1} \equiv 0$, $V_0^{M1}(c, i)$ is concave in c, and thus the assertion holds for $t = 0$. Now assume $V_t^{M1}(c, i)$ is concave in c for all $i \in I$ and some $t \ge 0$. At $t + 1$, we have

$$V_{t+1}^{M1}(c, i) = \max_{a \in A(c,i)} \{a\varphi_i + \hat{H}_t V_t^{M1}(c - a)\}. \tag{4.7}$$

The induction assumption in combination with the fact that a convex combination of concave functions is also concave yields that $\hat{H}_t V_t^{M1}(c - a)$ is concave in c. Thus, we can apply Lemma 4.2 to (4.7), which yields concavity of $V_{t+1}^{M1}(c)$ in c. Monotonicity of $V_t^{M1}(c, i)$ in c was already shown in Lemma 4.1, which completes the proof. □

We now have the necessary and sufficient conditions for ensuring that the optimal policy of M1 follows a monotone policy.

Theorem 4.1. *M1's optimal policy is a control limit policy π^* with decision rules*

$$f_t^*(c,i) = \begin{cases} 0 & c \leq c^*(t,i) \\ \min\{\gamma_i, c - c^*(t,i)\} & c > c^*(t,i). \end{cases}$$

We define $c^*(t,i) = \max\left\{c > 0 : \varphi_i < \hat{H}_{t-1}V_{t-1}^{M1}(c) - \hat{H}_{t-1}V_{t-1}^{M1}(c-1)\right\}$ as control limits. We further define $c^*(t,i) = 0$ if the set is empty.

Proof. Since $V_t^{M1}(c,i)$ is concave in c for all $t = T, ..., 0$, $\hat{H}_t V_t^{M1}(c)$ is also concave in c as a convex combination of concave functions. Concavity implies that

$$\hat{H}_{t-1}V_{t-1}^{M1}(c) - \hat{H}_{t-1}V_{t-1}^{M1}(c-1) \leq \hat{H}_{t-1}V_{t-1}^{M1}(c-1) - \hat{H}_{t-1}V_{t-1}^{M1}(c-2).$$

That means, $\hat{H}_{t-1}V_{t-1}^{M1}(c) - \hat{H}_{t-1}V_{t-1}^{M1}(c-1)$ is non-increasing in c which ensures the existence of the control limits

$$c^*(t,i) = \max\{c > 0 : \varphi_i < \hat{H}_{t-1}V_{t-1}^{M1}(c) - \hat{H}_{t-1}V_{t-1}^{M1}(c-1)\}. \qquad (4.8)$$

Now fix $c \in C$, $i \in I$, $t > 0$, and let $d \in \mathbb{N}_0$. Let a be the largest $a \in A(c,i)$ that maximizes the right hand side of (4.5) in t. Then, we have

$$a\varphi_i + \hat{H}_{t-1}V_{t-1}^{M1}(c-a) \geq d\varphi_i + \hat{H}_{t-1}V_{t-1}^{M1}(c-d) \text{ for } a > d \geq 0, \text{ and}$$
$$a\varphi_i + \hat{H}_{t-1}V_{t-1}^{M1}(c-a) > d\varphi_i + \hat{H}_{t-1}V_{t-1}^{M1}(c-d) \text{ for } a < d \leq \min\{\gamma_i, c\}.$$

Since $\hat{H}_{t-1}V_{t-1}^{M1}(c)$ is concave in c, we can rewrite the above inequalities as

$$a\varphi_i + \hat{H}_{t-1}V_{t-1}^{M1}(c-a) \geq (a-1)\varphi_i + \hat{H}_{t-1}V_{t-1}^{M1}(c-a+1),$$
$$a\varphi_i + \hat{H}_{t-1}V_{t-1}^{M1}(c-a) > (a+1)\varphi_i + \hat{H}_{t-1}V_{t-1}^{M1}(c-a-1),$$

where the expression reduces to the first (second) equation if $a = \min\{\gamma_i, c\}$ ($a = 0$). This can be rearranged as

$$\varphi_i \geq \hat{H}_{t-1} V_{t-1}^{M1}(c - a + 1) - \hat{H}_{t-1} V_{t-1}^{M1}(c - a), \tag{4.9}$$

$$\varphi_i < \hat{H}_{t-1} V_{t-1}^{M1}(c - a) - \hat{H}_{t-1} V_{t-1}^{M1}(c - a - 1). \tag{4.10}$$

Applying (4.8) to the above inequalities yields that $c^*(t, i) = c - a$. For $c \leq c^*(t, i)$, it follows that the optimal action is $a = 0$. For all $c > c^*(t, i)$, we have $a = c - c^*(t, i)$. The optimal action is only limited by the request size γ_i. Thus, we have $a = \min\{\gamma_i, c - c^*(t, i)\}$ if $c > c^*(t, i)$. $\qquad\square$

The optimal policy of M1 reveals that smaller portions of requests should be accepted as remaining capacity decreases (assuming constant time). This result is intuitive since a part of the capacity should be saved for later requests that may have a higher value. Note that $c^*(t, i)$ has a similar interpretation as *time-dependent protection levels*, which are used as control instruments in passenger revenue management: A control limit $c^*(t, i)$ tells a revenue manager that given a request in time period t for a shipment class $i \in I$, an amount of $c^*(t, i)$ capacity units should be protected for later bookings.

A further characteristic of M1 is that the control limits can be structured with respect to time.

Proposition 4.3. *The control limits $c^*(t, i)$ are non-decreasing in t for $i \in I$.*

Proof. In order to prove this proposition, we have to show that opportunity cost $\hat{H}_t V_t^{M1}(c) - \hat{H}_t V_t^{M1}(c - 1)$ is non-decreasing in time (for $c > 0$). We fix $c \in C$ with $c > 0$ as well as $t > 0$ and define $a_i^* = f_t^*(c - 1, i)$ as the optimal action depending on $i \in I$ at time t if $c - 1$ capacity units are remaining. Note that for all $i \in I$ we have $a_i^* \in A(c - 1, i)$ and $a_i^* \in A(c, i)$. Then, it follows

$$\Delta_c \hat{H}_t V_t^{M1}(c) := \hat{H}_t V_t^{M1}(c) - \hat{H}_t V_t^{M1}(c - 1)$$

$$= \sum_{i \in I} q_{t,i} \left[\max_{a \in A(c,i)} \left\{ a\varphi_i + \hat{H}_{t-1} V_{t-1}^{M1}(c - a) \right\} \right.$$

$$- \max_{a \in A(c-1,i)} \left\{ a\varphi_i + \hat{H}_{t-1} V_{t-1}^{M1}(c-1-a) \right\} \Bigg]$$

$$\geq \sum_{i \in I} q_{t,i} \left[\hat{H}_{t-1} V_{t-1}^{M1}(c - a_i^*) - \hat{H}_{t-1} V_{t-1}^{M1}(c - 1 - a_i^*) \right]$$

$$\geq \Delta_c \hat{H}_{t-1} V_{t-1}^{M1}(c).$$

The last inequality follows from concavity of $\hat{H}_{t-1} V_{t-1}^{M1}(c)$ in c. $\qquad \Box$

Since the control limits are non-increasing as departure approaches (assuming constant capacity), this result reveals that greater portions of requests should be accepted close to departure. This characteristic of M1 is reasonable since the less time is remaining until departure, the less likely is the arrival of a request which may generate revenue. Thus, a revenue manager should take advantage of remaining opportunities to sell capacity.

The following property of M1 additionally characterizes the structure of the control limits.

Proposition 4.4. *For $t = T, ..., 1$, we have $c^*(t, i_1) \leq c^*(t, i_2)$ with $\varphi_{i_1} \geq \varphi_{i_2}$ and $i_1, i_2 \in I$.*

Proof. Consider two shipment classes i_1 and i_2 with $\varphi_{i_1} \geq \varphi_{i_2}$. From Lemma 4.3 we know that $\hat{H}_{t-1} V_{t-1}^{M1}(c)$ is concave which implies that $\hat{H}_{t-1} V_{t-1}^{M1}(c) - \hat{H}_{t-1} V_{t-1}^{M1}(c-1)$ is non-increasing in c. This means that the maximum capacity level c that satisfies $\varphi_{i_1} < \hat{H}_{t-1} V_{t-1}^{M1}(c) - \hat{H}_{t-1} V_{t-1}^{M1}(c-1)$ cannot be greater than the maximum capacity level that satisfies $\varphi_{i_2} < \hat{H}_{t-1} V_{t-1}^{M1}(c) - \hat{H}_{t-1} V_{t-1}^{M1}(c-1)$. Therefore, it follows that $c^*(t, i_1) \leq c^*(t, i_2)$. $\qquad \Box$

This result's interpretation is that the higher the per unit revenue of a request, the greater is the portion of the request that should be accepted. Note that the requests' size does not affect this result since M1 allows for partial acceptance.

Since it is only necessary to compute control limits $c^*(t, i)$ in order to determine optimal actions and because the state space is one-dimensional, the computational load of M1 is reduced compared to the basic capacity control model. Furthermore, the intuitive structures offered by M1 make the acceptance policy comprehensible for revenue managers. This might yield a higher acceptance of decision support systems in practice.

Since M1 considers only one capacity dimension, a loss in accuracy occurs if neither loose cargo nor dense cargo is exclusively requested. Below, we study a further decision model which does not focus on a single resource. This model is applicable if requested shipments mainly feature the weight-volume ratio of a standard shipment.

A Decision Model for Standard Shipments

This decision model (which is hereafter referred to as *M2*) is similar to M1, which we described in the previous section. The differences to M1 are the following: First, in M2, we consider two capacity dimensions rather than one. Second, partially accepting requests is allowed, where the set of admissible actions is defined so that it is only possible to accept an equal number of capacity units of both resources. Third, we let the system state comprise remaining weight $c_w \in C_w = \{0, ..., \mathfrak{C}_w\}$ as well as dimensional weight $\tilde{c}_v \in \tilde{C}_v = \{0, ..., \lfloor \mathfrak{C}_v/\vartheta \rfloor\}$. Consequently, a decision lowers the system state by the same amount of weight and dimensional weight units. If largely standard shipments are requested, M2 will allow accepting any (integer) part of a request while exactly accounting for both capacity dimensions.

Note that the state space can be chosen arbitrarily in the way that multiples or fractions of weight and volume units can be considered. That means, if requested shipments are expected to follow a particular pattern regarding the weight-volume ratio, the state space can be chosen to represent this pattern, too.

We make the same assumptions in M2 as in the basic model except allowing for partial acceptance. The objective of M2 is to determine an optimal policy that maximizes total expected revenue. This can be modeled by means of an MDP $(T, S, E, A, p_t, r_t, V_0^{M2})$ with:

(i) *Planning horizon* $T \in \mathbb{N}_0$.

(ii) *State space* $S \times E = (C_w \times \tilde{C}_v) \times I$.

(iii) *Action space* $A \subset \mathbb{N}_0$ with $a \in A$ as the number of both accepted weight and dimensional weight units. The set of *admissible actions* is defined as $\hat{A}(c_w, \tilde{c}_v, i) := \{0, ..., \min\{\tilde{\gamma}_i, c_w, \tilde{c}_v\}\}$ for all $c_w \in C_w$ and $\tilde{c}_v \in \tilde{C}_v$ with $\tilde{\gamma}_i := \min\{w_i, v_i/\vartheta\}$.

This definition implies that any part of a request can be accepted, where the number of accepted capacity units is bounded by, first, the capacity dimension featuring the lowest inventory level (c_w or $\tilde{c}_v$), and second, the lowest capacity requirement ($\tilde{\gamma}_i$).

(iv) *Transition law* $p_t(c_w, \tilde{c}_v, i, a, c_w - a, \tilde{c}_v - a, i') = q_{t-1,i'}$
for all $t = T, ..., 1$, $c_w \in C_w$, $\tilde{c}_v \in \tilde{C}_v$, $i, i' \in I$, and $a \in \hat{A}(c_w, \tilde{c}_v, i)$.

(v) *One-stage reward function* $r_t(c_w, \tilde{c}_v, i, a) = \varphi_i a$
for all $t = T, ..., 1$, $c_w \in C_w$, $\tilde{c}_v \in \tilde{C}_v$, $i \in I$, and $a \in \hat{A}(c_w, \tilde{c}_v, i)$.

(vi) *Terminal reward function* $V_0^{M2} \equiv 0$.

The maximum expected revenue at time $t = T, ..., 1$, given remaining capacity $(c_w, \tilde{c}_v) \in C_w \times \tilde{C}_v$ and a request for shipment class $i \in I$, is the unique solution to the optimality equation

$$V_t^{M2}(c_w, \tilde{c}_v, i) = \max_{a \in \hat{A}(c_w, \tilde{c}_v, i)} \left\{ \varphi_i a + \sum_{i'=0}^{m} q_{t-1,i'} V_{t-1}^{M2}(c_w - a, \tilde{c}_v - a, i') \right\}.$$
(4.11)

Even though the system state is two-dimensional, the set of admissible actions causes M2 to simplify to M1 with a slightly different set of admissible actions.

Proposition 4.5. *For* $c_w \leq \tilde{c}_v$, *M2 is equal to M1 with optimality equation*

$$V_t^{M1}(c_w, i) = \max_{a \in A(c_w, i)} \{\varphi_i a + \hat{H}_{t-1} V_{t-1}^{M1}(c_w - a)\}$$

for $c_w \in C_w$, $i \in I$, $t = T, ..., 1$ and with $A(c_w, i) := \{0, ..., \min\{c_w, \tilde{\gamma}_i\}\}$. Further, for $c_w \geq \tilde{c}_v$, M2 is equal to M1 with

$$V_t^{M1}(\tilde{c}_v, i) = \max_{a \in A(\tilde{c}_v, i)} \{\varphi_i a + \hat{H}_{t-1} V_{t-1}^{M1}(\tilde{c}_v - a)\}$$

for $\tilde{c}_v \in \tilde{C}_v$, $i \in I$, $t = T, ..., 1$ and with $A(\tilde{c}_v, i) := \{0, ..., \min\{\tilde{c}_v, \tilde{\gamma}_i\}\}$.

Proof. If we have $c_w \leq \tilde{c}_v$, $\tilde{c}_v$ does never affect any action. Accordingly, $\hat{A}(c_w, \tilde{c}_v, i)$ reduces to $A(c_w, i) = \{0, ..., \min\{c_w, \tilde{\gamma}_i\}\}$. Furthermore, this also implies that once $c_w \leq \tilde{c}_v$, $\tilde{c}_v$ can never be lower than c_w, i.e. volume can never be the bottleneck. Therefore, only c_w must be considered as a state variable, and M2 reduces to M1 with a different set of admissible actions. The proof for the second part of the proposition follows analogously. Note that the total available capacity, $\mathfrak{C}_w$ and $\tilde{\mathfrak{C}}_v$, determines which capacity dimension can be neglected. □

Since M2 is equal to M1 with different admissible actions, its optimal policy features the same structures as the one of M1.

Theorem 4.2. *M2's optimal policy is a control limit policy π^* with decision rules,*

(i) if $c_w \leq \tilde{c}_v$,

$$f_t^*(c_w, i) = \begin{cases} 0 & c_w \leq c_w^*(t, i) \\ \min\{\tilde{\gamma}_i, c_w - c_w^*(t, i)\} & c_w > c_w^*(t, i), \end{cases}$$

with control limits $c_w^*(t, i) = \max\{c_w > 0 : \varphi_i < \hat{H}_{t-1} V_{t-1}^{M1}(c_w) - \hat{H}_{t-1} V_{t-1}^{M1}(c_w - 1)\}$ and $c_w^*(t, i) = 0$ if the set is empty.

(ii) if $\tilde{c}_v \leq c_w$,

$$f_t^*(\tilde{c}_v, i) = \begin{cases} 0 & \tilde{c}_v \leq \tilde{c}_v^*(t, i) \\ \min\{\tilde{\gamma}_i, \tilde{c}_v - \tilde{c}_v^*(t, i)\} & \tilde{c}_v > \tilde{c}_v^*(t, i), \end{cases}$$

with control limits $\tilde{c}_v^*(t, i) = \max\{\tilde{c}_v > 0 : \varphi_i < \hat{H}_{t-1}V_{t-1}^{M1}(\tilde{c}_v) - \hat{H}_{t-1}V_{t-1}^{M1}(\tilde{c}_v - 1)\}$ *and* $\tilde{c}_v^*(t, i) = 0$ *if the set is empty.*

The proof of this theorem can be done analogously to the one of Theorem 4.1 and is thus omitted.

Note that the properties in Propositions 4.3 and 4.4 also hold for the control limits outlined above. Therefore, the interpretation of all structural properties of M1 apply as well to M2. Since these structures alleviate computational load, M2 is able to solve large-scale problem instances very efficiently.

One might argue that the option to accept parts of a request contradicts the practice of several cargo carriers. If the only options are to entirely reject or to accept a request, one has to apply the basic capacity control model. As we already outlined, determining an optimal policy of a real-world problem might be computationally intractable in this case. Therefore, we propose heuristics in the next section that provide acceptance decisions which are easy to obtain.

4.3 Heuristics and Bounds

Our motivation for developing heuristics is that the basic capacity control problem suffers from the curse of dimensionality for large problems. The heuristics we propose provide control policies which are easy to obtain and have a low storage requirement. Since the maximum expected revenue cannot be determined for large problems either, we propose two different upper bounds. Comparing these bounds to the maximum expected revenue in our numerical experiments allows us to make a statement on the bounds' quality.

In this section, we propose three different heuristics. First, we outline the approach introduced by Amaruchkul et al. (2007) that just decomposes the underlying MDP into weight and volume subproblems. This heuristic is among the best for solving the single-leg cargo capacity control problem. Further, this approach provides also an upper bound on the optimal objective value. Second, we propose a new decomposition heuristic that is based on the insights gained from M1 yielding a comprehensible decision rule. Third, we describe a heuristic based

81

on a piecewise linear value function approximation. This approach provides an upper bound on the maximum expected revenue.

Heuristic based on Decomposition (HD)

This heuristic was first proposed by Amaruchkul et al. (2007) who applied it to a single-leg cargo capacity control problem which accounts for uncertain capacity requirement and overbooking. HD can also be used to determine a policy for the basic capacity control problem when overbooking and uncertain shipment capacity requirement are neglected. The heuristic's major idea is to split the two-dimensional MDP into two subproblems, one with weight as state space (indicated by superscript w), the other having volume as state space (indicated by superscript v). Since total revenue depends on both weight and volume, a one-dimensional revenue function for each capacity dimension has to be approximated in the subproblems. The revenue in each subproblem generated by accepting a request is defined as follows:

$$\rho_i^w := \varphi_i w_i$$
$$\rho_i^v := \rho_i - \varphi_i w_i.$$

Accordingly, accepting a request for class i in the weight subproblem generates a revenue ρ_i^w, which is defined as the revenue per chargeable weight unit times the weight requirement of class i. The revenue generated in the volume subproblem is equal to the difference between total revenue of i and the revenue of i in the weight subproblem. That means, accepting a request in the volume subproblem gives only revenue if dimensional weight is greater than weight. According to this definition, weight is the primary dimension, whereas volume is the supplementary dimension.

The weight subproblem is formulated as an MDP with one-dimensional system state c_w and the following optimality equation for all $c_w \in C_w$, $i \in I$, and $t = T, ..., 1$:

$$V_t^{HD,w}(c_w, i) = \max_{a \in \bar{A}(c_w, i)} \left\{ a\rho_i^w + \hat{H}_{t-1} V_{t-1}^{HD,w}(c_w - aw_i) \right\}$$

with $\bar{A}(c_w, i) := \{0\}$ if $c_w < w_i$ and $\bar{A}(c_w, i) := \{0, 1\}$ otherwise. Likewise, the volume subproblem's optimality equation with c_v as its system state can be formulated for all $c_v \in C_v$, $i \in I$, and $t = T, ..., 1$:

$$V_t^{HD,v}(c_v, i) = \max_{a \in \bar{A}(c_v, i)} \left\{ a\rho_i^v + \hat{H}_{t-1} V_{t-1}^{HD,v}(c_v - av_i) \right\}.$$

Note that we do not consider overbooking and thus let both terminal values $V_0^{HD,w}(c_w, i)$ and $V_0^{HD,v}(c_v, i)$ be equal to zero for $c_w \in C_w$, $c_v \in C_v$, and $i \in I$.

The decision rule of HD is to accept a request for shipment class $i \in I$ at time t given remaining capacity $c_w \geq w_i$ and $c_v \geq v_i$ if

$$\rho_i \geq \left[\hat{H}_{t-1} V_{t-1}^{HD,w}(c_w) - \hat{H}_{t-1} V_{t-1}^{HD,w}(c_w - w_i) \right]$$
$$+ \left[\hat{H}_{t-1} V_{t-1}^{HD,v}(c_v) - \hat{H}_{t-1} V_{t-1}^{HD,v}(c_v - v_i) \right].$$

Thus, the exact opportunity cost is approximated by the sum of the opportunity costs of the weight and the volume subproblem. We see from this result that it is necessary to compute all $\hat{H}_t V_t^{HD,w}(c_w)$ for any combination of t and c_w and all $\hat{H}_t V_t^{HD,v}(c_v)$ for any combination of t and c_v in order to obtain decision rules.

The sum of the maximum expected revenue of both subproblems gives an upper bound on the total maximum expected revenue determined in the basic capacity control model. This is stated in the following proposition (based on Amaruchkul et al., 2007).

Proposition 4.6. *For any $t = T, ..., 0$, $c_w \in C_w$, $c_v \in C_v$, and $i \in I$, we have*
$$V_t(c_w, c_v, i) \leq V_t^{HD,w}(c_w, i) + V_t^{HD,v}(c_v, i).$$

Proof. The proof follows by induction on t. At $t = 0$, we have $V_0(c_w, c_v, i) = V_0^{HD,w}(c_w, i) = V_0^{HD,v}(c_v, i) = 0$ for all $c_w \in C_w$, $c_v \in C_v$, and $i \in I$. Thus, the proposition holds for $t = 0$. Now assume the assertion holds for some $t \geq 0$.

Further, note that $\rho_i = \rho_i^w + \rho_i^v$. For $t + 1$, we then have for any $c_w \in C_w$, $c_v \in C_v$, and $i \in I$

$$V_{t+1}(c_w, c_v, i)$$

$$= \max_{a \in A(c_w, c_v, i)} \{\rho_i a + H_t V_t(c_w - aw_i, c_v - av_i)\}$$

$$= \max_{a \in A(c_w, c_v, i)} \{(\rho_i^w + \rho_i^v)a + H_t V_t(c_w - aw_i, c_v - av_i)\}$$

$$\leq \max_{a \in A(c_w, c_v, i)} \left\{ (\rho_i^w + \rho_i^v)a + \hat{H}_t V_t^{HD,w}(c_w - aw_i) + \hat{H}_t V_t^{HD,v}(c_v - av_i) \right\}$$

$$\leq \max_{a \in A(c_w, c_v, i)} \left\{ \rho_i^w a + \hat{H}_t V_t^{HD,w}(c_w - aw_i) \right\}$$

$$+ \max_{a \in A(c_w, c_v, i)} \left\{ \rho_i^v a + \hat{H}_t V_t^{HD,v}(c_v - av_i) \right\}$$

$$\leq \max_{a \in \bar{A}(c_w, i)} \left\{ \rho_i^w a + \hat{H}_t V_t^{HD,w}(c_w - aw_i) \right\}$$

$$+ \max_{a \in \bar{A}(c_v, i)} \left\{ \rho_i^v a + \hat{H}_t V_t^{HD,v}(c_v - av_i) \right\}$$

$$= V_{t+1}^{HD,w}(c_w, i) + V_{t+1}^{HD,v}(c_v, i).$$

The first inequality follows from the induction assumption and the second from subadditivity of the maximum function. The third inequality follows from the fact that $A(c_w, c_v, i) \subset \bar{A}(c_w, i)$ and $A(c_w, c_v, i) \subset \bar{A}(c_v, i)$. □

Note that this proposition is also valid if the optimality equation is written in observable-disturbance form. In this case, we define the upper bound given by the subproblems as $z_{ACG} := \hat{H}_T V_T^{HD,w}(\mathfrak{C}_w) + \hat{H}_T V_T^{HD,v}(\mathfrak{C}_v)$ (subscripts representing the initial letters of Amaruchkul, Cooper, and Gupta).

Heuristic based on Decomposition and Partial Acceptance (HDP)

This heuristic decomposes the two-dimensional MDP into two subproblems as done in HD. Moreover, the major idea is to pretend *any part* of a request can be accepted. By pretending partial acceptance, we obtain concavity of each sub-problem's value function in its capacity dimension. Note that this assumption is only made in the subproblems. The resulting heuristic control policy accepts or denies requests only in their entirety.

Decomposing the problem is associated with the question of how to assign revenue that is generated by accepting parts of a request to the weight and volume subproblem. We allocate revenues generated by accepting one capacity unit as follows:

$$\varphi_i^w := \varphi_i \tag{4.12}$$

$$\varphi_i^v := \varphi_i \frac{\left(\frac{v_i}{\vartheta} - w_i\right)}{v_i} \mathbf{1}_{\left\{\frac{v_i}{\vartheta} > w_i\right\}} = \varphi_i \left(\frac{1}{\vartheta} - \frac{w_i}{v_i}\right) \mathbf{1}_{\left\{\frac{v_i}{\vartheta} > w_i\right\}}. \tag{4.13}$$

The revenue generated by accepting one weight unit in the weight subproblem (4.12) is equal to the class i's revenue per chargeable weight unit. The revenue in the volume subproblem (4.13) is equal to the difference between the standard ratio of weight to volume and the particular ratio of the requested class times its per unit revenue. The term $\mathbf{1}_{\{B\}}$ in (4.13) is an indicator function which is equal to 1 if the expression B is true. Thus, accepting one volume unit in the volume subproblem only generates revenue if dimensional weight is greater than weight. According to this definition, weight is the primary dimension, whereas volume is the supplementary dimension. The whole expression in (4.13) can be considered as the additional revenue from accepting one volume unit of shipment class i. Consider the following example in order to get a better idea of how total revenue is partitioned and assigned to the subproblems. Accepting shipment class i with $\varphi_i = 1.2$, $w_i = 45$, and $v_i = 30$ generates a revenue $\varphi_i \max\{w_i, v_i/\vartheta\} = 60$. In the weight subproblem, the generated revenue from accepting one capacity unit is $\varphi_i^w = 1.2$. On the other hand, the generated revenue in the volume subproblem is $\varphi_i^v = 1.2(1.67 - 1.5)\mathbf{1}_{\{50>45\}} = 0.2$. That means, the sum of the revenues from accepting the entire request is $1.2 \times 45 + 0.2 \times 30 = 60$, which is equal to the total revenue. The difference is that additional revenue in the volume subproblem is only generated if dimensional weight exceeds actual weight.

The weight subproblem is a one-dimensional MDP like M1 with system state c_w. It features the following optimality equation for all $c_w \in C_w$, $i \in I$, and $t = T, ..., 1$:

$$V_t^{M1,w}(c_w, i) = \max_{a \in A(c_w, i)} \left\{ a\varphi_i^w + \hat{H}_{t-1} V_{t-1}^{M1,w}(c_w - a) \right\}.$$

Likewise, we can formulate the volume subproblem's optimality equation for all $c_v \in C_v$, $i \in I$, and $t = T, ..., 1$.

$$V_t^{M1,v}(c_v, i) = \max_{a \in A(c_v, i)} \left\{ a\varphi_i^v + \hat{H}_{t-1} V_{t-1}^{M1,v}(c_v - a) \right\}.$$

Again, both terminal values $V_0^{M1,w}(c_w, i)$ and $V_0^{M1,v}(c_v, i)$ are equal to zero for all $c_w \in C_w$, $c_v \in C_v$, and $i \in I$.

The heuristic decision rule based on HDP is to accept a request for shipment class $i \in I$ at time t if $c_w \geq w_i$ weight and $c_v \geq v_i$ volume is remaining and if

$$\rho_i \geq \underbrace{\left[\hat{H}_{t-1} V_{t-1}^{M1,w}(c_w) - \hat{H}_{t-1} V_{t-1}^{M1,w}(c_w - w_i) \right]}_{=\delta_{t-1}(c_w, i)} +$$

$$\underbrace{\left[\hat{H}_{t-1} V_{t-1}^{M1,v}(c_v) - \hat{H}_{t-1} V_{t-1}^{M1,v}(c_v - v_i) \right]}_{=\delta_{t-1}(c_v, i)}.$$

That means, a request is accepted if sufficient capacity is remaining and if opportunity cost of the weight subproblem plus opportunity cost of the volume subproblem is lower than the generated revenue. At first glance, it seems necessary to compute all $\hat{H}_t V_t^{M1,w}(c_w)$ for any combination of t and c_w and all $\hat{H}_t V_t^{M1,v}(c_v)$ for any combination of t and c_v in order to determine heuristic decisions. However, due to the value functions' special structure, computational load can be reduced. We know from M1 that $V_t^{M1,w}(c_w)$ and $V_t^{M1,v}(c_v)$ are concave and non-decreasing in their capacity dimension which implies that the opportunity costs $\delta_t(c_w, i)$ and $\delta_t(c_v, i)$, as differences in V^{M1}, are non-increasing in c_w and c_v, respectively. Therefore, we can formulate heuristic policies based on HDP as control limit policies with respect to weight or volume. Moreover, since $\delta_t(c_w, i) + \delta_t(c_v, i)$ is non-increasing in both c_w and c_v, these control limits are functions of c_w and c_v giving switching curves.

Proposition 4.7. *The heuristic policy based on HDP is a monotone (non-increasing) switching curve policy* $\pi = (f_T, f_{T-1}, ..., f_1)$ *with decision rules*

$$f_t(c_w, c_v, i) = \begin{cases} 1 & c_w > c_w(t, c_v, i), c_w \geq w_i, c_v \geq v_i \\ 0 & \text{otherwise} \end{cases}$$

and with switching curves $c_w(t, c_v, i) = \max\{c_w \geq w_i : \rho_i < \delta_{t-1}(c_w, i) + \delta_{t-1}(c_v, i), c_v \geq v_i\}$, *which are non-increasing in* c_v. *If the set is empty, we define* $c_w(t, c_v, i) = 0$.

The proof of this proposition follows directly from concavity of $\hat{H}_t V_t^{M1,w}(c_w)$ and $\hat{H}_t V_t^{M1,v}(c_v)$. Note that an analog policy can be formulated for volume with switching curves $c_v(t, c_w, i)$. The interpretation of this policy is that a request tends to be accepted, the more weight and/or volume is remaining.

Due to this structure, only switching curves need to be determined in order to derive decisions. Since $\delta_{t-1}(c_w, i) = \hat{H}_{t-1} V_{t-1}^{M1,w}(c_w) - \hat{H}_{t-1} V_{t-1}^{M1,w}(c_w - w_i)$ is monotone in c_w, not all values for $\hat{H}_{t-1} V_{t-1}^{M1,w}(c_w)$ have to be determined. This alleviates computational load significantly. Further, switching curves are much easier to implement and more comprehensible for revenue managers.

Heuristic based on Piecewise Linear Value Function Approximation (HPL)

Next, we propose a heuristic that is based on the linear programming approach to approximate dynamic programming as introduced in Section 3.3. We know that the maximum expected revenue can be computed by a linear program. For this purpose, we define $\boldsymbol{a} := (a_0, a_1, ..., a_m)$ with a_i as the action taken if class i is requested. We further define $A(c_w, c_v) := \{\boldsymbol{a} \in \{0\} \times \{0,1\}^m : c_w \geq a_i w_i, c_v \geq a_i v_i\}$ for all $c_w \in C_w = \{0, ..., \mathfrak{C}_w\}$ and $c_v \in C_v = \{0, ..., \mathfrak{C}_v\}$. We consider time-dependent system states $C_{w,t} := \{\max\{0, \mathfrak{C}_w - (T-t)w^{max}\}, ..., \mathfrak{C}_w\}$ and $C_{v,t} := \{\max\{0, \mathfrak{C}_v - (T-t)v^{max}\}, ..., \mathfrak{C}_v\}$ with $w^{max} := \max_{i \in I}\{w_i\}$ and $v^{max} := \max_{i \in I}\{v_i\}$ as the maximum weight and volume requirement, respectively. Note that we can use time-dependent system states here since we start with an initial system state. Thus, not all combinations of weight and volume can be realized in every decision period. More specifically, the remaining weight and volume in period t must be at least as high as the total available weight and volume minus $(T-t)$ times the maximum capacity requirement in weight and volume, respectively.

We can determine the maximum expected revenue at time T starting with capacity $\mathfrak{C}_w$ and $\mathfrak{C}_v$ by means of the following linear program:

$$(\mathbf{L}) \quad \min_{H_T V_T, ..., H_1 V_1} H_T V_T(\mathfrak{C}_w, \mathfrak{C}_v)$$

$$\text{s.t.} \quad H_t V_t(c_w, c_v) - \sum_{i \in I} q_{t,i} H_{t-1} V_{t-1}(c_w - a_i w_i, c_v - a_i v_i)$$

$$\geq \sum_{i \in I} q_{t,i} \rho_i a_i \quad \forall t = T, ..., 1, c_w \in C_{w,t}, c_v \in C_{v,t}, \boldsymbol{a} \in \boldsymbol{A}(c_w, c_v)$$

$$H_t V_t(c_w, c_v) \in \mathbb{R} \quad \forall t = T, ..., 1, c_w \in C_{w,t}, c_v \in C_{v,t}.$$

Note that we could simplify the problem by allowing only non-negative decision variables. Since terminal and one-stage rewards are non-negative, the value function has to be non-negative, too.

Now we approximate the value function by simpler functions in order to reduce its complexity. While a linear value function approximation is very common in currently available literature (e.g. Adelman, 2007 and Patrick et al., 2008), we use a *piecewise linear* approximation scheme in order to better reflect the value function's curvature. The underlying idea is that the value of remaining capacity is differently approximated depending on whether it is above or below a particular threshold. For weight, this threshold is $\bar{c}_w < \mathfrak{C}_w$, and for volume it is $\bar{c}_v < \mathfrak{C}_v$. Accordingly, we approximate the value function (in observable-disturbance form) in the following way for all $(c_w, c_v) \in C_w \times C_v$ and $t = T, ..., 1$:

$$H_t V_t(c_w, c_v) \approx \psi_t + \alpha_{w,t} c_w + \beta_{w,t}(c_w - \bar{c}_w)\mathbf{1}_{\{c_w > \bar{c}_w\}}$$
$$+\alpha_{v,t} c_v + \beta_{v,t}(c_v - \bar{c}_v)\mathbf{1}_{\{c_v > \bar{c}_v\}} \qquad (4.14)$$

with approximation parameters ψ, α, and β. In this approximation scheme, $\alpha_{w,t}$ and $\alpha_{v,t}$ measure the marginal value in period t of a remaining weight and volume unit that is equal to or below $\bar{c}_w$ and $\bar{c}_v$, respectively. $\alpha_{w,t} + \beta_{w,t}$ and $\alpha_{v,t} + \beta_{v,t}$ measure the marginal value in period t of a weight and volume unit that is above $\bar{c}_w$ and $\bar{c}_v$, respectively. ψ_t is a constant offset.

In order to determine the approximation parameters required for making decisions, we apply the linear programming approach to approximate dynamic programming. Plugging approximation (4.14) into (**L**) (with $\psi_0 = 0$, $\alpha_{w,0} = \beta_{w,0} = 0$, $\alpha_{v,0} = \beta_{v,0} = 0$) yields

(**P1**) $\quad \min\limits_{\alpha,\beta,\psi} \psi_T + \alpha_{w,T}\mathfrak{C}_w + \beta_{w,T}(\mathfrak{C}_w - \bar{c}_w) + \alpha_{v,T}\mathfrak{C}_v + \beta_{v,T}(\mathfrak{C}_v - \bar{c}_v)$

$\quad$ s.t. $\quad \psi_t + \alpha_{w,t} c_w + \beta_{w,t}(c_w - \bar{c}_w)\mathbf{1}_{\{c_w > \bar{c}_w\}} + \alpha_{v,t} c_v$

$$+ \beta_{v,t}(c_v - \bar{c}_v)\mathbf{1}_{\{c_v > \bar{c}_v\}} - \sum_{i \in I} q_{t,i} \left[\psi_{t-1} + \alpha_{w,t-1}(c_w - a_i w_i) \right.$$

$$+\beta_{w,t-1}(c_w - a_i w_i - \bar{c}_w)\mathbf{1}_{\{c_w - a_i w_i > \bar{c}_w\}} + \alpha_{v,t-1}(c_v - a_i v_i)$$

$$\left. +\beta_{v,t-1}(c_v - a_i v_i - \bar{c}_v)\mathbf{1}_{\{c_v - a_i v_i > \bar{c}_v\}} \right]$$

$$\geq \sum_{i \in I} q_{t,i}\rho_i a_i \quad \forall t = T, ..., 1, c_w \in C_{w,t}, c_v \in C_{v,t}, \boldsymbol{a} \in \boldsymbol{A}(c_w, c_v)$$

$$\alpha_{w,t}, \beta_{w,t}, \alpha_{v,t}, \beta_{v,t}, \psi_t \in \mathbb{R} \quad \forall t = T, ..., 1.$$

Note that we do not allow only non-negative decision variables here since a combination of negative and positive approximation parameters can also approximate a non-negative value function. The dual of (**P1**) is

(**D1**) $\quad \max \quad \sum\limits_{1 \leq t \leq T, c_w \in C_{w,t}, c_v \in C_{v,t}, \boldsymbol{a} \in \boldsymbol{A}(c_w, c_v)} X_{t,c_w,c_v,\boldsymbol{a}} \sum\limits_{i \in I} q_{t,i}\rho_i a_i \quad (4.15)$

s.t. $\quad \sum_{c_w,c_v,\boldsymbol{a}} X_{t,c_w,c_v,\boldsymbol{a}} c_w$

$$= \begin{cases} \mathfrak{C}_w & t=T \\ \sum_{c_w,c_v,\boldsymbol{a}} X_{t+1,c_w,c_v,\boldsymbol{a}} \sum_{i \in I} q_{t+1,i}(c_w - a_i w_i) & 1 \leq t < T \end{cases} \tag{4.16}$$

$\sum_{c_w,c_v,\boldsymbol{a}} X_{t,c_w,c_v,\boldsymbol{a}} c_v$

$$= \begin{cases} \mathfrak{C}_v & t=T \\ \sum_{c_w,c_v,\boldsymbol{a}} X_{t+1,c_w,c_v,\boldsymbol{a}} \sum_{i \in I} q_{t+1,i}(c_v - a_i v_i) & 1 \leq t < T \end{cases} \tag{4.17}$$

$\sum_{c_w,c_v,\boldsymbol{a}} X_{t,c_w,c_v,\boldsymbol{a}}(c_w - \bar{c}_w)\mathbf{1}_{\{c_w > \bar{c}_w\}}$

$$= \begin{cases} \mathfrak{C}_w - \bar{c}_w & t=T \\ \sum_{c_w,c_v,\boldsymbol{a}} X_{t+1,c_w,c_v,\boldsymbol{a}} \\ \qquad \cdot \sum_{i \in I} q_{t+1,i}(c_w - a_i w_i - \bar{c}_w)\mathbf{1}_{\{c_w - a_i w_i > \bar{c}_w\}} & 1 \leq t < T \end{cases}$$
$$\tag{4.18}$$

$\sum_{c_w,c_v,\boldsymbol{a}} X_{t,c_w,c_v,\boldsymbol{a}}(c_v - \bar{c}_v)\mathbf{1}_{\{c_v > \bar{c}_v\}}$

$$= \begin{cases} \mathfrak{C}_v - \bar{c}_v & t=T \\ \sum_{c_w,c_v,\boldsymbol{a}} X_{t+1,c_w,c_v,\boldsymbol{a}} \\ \qquad \cdot \sum_{i \in I} q_{t+1,i}(c_v - a_i v_i - \bar{c}_v)\mathbf{1}_{\{c_v - a_i v_i > \bar{c}_v\}} & 1 \leq t < T \end{cases} \tag{4.19}$$

$\sum_{c_w,c_v,\boldsymbol{a}} X_{t,c_w,c_v,\boldsymbol{a}}$

$$= \begin{cases} 1 & t=T \\ \sum_{c_w,c_v,\boldsymbol{a}} X_{t+1,c_w,c_v,\boldsymbol{a}} & 1 \leq t < T \end{cases} \tag{4.20}$$

$$X_{t,c_w,c_v,\boldsymbol{a}} \geq 0 \quad \forall 1 \leq t \leq T, c_w \in C_{w,t}, c_v \in C_{v,t}, \boldsymbol{a} \in \boldsymbol{A}(c_w,c_v) \tag{4.21}$$

Note that constraint (4.20) can be simply replaced by

$$\sum_{c_w, c_v, \boldsymbol{a}} X_{t, c_w, c_v, \boldsymbol{a}} = 1 \quad 1 \le t \le T. \tag{4.22}$$

Note that for an optimal solution, we have for each combination of $c_w \in C_{w,t}$ and $c_v \in C_{v,t}$ a vector of actions $(a_0, ..., a_m)$ with $X_{t, c_w, c_v, \boldsymbol{a}}^* > 0$ (cf. Waldmann & Stocker, 2012, p. 163). This in combination with (4.22) and (4.21) allows us to interpret the optimal solution $X_{t, c_w, c_v, \boldsymbol{a}}^*$ as the probability of choosing actions $\boldsymbol{a} = (a_0, ..., a_m) \in A(c_w, c_v)$ in state (c_w, c_v) at time t. Further, constraints (4.16)-(4.19) ensure that the remaining capacity at time t equals the capacity at time $t + 1$ minus the capacity sold in that period. Thus, this optimization problem maximizes total expected revenue in (4.15) subject to flow-balance constraints for weight and volume.

(**P1**) and (**D1**) give a feasible solution to (**L**), and we know from Proposition 3.5 that any feasible solution of (**L**) gives an upper bound on the maximum expected reward of the underlying MDP. Thus, with z_{PL} as the optimal objective value of (**P1**)-(**D1**), we can state the following proposition.

Proposition 4.8. *We have* $z_{PL} \ge H_T V_T(\mathfrak{C}_w, \mathfrak{C}_v)$.

That is, by determining the approximation parameters required for HPL, we obtain an upper bound on the maximum expected revenue when the optimality equation is written in observable-disturbance form.

(**P1**) is a linear problem with only $5 \times T$ decision variables but a very large number of constraints. Accordingly, (**D1**) features only $5 \times T$ constraints but a large number of decision variables. Thus, an appropriate solution approach is to solve (**D1**) by using column generation. The general idea of column generation is to start with a subset of all variables and add, during an iterative process, further variables that increase the objective value. Thereby, a reduced optimization problem can be considered. For an introduction to column generation, the reader is referred to Bertsimas & Tsitsiklis (1997, Chapter 6). We have the following pricing subproblem **(PS)** for fixed t, which maximizes the reduced revenue of variable $X_{t,c_w,c_v,\boldsymbol{a}}$.

$$
\textbf{(PS)} \quad \max_{c_w,c_v,\boldsymbol{a}} \sum_{i \in I} q_{t,i} \big[\rho_i a_i + \psi_{t-1} - \psi_t
$$

$$
+\alpha_{w,t-1}(c_w - a_i w_i) + \beta_{w,t-1}(c_w - a_i w_i - \bar{c}_w)\mathbf{1}_{\{c_w - a_i w_i > \bar{c}_w\}}
$$

$$
+\alpha_{v,t-1}(c_v - a_i v_i) + \beta_{v,t-1}(c_v - a_i v_i - \bar{c}_v)\mathbf{1}_{\{c_v - a_i v_i > \bar{c}_v\}} \big]
$$

$$
- \alpha_{w,t}c_w - \beta_{w,t}(c_w - \bar{c}_w)\mathbf{1}_{\{c_w > \bar{c}_w\}}
$$

$$
- \alpha_{v,t}c_v - \beta_{v,t}(c_v - \bar{c}_v)\mathbf{1}_{\{c_v > \bar{c}_v\}}
$$

$$
\text{s.t.} \quad c_w \in C_{w,t}, c_v \in C_{v,t}, \boldsymbol{a} \in \boldsymbol{A}(c_w, c_v)
$$

Note that the piecewise linear approximation causes the pricing subproblem to be non-linear. Therefore, we need to introduce a number of auxiliary variables and constraints in order to obtain the following equivalent linear problem.

$$
\textbf{(PS')} \quad \max_{c_w,c_v,\boldsymbol{a},\varsigma,\chi} \sum_{i \in I} q_{t,i} \big[\rho_i a_i + \psi_{t-1} + \alpha_{w,t-1}(c_w - a_i w_i) + \beta_{w,t-1}\chi_{w,i}
$$

$$
+\alpha_{v,t-1}(c_v - a_i v_i) + \beta_{v,t-1}\chi_{v,i} \big] - \psi_t - \alpha_{w,t}c_w - \beta_{w,t}\chi_{w,0}
$$

$$
- \alpha_{v,t}c_v - \beta_{v,t}\chi_{v,0}
$$

$$
\text{s.t.} \quad c_w - a_i w_i - \bar{c}_w \leq \varsigma_{w,i}M \quad \forall i \in I
$$

$$
c_w - a_i w_i - \bar{c}_w \geq -(1 - \varsigma_{w,i})M \quad \forall i \in I
$$

$$
c_v - a_i v_i - \bar{c}_v \leq \varsigma_{v,i}M \quad \forall i \in I
$$

$$
c_v - a_i v_i - \bar{c}_v \geq -(1 - \varsigma_{v,i})M \quad \forall i \in I
$$

$$
\chi_{w,i} \leq M\varsigma_{w,i} \quad \forall i \in I
$$

$$
\chi_{w,i} \leq c_w - a_i w_i - \bar{c}_w + (1 - \varsigma_{w,i})M \quad \forall i \in I
$$

$$
\chi_{w,i} \geq c_w - a_i w_i - \bar{c}_w \quad \forall i \in I
$$

$$
\chi_{v,i} \leq M\varsigma_{v,i} \quad \forall i \in I
$$

$$
\chi_{v,i} \leq c_v - a_i v_i - \bar{c}_v + (1 - \varsigma_{v,i})M \quad \forall i \in I
$$

$$\chi_{v,i} \geq c_v - a_i v_i - \bar{c}_v \quad \forall i \in I$$

$$c_w, \chi_{w,i} \in C_{w,t} \quad \forall i \in I$$

$$c_v, \chi_{v,i} \in C_{v,t} \quad \forall i \in I$$

$$\varsigma_{w,i}, \varsigma_{v,i} \in \{0, 1\} \quad \forall i \in I$$

$$a \in A(c_w, c_v)$$

with M as a very large integer.

(**PS'**) maximizes the reduced revenue of a variable $X_{t,c_w,c_v,a}$, which is the approximated expected revenue from accepting a shipment class less the approximated expected revenue from rejecting it. According to the complementary slackness condition (see Theorem 3.2), a variable can only be part of the optimal solution if the associated constraint is active; in other words, the associated reduced revenue has to be zero. Thus, if the reduced revenue is greater than zero, a solution containing the associated variable is not optimal. This relationship is used by column generation. The solution process is as follows:

(i) Use an initial feasible solution to (**D1**), which is $c_w = \mathfrak{C}_w$, $c_v = \mathfrak{C}_v$, and $a = \vec{0}$ for all t (i.e. offer nothing) to create an initial set of variables; then solve (**D1**).

(ii) Use dual prices of (**D1**) as input for (**PS'**) and solve (**PS'**) for all t.

(iii) If the objective value of (**PS'**) is greater than zero, the solution determined in (i) is not optimal. In other words, a constraint in the primal problem is violated. Thus, add the variable that is associated with the violated constraint to the existing set of variables for (**D1**).

(iv) Solve (**D1**) with updated set of variables.

(v) If the sum of the objective values of (**PS'**) from step (ii) is lower than a particular optimality tolerance times the objective value of (**D1**), an optimal solution is determined. Otherwise go back to step (ii).

The heuristic decision rule under this value function approximation is:

$$f_t(c_w, c_v, i) = \begin{cases} 1 & \rho_i \geq \alpha_{w,t-1} w_i + \alpha_{v,t-1} v_i \\ & \quad + \beta_{w,t-1} \left[(c_w - \bar{c}_w) \mathbf{1}_{\{c_w > \bar{c}_w\}} \right. \\ & \qquad \left. - (c_w - w_i - \bar{c}_w) \mathbf{1}_{\{c_w - w_i > \bar{c}_w\}} \right] \\ & \quad + \beta_{v,t-1} \left[(c_v - \bar{c}_v) \mathbf{1}_{\{c_v > \bar{c}_v\}} \right. \\ & \qquad \left. - (c_v - v_i - \bar{c}_v) \mathbf{1}_{\{c_v - v_i > \bar{c}_v\}} \right], \\ & c_w \geq w_i, c_v \geq v_i \\ 0 & \text{otherwise.} \end{cases}$$

The interpretation of this decision rule is as follows: Accept a request if its revenue is at least as high as the sum of the value of required weight and volume. If remaining capacity is below the threshold, the capacity requirement is weighted by α. If remaining capacity is above the threshold, the value is corrected by β. If remaining capacity is above the threshold before the request is accepted and below the threshold afterwards, the capacity requirement is weighted by β and α for units above the threshold and by α for units below the threshold. HPL applies this decision rule in the booking process.

In the following numerical experiments, we address the question of how well all proposed heuristics perform.

4.4 Numerical Experiments

In this section, we assess the quality of the described heuristics HD, HDP, and HPL. Additionally, we test a first-come-first-served policy (FCFS) which accepts requests as long as capacity is available. The approximation parameters in HPL are computed with $\bar{c}_w = \mathfrak{C}_w/2$ and $\bar{c}_v = \mathfrak{C}_v/2$. As a benchmark for the heuristics' achieved revenue over the simulated booking processes, we use the maximum average revenue determined in (4.3). We computed this value by means of a HP XC3000 high performance computer. We compare the upper bounds z_{PL} and z_{ACG} to the maximum expected revenue in order to make a statement on the bounds' quality. Initially, we present a numerical study that uses the data set provided in Huang & Chang (2010). The second study uses a modification of this data set which contains classes featuring a non-standard weight-volume ratio. All experiments were conducted on an Intel Core2 Quad CPU at 2.83 GHz and 8 GB RAM. In order to obtain the approximation parameters in HPL, we solved the linear program by means of Gurobi 5.0 (Gurobi Optimization, 2012). In the column generation procedure we used an optimality tolerance of 1%.

Setting 1: Base Case

The data set we consider contains shipment categories $b = 1, ..., 9$ that all have a different weight and volume requirement w_b, v_b as shown in Table 4.1.

Category b	1	2	3	4	5	6	7	8	9
Weight requirement w_b (kg)	80	160	400	100	200	500	100	200	500
Volume requirement v_b ($\times 10^4$ cm^3)	60	120	300	60	120	300	50	100	250

Table 4.1: Weight and volume requirement of shipment categories

Categories 1-3 represent loose cargo since the ratio of volume to weight is greater than the one of a standard shipment (0.6×10^4 cm^3/kg). Categories 7-9 represent dense cargo for the opposite reason. Categories 4-6 feature the volume-weight ratio of a standard shipment. In each time period t, either a shipment with revenue per chargeable weight φ or no shipment is requested. Table 4.2 shows the probabilities for incoming requests with revenue φ. Note that the probability for high-value requests increases as departure approaches. Given a shipment request, the probability that the shipment belongs to a particular category is constant in time as displayed in Table 4.3. We assume that the observed category is independent of the observed per-unit revenue. Thus, the request probability for a particular class $i = (b, \varphi)$ at time t (i.e. $q_{t,i}$) equals the probability of observing a revenue per chargeable weight φ multiplied by the probability of observing a

Revenue	Request probabilities in periods		
φ	1-20	21-40	41-60
1.2	0.25	0.1667	0.10
1.0	0.15	0.1666	0.15
0.8	0.10	0.1667	0.25

Table 4.2: Request probabilities for different revenues per chargeable weight

Category b	1-3	4	5	6	7-9
Request probability	0.0833	0.1667	0.1668	0.1667	0.0833

Table 4.3: Request probabilities for shipment categories

category b request at this time. For example, the probability for an arrival of a class with $\varphi = 1.0$ and $b = 4$ at $t = 45$ is $0.1667 \times 0.15 = 0.025$. Accepting a request for class i gives a revenue of $\varphi_i \max\{w_i, v_i/\vartheta\}$ with $\vartheta = 0.6$. Note that for $i = 0$, the request probability is $q_{t,0} = 1 - \sum_{i=1}^{m} q_{t,i}$. Thus, the probability for no request is 0.5 in each period. Combining nine shipment categories and three different revenues per chargeable weight results in 27 shipment classes that are considered in these experiments.

We consider a booking horizon of $T = 60$ time periods. Further, multiplying capacity requirements by request probabilities over the entire booking horizon yields expected demand in weight and volume of $\mathfrak{D}_w$=7600 kg and $\mathfrak{D}_v$=4600$\times 10^4$ cm^3, respectively. This corresponds to approximately 19% of a Boeing 757-200 freighter's payload and cargo volume (Boeing, 2012). While total demand is given, we let total available capacity $(\mathfrak{C}_w, \mathfrak{C}_v)$ vary in order to demonstrate the heuristics' performance for different capacity-demand ratios. We test different ratios for weight restricted, volume restricted, and both weight and volume restricted flights.

In order to determine the performance of our heuristics, we repeatedly simulated the arrival process and computed the average revenue gained in the selling process over all simulation runs. In order to obtain reliable results, we simulated

100,000 booking processes. Figure 4.3 displays the heuristics' performance relative to the maximum expected revenue for flights that are restricted with respect to both weight and volume (i.e. $\mathcal{C}_w/\mathfrak{D}_w=\mathcal{C}_v/\mathfrak{D}_v$). One major finding is that the

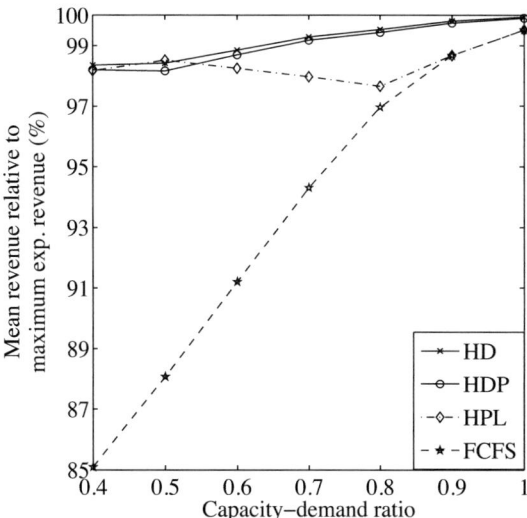

Figure 4.3: Heuristics' performance for both weight and volume restricted flights (relative to maximum expected revenue)

heuristics' performance relative to FCFS increases as less capacity is available. This result is intuitive since the optimal control policy in a situation with sufficient capacity is to simply accept every request. This policy becomes worse as less capacity is available. Another observation is that all heuristics (except FCFS) are quite close to the maximum expected revenue for all capacity-demand ratios. Further, HD and HDP outperform HPL for slightly restricted flights. On the other hand, if a flight is heavily restricted ($\mathcal{C}_w/\mathfrak{D}_w=\mathcal{C}_v/\mathfrak{D}_v < 0.6$), HPL performs as well as the other heuristics. The observed slight disadvantage of HDP relative to HD is caused by approximating actual non-monotone opportunity cost through monotone functions.

Figure 4.4 summarizes the heuristics' performance for flights with sufficient volume and scarce weight. Observe that, for all capacity-demand ratios, HDP

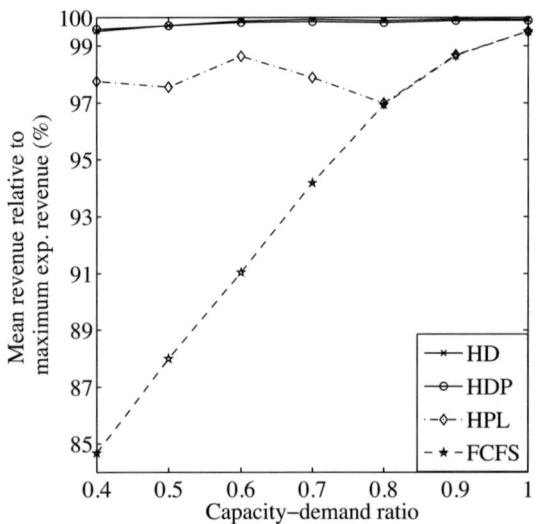

Figure 4.4: Heuristics' performance for weight restricted flights
(relative to maximum expected revenue)

and HD do better than all other heuristics. Since they both have a priority on weight, they demonstrate a strong performance if weight is the valuable resource. Another observation is that HPL performs quite well and is not very sensitive to the availability of weight.

Figure 4.5 shows the percent difference of the heuristics' achieved revenue relative to the maximum expected revenue when sufficient weight is available and volume is the bottleneck. Observe that HPL performs significantly better than HD and HDP. The reason for the poor performance of heuristics based on decomposition is that opportunity cost is miscalculated when volume is scarce since the availability of volume does not at all affect the calculation of weight opportunity cost. Further, the change in supplementary volume opportunity cost

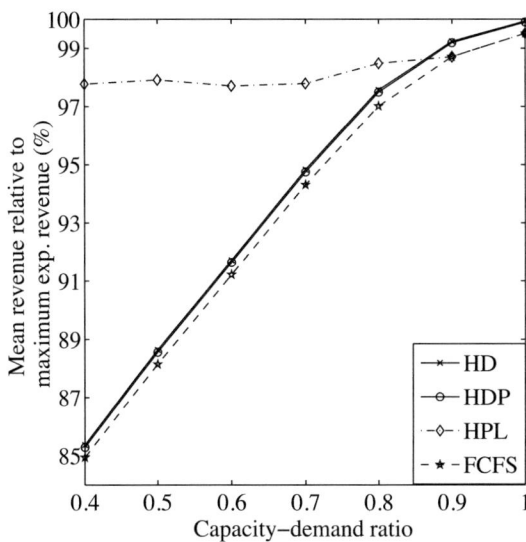

Figure 4.5: Heuristics' performance for volume restricted flights
(relative to maximum expected revenue)

does not have a significant impact on the heuristics' decision. Thus, total opportunity cost is too low, which leads to excessive acceptance of requests. HPL does not feature this drawback since it does not prioritize a capacity dimension. Thus, its performance is approximately the same as in case of insufficient weight as well as in case of flights that are both weight and volume restricted.

Tables 4.4, 4.5, and 4.6 report the relative difference between the upper bounds and the maximum expected revenue. If both weight and volume capacity is less than expected demand, z_{PL}'s quality is approximately constant, and z_{ACG} becomes less tight as capacity decreases (see Table 4.4). If either weight or volume capacity is insufficient, it can be observed that z_{PL} becomes tighter as available capacity decreases, whereas z_{ACG} becomes less tight (see Tables 4.5 and 4.6). Further, z_{ACG} shows a better quality than z_{PL} for most scenarios of weight restricted flights (see Table 4.5). If very little weight is available, z_{PL} is again tighter than z_{ACG}. The quality of z_{ACG} in case of volume restricted flights is particularly poor because of the already mentioned shortcomings of ACG (see Table 4.6).

$\mathcal{C}_w/\mathcal{D}_w$	$\mathcal{C}_v/\mathcal{D}_v$	$\frac{z_{PL}}{H_T V_T(\mathcal{C}_w,\mathcal{C}_v)}$ %	$\frac{z_{ACG}}{H_T V_T(\mathcal{C}_w,\mathcal{C}_v)}$ %
1.0	1.0	106.42	100.98
0.9	0.9	105.00	101.50
0.8	0.8	104.89	102.06
0.7	0.7	104.78	102.79
0.6	0.6	104.95	103.98
0.5	0.5	104.83	105.39
0.4	0.4	105.07	106.96

Table 4.4: Upper bound quality depending on both available weight and volume (relative to maximum expected revenue)

In summary, this example demonstrates that HPL provides a very constant and reliable performance. While HPL is not sensitive to the availability of a particular capacity dimension, HD's and HDP's performance significantly depends on the

$\mathfrak{C}_w/\mathfrak{D}_w$	$\mathfrak{C}_v/\mathfrak{D}_v$	$\frac{z_{PL}}{H_T V_T(\mathfrak{C}_w,\mathfrak{C}_v)}$ %	$\frac{z_{ACG}}{H_T V_T(\mathfrak{C}_w,\mathfrak{C}_v)}$ %
1.0	1.0	106.42	100.98
0.9	1.0	104.02	100.52
0.8	1.0	103.74	100.78
0.7	1.0	104.06	101.12
0.6	1.0	103.04	102.08
0.5	1.0	103.00	103.41
0.4	1.0	103.81	104.69

Table 4.5: Upper bound quality depending on available weight (relative to maximum expected revenue)

$\mathfrak{C}_w/\mathfrak{D}_w$	$\mathfrak{C}_v/\mathfrak{D}_v$	$\frac{z_{PL}}{H_T V_T(\mathfrak{C}_w,\mathfrak{C}_v)}$ %	$\frac{z_{ACG}}{H_T V_T(\mathfrak{C}_w,\mathfrak{C}_v)}$ %
1.0	1.0	106.42	100.98
1.0	0.9	104.06	107.02
1.0	0.8	103.76	116.62
1.0	0.7	104.05	129.28
1.0	0.6	103.37	146.60
1.0	0.5	103.19	171.40
1.0	0.4	103.91	208.03

Table 4.6: Upper bound quality depending on available volume (relative to maximum expected revenue)

particular capacity-demand scenario. Thus, HD and HDP are only appropriate if the short capacity dimension is known in advance. Further, for all tested capacity-demand ratios, the upper bound z_{PL} features a very good quality.

Setting 2: Non-Standard Capacity Requirement

In these experiments, we modify the previously presented data in the way that we change the resource requirement of shipment categories 2 and 7, as shown in Table 4.7 (changes in bold). Now the data set contains two shipment classes that have a capacity requirement with a weight-volume ratio which we hereafter refer to as "non-standard". All other data remains unchanged.

Category	1	2	3	4	5	6	7	8	9
Weight requirement ($\times$ 10 kg)	80	160	400	100	200	500	**660**	200	500
Volume requirement ($\times 10^5$ cm^3)	60	**680**	300	60	120	300	50	100	250

Table 4.7: Non-standard capacity requirement - weight and volume of shipment categories

These changes yield an expected demand in weight and volume of $\mathfrak{D}_w$=9000 kg and $\mathfrak{D}_v$=6000$\times 10^4$ cm^3, respectively. We conducted the same experiments as described in the previous section. For weight and volume restricted flights (see Figure 4.6), we discover the following differences to the situation without non-standard capacity requirement: First, observe that HD and HDP are inferior to HPL if capacity is scarce. This result demonstrates the disadvantage of prioritizing a capacity dimension if capacity requirement is extremely uneven. For instance, if a class has a very high volume requirement, accepting it in the volume subproblem gives little revenue while remaining volume is decreased significantly. Thus, such a request is likely to be rejected which yields miscalculated opportunity cost in the heuristic decision rule.

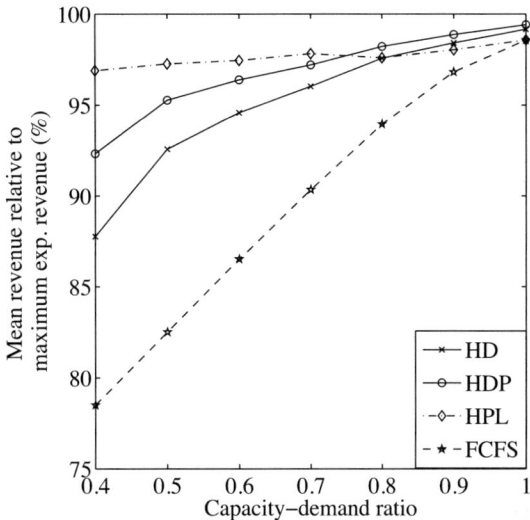

Figure 4.6: Heuristics' performance for both weight and volume restricted flights (relative to maximum expected revenue)

Observe that now HDP outperforms HD. Since the characteristics of HD and HDP do not offer an intuitive explanation for this observation, a detailed investigation is necessary. A closer look at the opportunity cost of both heuristics shows that volume opportunity cost of HDP is significantly higher than HD's volume opportunity cost for all shipment classes that feature a standard capacity requirement. This observation cannot be made when the data set does not contain non-standard shipments. This result suggests that HD underestimates volume opportunity cost of regular shipments yielding a worse performance compared to the case without non-standard shipments. This result is confirmed by Figure 4.7 which shows a comparison between the basic model's, HD's, and HDP's opportunity cost for a particular regular shipment class. Moreover, the figure provides

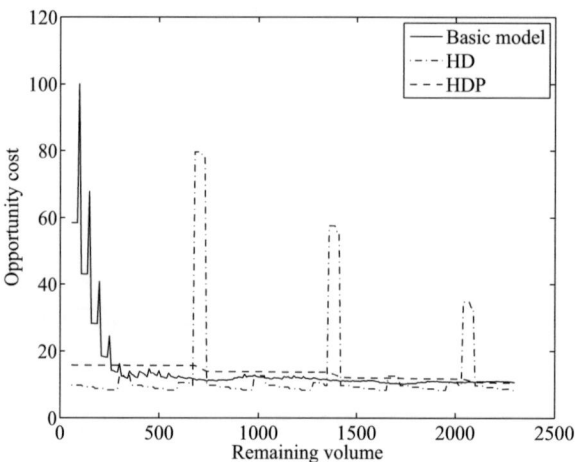

Figure 4.7: Comparison of opportunity costs

a further explanation why HDP outperforms HD. Observe that HD tends to overestimate opportunity cost significantly when remaining capacity is just sufficient to accommodate an additional shipment with non-standard capacity requirement (approximately when remaining volume is 700, 1400, and 2100). HDP does not feature such "peaks" since opportunity cost is monotone. The effect of overestimating opportunity cost for particular values of remaining volume additionally contributes to the bad performance of HD compared to HDP.

The difference between the heuristics' performance and the maximum expected revenue for weight restricted flights is depicted in Figure 4.8. Again, HDP

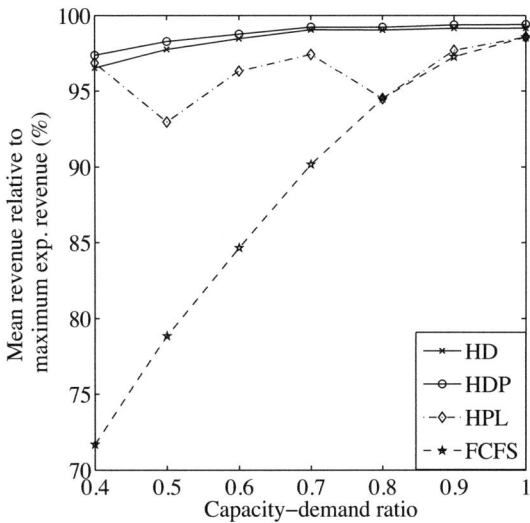

Figure 4.8: Heuristics' performance for weight restricted flights (relative to maximum expected revenue)

outperforms HD, and HPL performs well. The explanation for both observations is analog to the ones given in the case of equally restricted flights. Moreover, the observations of HDP outperforming HD and HPL performing well can also be made for volume restricted flights (see Figure 4.9).

Tables 4.8, 4.9, and 4.10 summarize the relative difference between the upper bounds and the maximum expected revenue. The same observations as in the base case can be made. The only difference is that if both weight and volume is scarce, z_{PL}'s quality slightly decreases as available capacity decreases (see Table 4.8). However, z_{PL}'s overall quality is very good.

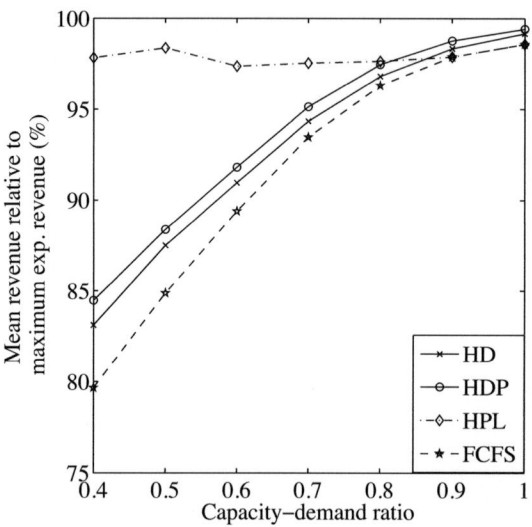

Figure 4.9: Heuristics' performance for volume restricted flights
(relative to maximum expected revenue)

$\mathfrak{C}_w/\mathfrak{D}_w$	$\mathfrak{C}_v/\mathfrak{D}_v$	$\frac{z_{PL}}{H_T V_T(\mathfrak{C}_w,\mathfrak{C}_v)}$ %	$\frac{z_{ACG}}{H_T V_T(\mathfrak{C}_w,\mathfrak{C}_v)}$ %
1.0	1.0	108.23	105.36
0.9	0.9	108.27	107.45
0.8	0.8	108.84	109.40
0.7	0.7	109.39	111.65
0.6	0.6	110.01	114.37
0.5	0.5	110.74	117.07
0.4	0.4	111.72	120.22

Table 4.8: Upper bound quality depending on both available weight and volume
(relative to maximum expected revenue)

$\mathfrak{C}_w/\mathfrak{D}_w$	$\mathfrak{C}_v/\mathfrak{D}_v$	$\frac{z_{PL}}{H_T V_T(\mathfrak{C}_w,\mathfrak{C}_v)}$ %	$\frac{z_{ACG}}{H_T V_T(\mathfrak{C}_w,\mathfrak{C}_v)}$ %
1.0	1.0	108.23	105.36
0.9	1.0	106.69	103.99
0.8	1.0	105.13	102.91
0.7	1.0	104.60	102.43
0.6	1.0	103.33	102.70
0.5	1.0	103.05	103.40
0.4	1.0	103.45	104.29

Table 4.9: Upper bound quality depending on available weight (relative to maximum expected revenue)

$\mathfrak{C}_w/\mathfrak{D}_w$	$\mathfrak{C}_v/\mathfrak{D}_v$	$\frac{z_{PL}}{H_T V_T(\mathfrak{C}_w,\mathfrak{C}_v)}$ %	$\frac{z_{ACG}}{H_T V_T(\mathfrak{C}_w,\mathfrak{C}_v)}$ %
1.0	1.0	108.23	105.36
1.0	0.9	106.32	109.99
1.0	0.8	104.86	117.07
1.0	0.7	104.64	126.64
1.0	0.6	103.72	138.96
1.0	0.5	103.26	155.40
1.0	0.4	103.66	177.71

Table 4.10: Upper bound quality depending on available volume (relative to maximum expected revenue)

107

In summary, HPL gives in most scenarios the highest revenue in the presence of shipments having a non-standard capacity requirement. Further, HDP outperforms HD for all tested scenarios. Even though HD and HDP perform well for weight restricted flights, their overall performance is lower than the one of HPL. Furthermore, z_{PL} gives a good upper bound on the maximum expected revenue.

CHAPTER 5

Integrated Capacity Control of Cargo Space and Passenger Seats

In this chapter, we model the decision problem that maximizes the total revenue from selling both cargo space and passenger seats. Thus, the whole aircraft's capacity is controlled. Note that this implies that passenger demand can be rejected in favor of cargo. In Section 5.1, we propose a basic integrated decision model for simultaneously controlling a combination carrier's cargo and seat capacity. Since this model does not offer monotone optimal decision rules, we propose a further decision model in Section 5.2 that makes specific assumptions and thereby provides a simply structured optimal control policy. Section 5.3 outlines two different heuristics that can be applied to determine a solution to the basic decision model, which suffers from the curse of dimensionality. Further, we provide an upper bound on the maximum expected revenue of the basic model. In Section 5.4, the heuristics' performance and the bound's quality are assessed using numerical experiments.

5.1 Basic Integrated Capacity Control Model

We consider an airline that operates flights on single legs like in Chapter 4. Contrary to the cargo capacity control models, we now take into account the entire capacity of an aircraft, that is both passenger seats on the upper deck and cargo space on the lower deck. A combination carrier on a particular leg has a remaining weight capacity $c_w \in C_w = \{0, 1, ..., \mathfrak{C}_w\}$, volume capacity $c_v \in C_v = \{0, 1, ..., \mathfrak{C}_v\}$, and seats $c_s \in C_s = \{0, 1, ..., \mathfrak{C}_s\}$. While $\mathfrak{C}_w$ and $\mathfrak{C}_v$ denote the aircraft's total weight and volume capacity, respectively, $\mathfrak{C}_s$ represents the total number of passenger seats. In each of T decision periods, at most one request for either a particular cargo shipment class $i \in I_c = \{1, ..., m_1\}$, or for a particular passenger booking class $i \in I_s = \{m_1 + 1, ..., m_2\}$, or no request may arrive. We let $i = 0$ represent the event of no arriving request. Like in the cargo capacity control models, each shipment class $i \in I_c$ is characterized by its weight and volume requirement $w_i \in \mathbb{N}_0$ and $v_i \in \mathbb{N}_0$, respectively, and its per unit revenue $\varphi_i \geq 0$. For $i = 0$, we define $w_0 = 0$, $v_0 = 0$, and $\varphi_0 = 0$. Each passenger booking class $i \in I_s$ requires exactly one seat, and we define the seat requirement as $\sigma_i := 1$ if $i \in I_s$ and $\sigma_i := 0$ otherwise. A passenger booking class is further characterized by revenue per seat $\varphi_i \geq 0$ and a particular weight and volume requirement $w_i \in \mathbb{N}_0$ and $v_i \in \mathbb{N}_0$, respectively, which is assumed to be constant for all $i \in I_s$. Note that a passenger requires weight due to his or her body weight and luggage, and the volume requirement is only caused by luggage. If an aircraft is equipped with a particular luggage compartment, which cannot be used by other cargo shipments, volume requirement can be neglected. Further, note that we denote the per-unit revenue of both passenger and cargo requests as φ. In case of a cargo request the unit is one chargeable weight unit, and in case of a passenger request the unit is one seat.

We count time backwards with time period T denoting the beginning of the booking process and $t = 0$ representing the departure of the aircraft. We choose T sufficiently large to ensure that the probability of more than one arrival per time period can be neglected. At each time $t = T, ..., 0$, the probability of an arriving class-i request is denoted by $q_{t,i} \geq 0$. The probability that no request arrives is given by $q_{t,0} = 1 - \sum_{i=1}^{m_2} q_{t,i} \geq 0$. We further define $q_{0,0} = 1$ and $q_{0,i} = 0$ for $i = 1, ..., m_2$. That means, no request arrives at $t = 0$.

In each period, in which a request for $i \in \hat{I} = \{0, ..., m_2\}$ is observed, the decision maker has to decide if the incoming request is accepted or rejected. We assume that at the time the decision is made, weight and volume requirement is known. Thus, accepting a request for a shipment class $i = 1, ..., m_1$ gives a revenue $\varphi_i \max\{w_i, v_i/\vartheta\}$, where ϑ denotes a constant representing the ratio of volume to weight of a standard shipment. Further, accepting a request for a passenger booking class $i = m_1 + 1, ..., m_2$ yields a revenue φ_i which is the price of class i.

We make the same assumptions as in the basic model in the previous chapter, which are the following: Demand is independent between booking classes, demand is independent of the availability of other classes, the arrival process follows a (discretized) Poisson process, neither cancellations nor no-shows occur (thus, overbooking is not required), the decision maker is risk-neutral, customers do not behave strategically and request only single-leg flights. In this model, we make the additional assumption that passenger group bookings do not occur. That is, at most one seat is requested within one decision period.

The decision problem that needs to be solved is the following: The decision maker faces the problem of whether to generate revenue by accepting a request or saving capacity for later requests that may have a higher revenue. This problem implies that the revenue manager has to decide whether to deny passenger requests in order to save weight and volume for later high-value cargo bookings. The objective is to identify an optimal control policy that maximizes total expected revenue over the entire booking horizon. This can be reduced to solving the optimality equation of a finite-horizon MDP $(T, S, E, A, p_t, r_t, V_0)$ with:

(i) *Planning horizon* $T \in \mathbb{N}_0$, indexed by t.

(ii) *State space* $S \times E = (C_w \times C_v \times C_s) \times \hat{I}$
with $\hat{I} = \{0, ..., m_2\}$. The state space comprises remaining weight, volume, and seats as system states (all integer values) and the requested shipment or booking class as an environmental state.

111

(iii) *Action space* $A \in \{0, 1\}$ indicates whether a request is rejected or accepted. The set of admissible actions is defined as

$$A(c_w, c_v, c_s, i) := \begin{cases} \{0, 1\} & c_w \geq w_i, c_v \geq v_i, c_s \geq \sigma_i, i \in \hat{I} \\ \{0\} & \text{otherwise.} \end{cases}$$

(iv) *Transition law* $p_t(c_w, c_v, c_s, i, a, c_w - aw_i, c_v - av_i, c_s - a\sigma_i, i') = q_{t-1,i'}$ for all $t = T, ..., 1$, $c_w \in C_w$, $c_v \in C_v$, $c_s \in C_s$, $i, i' \in \hat{I}$, and $a \in A(c_w, c_v, c_s, i)$. That means, the transition probability represents the probability of a class-i' request arriving in the next decision period.

(v) *One-stage reward function*

$$r_t(c_w, c_v, c_s, i, a) = a\rho_i := \begin{cases} a\varphi_i \max\{w_i, v_i/\vartheta\} & 0 \leq i \leq m_1 \\ a\varphi_i & m_1 < i \leq m_2 \end{cases}$$

for all $t = T, ..., 1$, $c_w \in C_w$, $c_v \in C_v$, $c_s \in C_s$, $i \in \hat{I}$, and $a \in A(c_w, c_v, c_s, i)$.

(vi) *Terminal reward function* $V_0 \equiv 0$.

The maximum expected revenue in $t = T, ..., 1$, given remaining capacity $c_w \in C_w$, $c_v \in C_v$, $c_s \in C_s$ and a request for $i \in \hat{I}$, is the unique solution to the optimality equation

$$V_t(c_w, c_v, c_s, i) =$$

$$\max_{a \in A(c_w, c_v, c_s, i)} \left\{ a\rho_i + \sum_{i' \in \hat{I}} q_{t-1,i'} V_{t-1}(c_w - aw_i, c_v - av_i, c_s - a\sigma_i, i') \right\}.$$

$$(5.1)$$

For an arbitrary real-valued function u on $C_w \times C_v \times C_s \times \hat{I}$, we define the operator Q as

$$Q_t u(c_w, c_v, c_s) := \sum_{i \in \hat{I}} q_{t,i} u(c_w, c_v, c_s, i) \quad \forall t = T, ..., 0.$$

Then, we can write (5.1) as

$$
\begin{aligned}
V_t(c_w, c_v, c_s, i) = \\
\max_{a \in A(c_w, c_v, c_s, i)} \{a\rho_i + Q_{t-1}V_{t-1}(c_w - aw_i, c_v - av_i, c_s - a\sigma_i)\}.
\end{aligned}
\tag{5.2}
$$

The observable-disturbance form of (5.2) is

$$
\begin{aligned}
Q_t V_t(c_w, c_v, c_s) = \\
\sum_{i \in \hat{I}} q_{t,i} \max_{a \in A(c_w, c_v, c_s, i)} \{a\rho_i + Q_{t-1}V_{t-1}(c_w - aw_i, c_v - av_i, c_s - a\sigma_i)\}.
\end{aligned}
\tag{5.3}
$$

The maximum expected revenue determined in (5.3) will be used later in the numerical experiments.

In case of an arriving request and sufficient available capacity (i.e. $c_w \geq w_i$, $c_v \geq v_i$, and $c_s \geq \sigma_i$), we can write (5.2) as

$$
\begin{aligned}
V_t(c_w, c_v, c_s, i) = \\
\max \{\rho_i + Q_{t-1}V_{t-1}(c_w - w_i, c_v - v_i, c_s - \sigma_i), Q_{t-1}V_{t-1}(c_w, c_v, c_s)\}.
\end{aligned}
\tag{5.4}
$$

The optimal decision rule can be directly inferred: If a request for $i \in \hat{I}$ is accepted at time t, the expected revenue is $\rho_i + Q_{t-1}V_{t-1}(c_w - w_i, c_v - v_i, c_s - \sigma_i)$. If it is rejected, the expected revenue is $Q_{t-1}V_{t-1}(c_w, c_v, c_s)$. Thus, the optimal decision rule in t is

$$
f_t^*(c_w, c_v, c_s, i) = \begin{cases} 1 & \rho_i \geq Q_{t-1}V_{t-1}(c_w, c_v, c_s) \\ & \quad -Q_{t-1}V_{t-1}(c_w - w_i, c_v - v_i, c_s - \sigma_i), \\ & \quad c_w \geq w_i, c_v \geq v_i, c_s \geq \sigma_i, i \in \hat{I} \\ 0 & \text{otherwise.} \end{cases}
$$

That means, a request is accepted if its revenue is at least as high as the opportunity cost of the capacity the request requires. For the ease of notation, we define opportunity cost $\delta_{t-1}(c_w, c_v, c_s, i) := Q_{t-1}V_{t-1}(c_w, c_v, c_s) - Q_{t-1}V_{t-1}(c_w - w_i, c_v - v_i, c_s - \sigma_i)$. Note that in order to determine optimal actions in t, all values $Q_{t-1}V_{t-1}(c_w, c_v, c_s)$ for $c_w \in C_w$, $c_v \in C_v$, and $c_s \in C_s$ are required. Determining these values for real world problems is computationally infeasible. For example, consider 60 time periods and an A320 combination carrier having 150 seats and approximately a cargo capacity of 32 m^3 and total payload of 16600 kg. In this example, 4.8×10^9 different values need to be computed. As we remarked earlier, a potential way out of this curse of dimensionality might be the identification of monotone policies. Unfortunately, since opportunity cost is not monotone, the integrated capacity control model does not feature an optimal control policy which is structured with respect to capacity or time. This is outlined below.

Proposition 5.1. *For $(c_w, c_v, c_s, i) \in C_w \times C_v \times C_s \times \hat{I}$ and $t = T - 1, ..., 0$, $\delta_t(c_w, c_v, c_s, i)$ is not monotone in c_w, neither in c_v, and neither in c_s.*

Due to the same reasons given for the cargo capacity control model in Section 4.1, opportunity cost is neither monotone in c_w nor in c_v. A similar example as in the pure cargo case can be easily constructed. Moreover, opportunity cost is not monotone in c_s as the following example demonstrates.

Example 5.1. Consider a combination carrier with remaining capacity of $c_w = 3$, $c_v = 3$, and $c_s = 3$. In each period a request for one of three different request classes arrives. Classes 1 and 2 are cargo booking classes with $\varphi_1 = \varphi_2 = 9$, $w_1 = v_1 = 1$, $w_2 = v_2 = 2$, $q_{t,1} = 0.01$, and $q_{t,2} = 0.89$ for all $t = T, ..., 1$. Class 3 is a passenger booking class with $\varphi_3 = 16$, $w_3 = v_3 = 1$, and $q_{t,3} = 0.1$ for all $t = T, ..., 1$. For the sake of simplicity, we let $\vartheta = 1$. Accordingly, we have $\rho_1 = 9$, $\rho_2 = 18$, and $\rho_3 = 16$. Now consider the opportunity cost of a class-3 request in period $t = 4$, which is required if a decision is made at $t = 5$. This is computed as $\delta_4(3, 3, 3, 3) = Q_4V_4(3, 3, 3) - Q_4V_4(2, 2, 2) = 5.3767$. Now assume only 2 seats are remaining, i.e. $c_s = 2$. We expect opportunity cost not to decrease since capacity becomes more valuable if it is scarce. Indeed, opportunity cost is $\delta_4(3,3,2,3) = 5.7254$. Now assume only one seat is remaining ($c_s = 1$). We again expect opportunity cost not to decrease; however, it is computed as $\delta_4(3,3,1,3) = 5.7243$. That means, opportunity cost decreases even though less capacity is available.

The reason for the observed non-monotonicity is that cargo requests have to be accepted in their entirety. This is also the reason for the non-monotone behavior in time.

Proposition 5.2. *For $(c_w, c_v, c_s, i) \in C_w \times C_v \times C_s \times \hat{I}$, $\delta_t(c_w, c_v, c_s, i)$ is not monotone in time.*

Example 4.2 in Section 4.1 can be considered as a special case for the integrated capacity control model when assuming no customer requests arrive. This demonstrates the above proposition's validity.

We now turn to an integrated capacity control model that features an optimal monotone policy.

5.2 A Capacity Control Model featuring a Structured Control Policy

The decision model introduced in the previous section is very complex since its system state comprises three dimensions. Further, the model lacks a monotone optimal policy which could potentially decrease computational complexity. Thus, we propose a decision model in this section which overcomes these drawbacks. We refer to this decision model hereafter as $\tilde{M}$.

In $\tilde{M}$, we make the following assumptions: Cargo capacity is assumed to be one-dimensional as done in M1. We already mentioned in Section 4.2 that this approach is reasonable if the expected ratio of capacity to demand is much lower for one capacity dimension than for the other one (e.g. an aircraft carrying largely flowers). A further assumption we make in this model is that cargo requests can be partially accepted. This assumption is not unrealistic for the same reasons given for the cargo capacity control model M1. We also assume that a passenger request requires exactly one cargo unit. This can be easily achieved by adjusting the cargo space's scale. Furthermore, we make the same assumptions as in the basic integrated model.

We again consider a carrier that operates flights on single legs. Now a combination carrier has a remaining cargo capacity $c \in C = \{0, 1, , ..., \mathfrak{C}\}$ with $\mathfrak{C}$ as the aircraft's total capacity. It further has a number of remaining seats $c_s \in C_s = \{0, 1, ..., \mathfrak{C}_s\}$. Each cargo shipment class, which may be requested, is characterized by its capacity requirement $\gamma_i \in \mathbb{N}_0$ and its per unit revenue $\varphi_i \geq 0$. Further, we define $\gamma_0 = 0$ and $\varphi_0 = 0$. The cargo capacity requirement of a passenger request is defined as $\gamma_i := 1$ for all $i \in I_s$. All other notations are equal to the notation of the basic model described in the previous section.

In each period, in which a passenger request arrives, the decision maker has to decide if the incoming request is accepted or rejected. Accepting a passenger request for class $i \in I_s$ yields a revenue φ_i. In case of an arriving cargo request, the decision maker has to decide which part of the request to accept. Accepting an amount of a capacity units of a request $i \in I_c$ gives a revenue $\varphi_i a$.

The objective is to identify an optimal control policy that maximizes the total expected revenue over the entire booking horizon. This can be reduced to solving the optimality equation of a finite-horizon MDP $(T, S, E, A, p_t, r_t, \tilde{V}_0)$ with:

(i) *Planning horizon $T \in \mathbb{N}_0$.*

(ii) *State space $S \times E = (C \times C_s) \times \hat{I}$.*

(iii) *Action space $A \subset \mathbb{N}_0$ with $a \in A$ as the number of accepted capacity units in case of a cargo request and the accept/reject decision in case of a passenger request. The set of admissible actions is defined as*

$$A(c, c_s, i) := \begin{cases} \{0, ..., \min\{c, \gamma_i\}\} & i \in \{0, ..., m_1\}, c \in C, c_s \in C_s \\ \{0, 1\} & i \in I_s, c \geq 1, c_s \geq 1 \\ \{0\} & \text{otherwise.} \end{cases}$$

(iv) *Transition law* $p_t(c, c_s, i, a, c - a, c_s - a\sigma_i, i') = q_{t-1,i'}$
for all $t = T, ..., 1, c \in C, c_s \in C_s, i, i' \in \hat{I}$, and $a \in A(c, c_s, i)$.

(v) *One-stage reward function* $r_t(c, c_s, i, a) = a\varphi_i$
for all $t = T, ..., 1, c \in C, c_s \in C_s, i \in \hat{I}$, and $a \in A(c, c_s, i)$.

(vi) *Terminal reward function* $\tilde{V}_0 \equiv 0$.

The maximum expected revenue at time $t = T, ..., 1$, given remaining capacity $c \in C$, $c_s \in C_s$ and a request for class $i \in \hat{I}$, is the unique solution to the optimality equation

$$\tilde{V}_t(c, c_s, i) = \max_{a \in A(c, c_s, i)} \left\{ a\varphi_i + \sum_{i' \in \hat{I}} q_{t-1,i'} \tilde{V}_{t-1}(c - a, c_s - a\sigma_i, i') \right\}. \quad (5.5)$$

Using the operator $\tilde{Q}_t u(c, c_s) := \sum_{i \in \hat{I}} q_{t,i} u(c, c_s, i)$ for any real-valued function u defined on $C \times C_s \times \hat{I}$ and $t = T, ..., 0$, we can write (5.5) as

$$\tilde{V}_t(c, c_s, i) = \max_{a \in A(c, c_s, i)} \left\{ a\varphi_i + \tilde{Q}_{t-1} \tilde{V}_{t-1}(c - a, c_s - a\sigma_i) \right\}.$$

We now explore structural properties of $\tilde{M}$, which lead to the optimal policy.

Structural Properties

Lemma 5.1. *For all* $i \in \hat{I}$ *and* $t = T, ..., 0$, *we have*

(i) $\tilde{V}_t(c, c_s, i)$ *is non-decreasing in* c *for all* $c_s \in C_s$,

(ii) $\tilde{V}_t(c, c_s, i)$ *is non-decreasing in* c_s *for all* $c \in C$.

Proof. The proof can be done analogously to the one of Lemma 4.1. □

Due to the two-dimensional system state and the chosen set of admissible actions, the value function is multimodular in cargo capacity and the number of seats as is stated below.

Lemma 5.2. *For any $t = T, ..., 0$ and $i \in \hat{I}$, $\tilde{V}_t(c, c_s, i)$ is multimodular in c and c_s in the context of concavity. Thus, $\tilde{V}_t(c, c_s, i)$ is supermodular and superconcave in c and c_s.*

Proof. See Appendix A. □

Even though $\tilde{M}$'s system state is two-dimensional, it reduces to one dimension once cargo capacity becomes the bottleneck. The reason for this characteristic is that from this point on, capacity is always shorter than the number of remaining seats. In other words, there are more seats remaining than could be sold. Thus, the number of seats will never affect the acceptance decision.

Proposition 5.3. *For $c \leq c_s$, $\tilde{M}$ reduces to M1 with optimality equation*

$$V_t^{M1}(c, i) = \max_{a \in A(c,i)} \left\{ \varphi_i a + \hat{H}_{t-1} V_{t-1}^{M1}(c - a) \right\}$$

for all $i \in \hat{I}$, $t = T, ..., 1$, and $A(c, i) = \{0, ..., \min\{c, \gamma_i\}\}$.

Proof. The proof can be done analogously to the one of Proposition 4.5. □

We are now able to formulate the decision model's optimal policy. For the sake of exposition, we distinguish between cargo and passenger requests and describe the policy in two different theorems.

Theorem 5.1. *The optimal policy of $\tilde{M}$ is a policy $\pi^* = (f_T^*, f_{T-1}^*, ..., f_1^*)$ with decision rules,*

(i) if $c > c_s$ and $i \in \{0, ..., m_1\}$,

$$f_t^*(c, c_s, i) = \begin{cases} 0 & c \leq c^*(t, c_s, i) \\ \min\{\gamma_i, c - c^*(t, c_s, i)\} & c > c^*(t, c_s, i), \end{cases}$$

with switching curves $c^*(t, c_s, i) = \max\{c > 0 : \varphi_i < \tilde{Q}_{t-1}\tilde{V}_{t-1}(c, c_s) - \tilde{Q}_{t-1}\tilde{V}_{t-1}(c - 1, c_s)\}$ which are non-decreasing in c_s. We further define $c^*(t, c_s, i) = 0$ if the set is empty;

(ii) if $c \leq c_s$ and $i \in \{0, ..., m_1\}$,

$$f_t^*(c, i) = \begin{cases} 0 & c \leq c^*(t, i) \\ \min\{\gamma_i, c - c^*(t, i)\} & c > c^*(t, i). \end{cases}$$

We define control limits $c^*(t, i) = \max\{c > 0 : \varphi_i < \hat{H}_{t-1} V_{t-1}^{M1}(c) - \hat{H}_{t-1} V_{t-1}^{M1}(c-1)\}$ and $c^*(t, i) = 0$ if the set is empty.

Proof. We start with the case $c > c_s$. Since $\tilde{V}_t(c, c_s, i)$ is multimodular in c and c_s for $t = T, ..., 0$ and $i \in \{0, ..., m_1\}$, $\tilde{Q}_t \tilde{V}_t(c, c_s)$ is multimodular, too. This does also imply concavity in c, which is (for $c \geq 2$)

$$\tilde{Q}_{t-1} \tilde{V}_{t-1}(c, c_s) - \tilde{Q}_{t-1} \tilde{V}_{t-1}(c-1, c_s)$$
$$\leq \tilde{Q}_{t-1} \tilde{V}_{t-1}(c-1, c_s) - \tilde{Q}_{t-1} \tilde{V}_{t-1}(c-2, c_s).$$

That means, $\tilde{Q}_{t-1} \tilde{V}_{t-1}(c, c_s) - \tilde{Q}_{t-1} \tilde{V}_{t-1}(c-1, c_s)$ is non-increasing in c. Thus, there are thresholds

$$c^*(t, i) = \max\{c > 0 : \varphi_i < \tilde{Q}_{t-1} \tilde{V}_{t-1}(c, c_s) - \tilde{Q}_{t-1} \tilde{V}_{t-1}(c-1, c_s)\}. \quad (5.6)$$

Now fix $c \in C$, $c_s \in C_s$, $t > 0$, $i \in \{0, ..., m_1\}$ and let $d \in \mathbb{N}_0$. If an action a is the largest $a \in A(c, c_s, i)$ that maximizes the right hand side of (5.5) in t, we have

$$a\varphi_i + \tilde{Q}_{t-1} \tilde{V}_{t-1}(c - a, c_s) \geq d\varphi_i + \tilde{Q}_{t-1} \tilde{V}_{t-1}(c - d, c_s) \text{ for } a > d \geq 0, \text{ and}$$
$$a\varphi_i + \tilde{Q}_{t-1} \tilde{V}_{t-1}(c - a, c_s) > d\varphi_i + \tilde{Q}_{t-1} \tilde{V}_{t-1}(c - d, c_s) \text{ for } a < d \leq \gamma_i.$$

Since $\tilde{Q}_{t-1} \tilde{V}_{t-1}$ is concave, we can rewrite the above inequalities as

$$a\varphi_i + \tilde{Q}_{t-1} \tilde{V}_{t-1}(c - a, c_s) \geq (a-1)\varphi_i + \tilde{Q}_{t-1} \tilde{V}_{t-1}(c - (a-1), c_s)$$
$$a\varphi_i + \tilde{Q}_{t-1} \tilde{V}_{t-1}(c - a, c_s) > (a+1)\varphi_i + \tilde{Q}_{t-1} \tilde{V}_{t-1}(c - (a+1), c_s),$$

where the expression reduces to the first (second) equation if $a = \gamma_i$ $(a = 0)$. This can be rearranged as

$$\varphi_i \geq \tilde{Q}_{t-1}\tilde{V}_{t-1}(c - a + 1, c_s) - \tilde{Q}_{t-1}\tilde{V}_{t-1}(c - a, c_s) \qquad (5.7)$$

$$\varphi_i < \tilde{Q}_{t-1}\tilde{V}_{t-1}(c - a, c_s) - \tilde{Q}_{t-1}\tilde{V}_{t-1}(c - a - 1, c_s). \qquad (5.8)$$

Applying (5.6) to the above inequalities yields that $c^*(t, i) = c - a$. For $c \leq c^*(t, i)$, it follows that the optimal action is $a = 0$. For all $c > c^*(t, i)$, we have $a = c - c^*(t, i)$. The optimal action is only limited by the request size γ_i. Thus, we have $a = \min\{\gamma_i, c - c^*(t, i)\}$ if $c > c^*(t, i)$.

Moreover, supermodularity of $\tilde{Q}_{t-1}\tilde{V}_{t-1}(c, c_s)$ gives (for $c \geq 1$)

$$\tilde{Q}_{t-1}\tilde{V}_{t-1}(c, c_s) - \tilde{Q}_{t-1}\tilde{V}_{t-1}(c - 1, c_s)$$
$$\leq \tilde{Q}_{t-1}\tilde{V}_{t-1}(c, c_s + 1) - \tilde{Q}_{t-1}\tilde{V}_{t-1}(c - 1, c_s + 1)$$

Thus, $\tilde{Q}_{t-1}\tilde{V}_{t-1}(c, c_s) - \tilde{Q}_{t-1}\tilde{V}_{t-1}(c - 1, c_s)$ is non-decreasing in c_s. Consequently, the thresholds $c^*(t, i)$ are also non-decreasing in c_s and can thus be extended to monotone switching curves $c^*(t, c_s, i)$.

The proof for $c \leq c_s$ is analog to the proof of Theorem 4.1. $\qquad \square$

For an example of the described policy, see Figure 5.1. We can use this example to interpret the switching curves' shape. For $c > c_s$, the decision rule says that a greater fraction of a request should be accepted the more cargo capacity is remaining. The decision rule also suggests that less capacity should be sold the more seats are remaining. That is, if there are still a lot of seats available for sale, cargo capacity should be saved so that these seats can be sold later in the booking process. If $c < c_s$, decisions are independent of the number of remaining seats since more seats are remaining than could be sold. The decision rule then says that more units of a cargo request should be accepted the more capacity is remaining.

We now turn to the optimal policy in case a passenger request arrives.

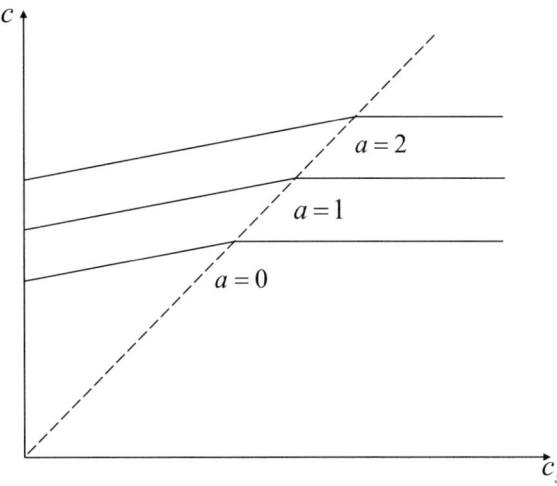

Figure 5.1: Example for a switching curve in case of a cargo request

Theorem 5.2. *The optimal policy of $\tilde{M}$ is a policy $\pi^* = (f_T^*, f_{T-1}^*, ..., f_1^*)$ with decision rules,*

(i) if $c > c_s$ and $i \in \{m_1 + 1, ..., m_2\}$,

$$f_t^*(c, c_s, i) = \begin{cases} 0 & c_s \leq c_s^*(t, c, i) \\ 1 & c_s > c_s^*(t, c, i), \end{cases}$$

with switching curves $c_s^*(t, c, i) = \max\{c_s > 0 : \varphi_i < \tilde{Q}_{t-1}\tilde{V}_{t-1}(c, c_s) - \tilde{Q}_{t-1}\tilde{V}_{t-1}(c - 1, c_s - 1)\}$ which are non-increasing in $c > 0$. We further define $c_s^*(t, c, i) = 0$ if the set is empty;

(ii) if $c \leq c_s$ and $i \in \{m_1 + 1, ..., m_2\}$,

$$f_t^*(c, i) = \begin{cases} 0 & c \leq c^*(t, i) \\ 1 & c > c^*(t, i). \end{cases}$$

We define control limits $c^*(t,i) = \max\{c > 0 : \varphi_i < \hat{H}_{t-1}V_{t-1}^{M1}(c) - \hat{H}_{t-1}V_{t-1}^{M1}(c-1)\}$ *and* $c^*(t,i) = 0$ *if the set is empty.*

Proof. We begin the proof for the case $c > c_s$: Since $\tilde{V}_t(c, c_s, i)$ is multimodular in c and c_s, $\tilde{Q}_{t-1}\tilde{V}_{t-1}(c, c_s)$ is also multimodular for $t = T, ..., 1$. It follows from superconcavity that (for $c \geq 1$ and $c_s \geq 2$)

$$\tilde{Q}_{t-1}\tilde{V}_{t-1}(c, c_s) - \tilde{Q}_{t-1}\tilde{V}_{t-1}(c, c_s - 1)$$
$$\leq \tilde{Q}_{t-1}\tilde{V}_{t-1}(c-1, c_s - 1) - \tilde{Q}_{t-1}\tilde{V}_{t-1}(c-1, c_s - 2),$$

which can be rearranged as

$$\tilde{Q}_{t-1}\tilde{V}_{t-1}(c, c_s) - \tilde{Q}_{t-1}\tilde{V}_{t-1}(c-1, c_s - 1)$$
$$\leq \tilde{Q}_{t-1}\tilde{V}_{t-1}(c, c_s - 1) - \tilde{Q}_{t-1}\tilde{V}_{t-1}(c-1, c_s - 2).$$

That means, $\tilde{Q}_{t-1}\tilde{V}_{t-1}(c, c_s) - \tilde{Q}_{t-1}\tilde{V}_{t-1}(c-1, c_s - 1)$ is non-increasing in c_s. Accordingly, there exist thresholds

$$c_s^*(t,i) := \max\{c_s > 0 : \varphi_i < \tilde{Q}_{t-1}\tilde{V}_{t-1}(c, c_s) - \tilde{Q}_{t-1}\tilde{V}_{t-1}(c-1, c_s - 1)\}$$

(5.9)

for all $i \in \{m_1 + 1, ..., m_2\}$ and $t = T, ..., 1$. If a request for class $i \in \{m_1 + 1, ..., m_2\}$ arrives at t, action $a = 1$ is optimal for $c_s > c_s^*(t,i)$, and $a = 0$ is optimal for $c_s \leq c_s^*(t,i)$.

Furthermore, superconcavity implies that (for $c \geq 2$ and $c_s \geq 1$)

$$\tilde{Q}_{t-1}\tilde{V}_{t-1}(c, c_s) - \tilde{Q}_{t-1}\tilde{V}_{t-1}(c-1, c_s)$$
$$\leq \tilde{Q}_{t-1}\tilde{V}_{t-1}(c-1, c_s - 1) - \tilde{Q}_{t-1}\tilde{V}_{t-1}(c-2, c_s - 1),$$

which can be rearranged as

$$\tilde{Q}_{t-1}\tilde{V}_{t-1}(c, c_s) - \tilde{Q}_{t-1}\tilde{V}_{t-1}(c-1, c_s - 1)$$
$$\leq \tilde{Q}_{t-1}\tilde{V}_{t-1}(c-1, c_s) - \tilde{Q}_{t-1}\tilde{V}_{t-1}(c-2, c_s - 1).$$

That means, $\tilde{Q}_{t-1}\tilde{V}_{t-1}(c,c_s) - \tilde{Q}_{t-1}\tilde{V}_{t-1}(c-1,c_s-1)$ is also non-increasing in c. Consequently, the thresholds $c_s^*(t,i)$ can be extended to switching curves $c_s^*(t,c,i)$ which are non-increasing in c.

We now consider the case for $c \leq c_s$. Due to concavity of $\hat{H}_{t-1}V_{t-1}^{M1}(c)$ in c (for $c \geq 2$) we have

$$\hat{H}_{t-1}V_{t-1}^{M1}(c) - \hat{H}_{t-1}V_{t-1}^{M1}(c-1) \leq \hat{H}_{t-1}V_{t-1}^{M1}(c-1) - \hat{H}_{t-1}V_{t-1}^{M1}(c-2)$$

That means, $\hat{H}_{t-1}V_{t-1}^{M1}(c) - \hat{H}_{t-1}V_{t-1}^{M1}(c-1)$ is non-increasing in c, which ensures the existence of the thresholds

$$c^*(t,i) := \max\{c > 0 : \varphi_i < \hat{H}_{t-1}V_{t-1}^{M1}(c) - \hat{H}_{t-1}V_{t-1}^{M1}(c-1)\},$$

and with $c^*(t,i) = 0$ if the set is empty. If a request for class $i \in \{m_1+1,...,m_2\}$ arrives at time t, action $a = 1$ is optimal for $c > c^*(t,i)$, and $a = 0$ is optimal for $c \leq c^*(t,i)$. $\qquad\Box$

In order to get an idea of the switching curves' shape, see Figure 5.2 as an example. This figure does also help to interpret the optimal policy. Consider first the area $c > c_s$. The policy suggests that if many seats are remaining, a passenger request should be accepted. That means, if only a few seats are remaining, capacity is saved for later passenger requests. This reflects the typical rationale in revenue management which is to save capacity for later requests which might have a higher revenue. Further, if much cargo capacity is remaining, a passenger request should be accepted. That is, if cargo capacity is scarce, passenger requests tend to be rejected in order to save capacity for profitable cargo requests. For $c \leq c_s$, decisions are independent of the number of available seats because there are more seats remaining than could be sold. The decision rule says that a passenger request should be accepted if much cargo capacity is remaining.

Note that we might as well define switching curves $c^*(t,c_s,i)$, which are non-increasing in c_s, and define optimal decisions based on them.

The optimal policy can also be structured with respect to time. In order to show this, we need the following lemma.

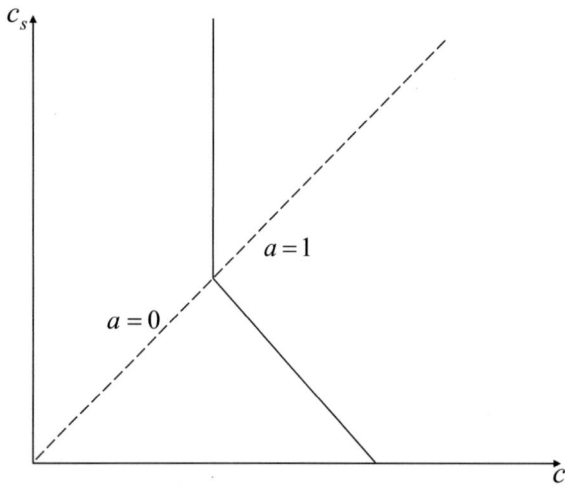

Figure 5.2: Example for a switching curve in case of a passenger request

Lemma 5.3. *For all $c \in C$, $c_s \in C_s$, $a_i^* = f_{t+1}^*(c, c_s, i)$ for some $i \in \hat{I}$, and $t = T - 1, ..., 0$, we have*

$$
\begin{aligned}
&\tilde{Q}_t \tilde{V}_t(c, c_s) - \tilde{Q}_t \tilde{V}_t(c - 1, c_s - 1) \\
&\leq \tilde{Q}_t \tilde{V}_t(c - a_i^*, c_s - a_i^* \sigma_i) - \tilde{Q}_t \tilde{V}_t(c - 1 - a_i^*, c_s - 1 - a_i^* \sigma_i).
\end{aligned}
\tag{5.10}
$$

Proof. It is easy to see that (5.10) holds for $a_i^* = 0$. We now consider (5.10) for some $i \neq 0$, $a_i^* > 0$, and $t \geq 0$:

(i) For cargo requests ($i \in I_c$), it follows from subconcavity that

$$
\begin{aligned}
&\tilde{Q}_t \tilde{V}_t(c, c_s) - \tilde{Q}_t \tilde{V}_t(c - 1, c_s - 1) \\
\leq &\tilde{Q}_t \tilde{V}_t(c - 1, c_s) - \tilde{Q}_t \tilde{V}_t(c - 2, c_s - 1) \\
\leq &\tilde{Q}_t \tilde{V}_t(c - 2, c_s) - \tilde{Q}_t \tilde{V}_t(c - 3, c_s - 1) \\
&\vdots
\end{aligned}
$$

$$\leq \tilde{Q}_t \tilde{V}_t(c - a^*, c_s) - \tilde{Q}_t \tilde{V}_t(c - 1 - a^*, c_s - 1).$$

(ii) For passenger requests ($i \in I_s$), the only action greater zero is $a_i^* = 1$. It follows from subconcavity that

$$\tilde{Q}_t \tilde{V}_t(c, c_s) - \tilde{Q}_t \tilde{V}_t(c - 1, c_s - 1)$$
$$\leq \tilde{Q}_t \tilde{V}_t(c - 1, c_s) - \tilde{Q}_t \tilde{V}_t(c - 2, c_s - 1)$$
$$\leq \tilde{Q}_t \tilde{V}_t(c - 1, c_s - 1) - \tilde{Q}_t \tilde{V}_t(c - 2, c_s - 2).$$

The two cases together complete the proof. $\qquad\qquad\square$

Proposition 5.4. *For any $i \in \{m_1 + 1, ..., m_2\}$ and $c > c_s$, the switching curves $c_s^*(t, c, i)$ are non-decreasing in t.*

Proof. In order to prove this proposition, we have to show that opportunity cost $\tilde{Q}_t \tilde{V}_t(c, c_s) - \tilde{Q}_t \tilde{V}_t(c - 1, c_s - 1)$ is non-decreasing in time. We fix $c > 0$ and $c_s > 0$ as well as $t > 0$. Further, we let $a_i^* = f_t^*(c - 1, c_s - 1, i)$ be the optimal action at time t if class $i \in \hat{I}$ is requested, $c - 1$ capacity and $c_s - 1$ seats are remaining. Note that we have $a_i^* \in A(c - 1, c_s - 1, i)$ and $a_i^* \in A(c, c_s, i)$. It follows that

$$\tilde{Q}_t \tilde{V}_t(c, c_s) - \tilde{Q}_t \tilde{V}_t(c - 1, c_s - 1)$$
$$= \sum_{i \in \hat{I}} q_{t,i} \left[\max_{a \in A(c, c_s, i)} \left\{ a\varphi_i + \tilde{Q}_{t-1} \tilde{V}_{t-1}(c - a, c_s - a\sigma_i) \right\} \right.$$
$$\left. - \max_{a \in A(c-1, c_s-1, i)} \left\{ a\varphi_i + \tilde{Q}_{t-1} \tilde{V}_{t-1}(c - 1 - a, c_s - 1 - a\sigma_i) \right\} \right]$$
$$\geq \sum_{i \in \hat{I}} q_{t,i} \left[\tilde{Q}_{t-1} \tilde{V}_{t-1}(c - a_i^*, c_s - a_i^* \sigma_i) \right.$$
$$\left. - \tilde{Q}_{t-1} \tilde{V}_{t-1}(c - 1 - a_i^*, c_s - 1 - a_i^* \sigma_i) \right]$$
$$\geq \tilde{Q}_{t-1} \tilde{V}_{t-1}(c, c_s) - \tilde{Q}_{t-1} \tilde{V}_{t-1}(c - 1, c_s - 1).$$

The last inequality follows from Lemma 5.3. Accordingly, the switching curves $c_s^*(t, c, i)$ are non-decreasing in time. $\square$

Proposition 5.5. *For any $i \in \{0, ..., m_1\}$ and $c > c_s$, the switching curves $c^*(t, c_s, i)$ are non-decreasing in t.*

Proof. The proof can be done analogously to the one shown above, but the last inequality follows from concavity. $\square$

Note that for $c \leq c_s$, the control limits $c^*(t, i)$ are also non-decreasing in time as it was shown in Proposition 4.3. This property implies that requests (or parts of them) should be accepted as departure approaches.

The policy can be further characterized by the following property.

Proposition 5.6. *For $t = T, ..., 1$ we have $c^*(t, c_s, i_1) \leq c^*(t, c_s, i_2)$ with $\varphi_{i_1} \geq \varphi_{i_2}$ and $i_1, i_2 \in \{0, ..., m_1\}$. Further, for $t = T, ..., 1$, we have $c_s^*(t, c, i_1) \leq c_s^*(t, c, i_2)$ with $\varphi_{i_1} \geq \varphi_{i_2}$ and $i_1, i_2 \in \{m_1 + 1, ..., m_2\}$.*

Proof. The proof can be done analogously to the one of Proposition 4.4. $\square$

Note that this property applies as well to the control limits $c^*(t, i)$ for $c \leq c_s$ (cf. Proposition 4.4). The implication of this property is that a request with a higher revenue is rather (partially) accepted than a request with a lower revenue.

The model $\tilde{M}$ provides a very comprehensible decision rule, which increases acceptance of the model in practice. However, if an airline's business policy only allows for entirely accepting requests or if both weight and volume have to be considered, $\tilde{M}$ cannot be applied. For this case, we provide, in the next section, two efficient heuristics that can be applied to determine a solution to the basic model outlined in Section 5.1.

5.3 Heuristics and Bounds

Optimal policies of the basic integrated capacity control model cannot be determined directly for real-world problems. Since the system state comprises three dimensions, the model suffers from the curse of dimensionality. Thus, we provide two different heuristics that efficiently find feasible solutions. The first heuristic decomposes the decision problem into three one-dimensional subproblems and allows for partially accepting cargo requests. This yields that the heuristic's decision rule is simply structured. The second heuristics makes decisions based on bid prices for weight, volume, and seats, which are determined by a deterministic linear program. This linear program provides an upper bound on the maximum expected revenue.

Heuristic based on Decomposition into Three Subproblems (HD3)

This heuristic decomposes the three-dimensional MDP into three one-dimensional subproblems. Thereby, the well-known passenger capacity control problem is obtained. Further, the two cargo subproblems are almost identical to the ones described in Section 4.3. The difference is the way the revenue generated by accepting one unit of a request is allocated among the subproblems. This is outlined below.

$$
\varphi_i^w := \begin{cases} \bar{\varphi} & i \in I_s \\ \varphi_i & \text{otherwise} \end{cases}
$$

$$
\varphi_i^v := \begin{cases} \varphi_i \dfrac{\left(\frac{v_i}{\vartheta} - w_i\right)}{v_i} \mathbf{1}_{\{\frac{v_i}{\vartheta} > w_i\}} = \varphi_i \left(\dfrac{1}{\vartheta} - \dfrac{w_i}{v_i}\right) \mathbf{1}_{\{\frac{v_i}{\vartheta} > w_i\}} & i \in I_c \\ 0 & \text{otherwise} \end{cases}
$$

$$
\varphi_i^s := \begin{cases} \max\{\varphi_i - \bar{\varphi} w_i, 0\} & i \in I_s \\ 0 & \text{otherwise} \end{cases}
$$

with $\bar{\varphi} = (\sum_{t=1}^{T} \sum_{i \in I_c} q_{t,i} \varphi_i) / (\sum_{t=1}^{T} \sum_{i \in I_c} q_{t,i})$ as the expected average revenue per chargeable weight unit over all cargo requests. This allocation implies that a passenger request generates revenue in both the seat subproblem and in the weight subproblem. This ensures that a passenger request is not always rejected in the weight subproblem; note that this would happen if its acceptance did not generate revenue. We only account for passengers requiring cargo capacity in the weight subproblem because weight requirement is relatively high compared to volume requirement.

All subproblems can be formulated as an MDP of the form of M1 as described in Section 4.2. Thus, the weight subproblem has the following optimality equation for all $c_w \in C_w$, $i \in \hat{I}$, and $t = T, ..., 1$:

$$V_t^{M1,w}(c_w, i) = \max_{a \in A(c_w, i)} \left\{ a\varphi_i^w + \hat{H}_{t-1} V_{t-1}^{M1,w}(c_w - a) \right\}.$$

The volume subproblem's optimality equation is for all $c_v \in C_v$, $i \in \hat{I}$, and $t = T, ..., 1$

$$V_t^{M1,v}(c_v, i) = \max_{a \in A(c_v, i)} \left\{ a\varphi_i^v + \hat{H}_{t-1} V_{t-1}^{M1,v}(c_v - a) \right\}.$$

And the seat subproblem's optimality equation for all $c_s \in C_s$, $i \in \hat{I}$, and $t = T, ..., 1$ is

$$V_t^{M1,s}(c_s, i) = \max_{a \in A(c_s, i)} \left\{ a\varphi_i^s + \hat{H}_{t-1} V_{t-1}^{M1,s}(c_s - a) \right\}.$$

In the seat subproblem, we have $A(c_s, i) = \{0, ..., \min\{\sigma_i, c_s\}\}$. We set all terminal values of the subproblems to zero since we do not consider overbooking.

The decision rule based on HD3 says that a request for shipment type $i \in \hat{I}$ should be accepted at time t when $c_w \geq w_i$, $c_v \geq v_i$, and $c_s \geq \sigma_i$ weight, volume, and seats, respectively, are remaining and if

$$\rho_i \geq \underbrace{\left[\hat{H}_{t-1}V_{t-1}^{M1,w}(c_w) - \hat{H}_{t-1}V_{t-1}^{M1,w}(c_w - w_i)\right]}_{=\delta_{t-1}(c_w,i)}$$

$$+ \underbrace{\left[\hat{H}_{t-1}V_{t-1}^{M1,v}(c_v) - \hat{H}_{t-1}V_{t-1}^{M1,v}(c_v - v_i)\right]}_{=\delta_{t-1}(c_v,i)}$$

$$+ \underbrace{\left[\hat{H}_{t-1}V_{t-1}^{M1,s}(c_s) - \hat{H}_{t-1}V_{t-1}^{M1,s}(c_s - \sigma_i)\right]}_{=\delta_{t-1}(c_s,i)}.$$

This decision rule suggests that a cargo request is accepted if sufficient capacity is available and if the generated revenue is at least as high as the opportunity cost of the weight plus the opportunity cost of the volume subproblem. Further, a passenger request should be accepted if at least one seat is remaining and if the sum of the opportunity costs of all three subproblems is not greater than the price associated with the booking class.

We know from Section 4.3 that the opportunity costs $\delta_t(c_w, i)$, $\delta_t(c_v, i)$, and $\delta_t(c_s, i)$ are non-increasing in c_w, c_v, and c_s, respectively. This monotonicity property applies as well to the sum of the opportunity costs, $\delta_t(c_w, i) + \delta_t(c_v, i) + \delta_t(c_s, i)$. This allows us to make a statement on the structure of the policy based on HD3.

Proposition 5.7. *The heuristic policy based on HD3 is a structured policy* $\pi = (f_T, f_{T-1}, ..., f_1)$ *with decision rules*

$$f_t(c_w, c_v, c_s, i) = \begin{cases} 1 & c_s > c_s(t, c_w, c_v, i), c_w \geq w_i, c_v \geq v_i, c_s \geq \sigma_i \\ 0 & otherwise \end{cases}$$

and with thresholds $c_s(t, c_w, c_v, i) = \max\{c_s > 0 : \rho_i < \delta_{t-1}(c_w, i) + \delta_{t-1}(c_v, i) + \delta_{t-1}(c_s, i), c_w \geq w_i, c_v \geq v_i\}$ *which are non-increasing in* c_w *and* c_v. *If the set is empty, we define* $c_s(t, c_w, c_v, i) = 0$ *for all* $i \in I_s$ *and* $c_s(t, c_w, c_v, i) = -1$ *for all* $i \in I_c$.

129

Note that the policy based on this heuristic might as well be defined with respect to volume or weight. Note further that the thresholds depend on two variables, and thus the concept of switching curves is not applicable in this context. The interpretation of the policy is that, first, if many seats are remaining, a request should be accepted, and second, if much cargo capacity (weight and/or volume) is remaining, a request should be accepted. Note that this contradicts the optimal policy of $\tilde{M}$ which saves cargo capacity if a lot of seats are remaining in order to sell these seats at a later time. This contradiction is caused by the decomposition of the state space.

Heuristic based on Bid Prices (HBP)

The capacity control problem can be simplified by considering the number of incoming requests for each class over the entire booking horizon as deterministic. Letting them be equal to the expected number of requests, the decision problem is then to maximize the revenue from accepting requests subject to the available capacity. Allowing for partially accepting requests (both cargo and passengers), this yields the following LP:

$$(\textbf{BP}) \quad \max_{\boldsymbol{y}} \sum_{i=1}^{m_2} y_i \rho_i \tag{5.11}$$

$$\text{s.t.} \quad \sum_{i=1}^{m_2} y_i w_i \leq \mathfrak{C}_w \tag{5.12}$$

$$\sum_{i=1}^{m_2} y_i v_i \leq \mathfrak{C}_v \tag{5.13}$$

$$\sum_{i=m_1+1}^{m_2} y_i \leq \mathfrak{C}_s \tag{5.14}$$

$$y_i \leq \sum_{t=1}^{T} q_{t,i} \quad \forall i = 1, ..., m_2 \tag{5.15}$$

$$y_i \geq 0 \quad \forall i = 1, ..., m_2. \tag{5.16}$$

Let z_{BP} denote the maximum objective value of the optimization problem. It gives an upper bound on the maximum expected revenue determined in (5.3).

Proposition 5.8. *We have* $Q_T V_T(\mathfrak{C}_w, \mathfrak{C}_v, \mathfrak{C}_s) \leq z_{BP}$.

Proof. The proof can be done very similarly to the proof of Proposition 2 in Amaruchkul et al. (2007) and is thus omitted. $\qquad\square$

We denote the dual variables of (5.12), (5.13), and (5.14) as λ_w, λ_v, and λ_s which are interpreted as the marginal value (bid price) of one weight unit, volume unit, and seat, respectively. These bid prices can be utilized to construct the following heuristic decision rule at time t:

$$f_t(c_w, c_v, c_s, i) = \begin{cases} 1 & \rho_i \geq \lambda_w w_i + \lambda_v v_i + \lambda_s \sigma_i, c_w \geq w_i, c_v \geq v_i, c_s \geq \sigma_i \\ 0 & \text{otherwise.} \end{cases}$$

Note that this approach is very similar to the deterministic linear programming approach that is used in passenger network revenue management (see Talluri & van Ryzin, 2004, pp. 93-95). The decision rule's advantage is that it is very comprehensible, and the bid prices can be obtained easily. However, it is not time-dependent and does not consider remaining capacity. The following numerical experiments demonstrate its performance in comparison to the decomposition heuristic HD3.

5.4 Numerical Experiments

We now assess the quality of HD3 and HBP. Further, the revenue of one more heuristic is evaluated. This heuristic accepts cargo as long as sufficient capacity is available, and it accepts passenger requests according to the optimal policy of the one-dimensional passenger decision problem. This heuristic is hereafter referred to as *IFCFS* since it integrates a cargo first-come-first-served policy and optimal passenger acceptance decisions. As a benchmark for the heuristics' achieved revenue over the simulated booking processes, we use the maximum expected revenue as determined in (5.3). This value was computed by means of a HP XC3000 high performance computer. Further, the upper bound z_{BP} is compared to the maximum expected revenue in order to assess its quality. All experiments were conducted on an Intel Core2 Quad CPU at 2.83 GHz and 8 GB RAM. In order to obtain the bid prices for HBP, we solved the linear program by means of Gurobi 5.0 (Gurobi Optimization, 2012).

In the experiments, we use the same shipment categories as in Section 4.4 (see Table 4.1). Thus, we consider shipment categories $b = 1, ..., 9$ that all have a different weight and volume requirement w_b, v_b. In each time period, either a shipment with revenue per chargeable weight φ, a passenger seat with revenue φ, or neither a shipment nor a seat is requested. Table 5.1 outlines the probabilities for an incoming request with a per unit revenue φ. The rationale behind this setting is that it is more likely that a passenger rather than a cargo request arrives at the beginning of the booking period. On the other hand, close to departure the arrival of a cargo request becomes more likely. Note that the probability of no arrival is 0.25 and 0.5 in periods 1-20 and 21-40, respectively. Further, note that the probability for high-value requests increases as departure approaches.

Given a cargo request, the probability that an incoming request belongs to a particular category is the same as in the cargo experiments (see Table 4.3). If a passenger request is observed, it belongs to category $b = 10$, which requires one seat, 100 kg, and 10×10^4 cm^3. The request probability for a particular class $i = (b, \varphi)$ at time t equals the probability of observing a revenue φ multiplied by the probability of observing a category b request at this time (since we assume independence between requested categories and per-unit revenues). For example, the probability of an arrival of a cargo shipment class with $\varphi = 0.8$ and $b = 8$ at $t = 10$ is $0.0833 \times 0.1 = 0.00833$. The probability for an arrival of a passenger booking class with $\varphi = 110$ at $t = 35$ equals the probability of the revenue at this time, which is 0.04 since only one passenger category is considered. Accepting a request for class $i \in I_c$ gives a revenue of $\varphi_i \max\{w_i, v_i/\vartheta\}$ with $\vartheta = 0.6$. Accepting a request for class $i \in I_s$ gives a revenue of φ_i.

We consider a booking horizon of $T = 40$ time periods. Multiplying capacity requirements by request probabilities over the entire booking horizon yields

Cargo requests Revenue	Request probabilities			
	Period 1-10	Period 11-20	Period 21-30	Period 31-40
1.2	0.25	0.1667	0.04	0
1.0	0.15	0.1666	0.06	0
0.8	0.1	0.1667	0.1	0
Passenger requests Revenue				
140	0.035	0.03	0.03	0.04
130	0.035	0.03	0.03	0.04
120	0.035	0.03	0.03	0.04
110	0.03	0.03	0.03	0.04
100	0.03	0.03	0.036	0.06
90	0.03	0.03	0.036	0.06
80	0.02	0.025	0.036	0.06
70	0.02	0.025	0.036	0.08
60	0.015	0.02	0.036	0.08

Table 5.1: Request probabilities for different revenues

expected demand in weight, volume, and seats of $\mathfrak{D}_w$=4340 kg, $\mathfrak{D}_v$=1970×10⁴ cm³, and $\mathfrak{D}_s$=13, respectively. We let total available capacity ($\mathfrak{C}_w,\mathfrak{C}_v,\mathfrak{C}_s$) vary in order to assess the heuristics' performance for different capacity-demand ratios. These ratios represent two different scenarios: First, a flight that is both weight and volume restricted, and second, a flight that is restricted with respect to weight, volume, and passenger seats.

In order to determine the performance of our heuristics, we repeatedly simulated the arrival process and computed the average revenue gained in the selling process over all simulation runs. In order to obtain reliable results, we simulated 100,000 booking processes. The heuristics' performance relative to the maximum expected revenue in case of a both weight and volume restricted flight is display in Figure 5.3. Observe that HD3 outperforms HBP and IFCFS for all

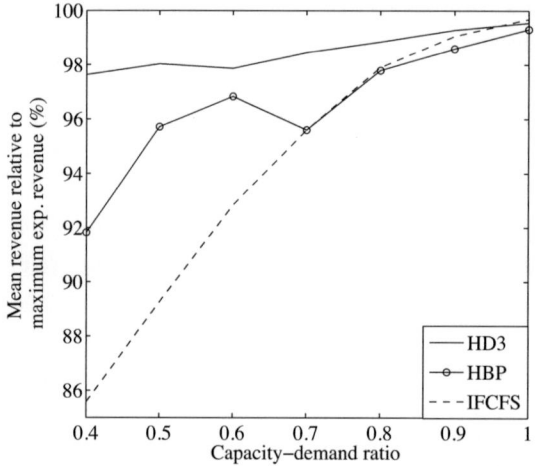

Figure 5.3: Heuristics' performance for both weight and volume restricted flights (relative to maximum expected revenue)

capacity-demand ratios lower than 1. Furthermore, the performance of HD3 is relatively constant and revenues are very close to the maximum expected revenue for all scenarios. Another observation is that the performance of IFCFS decreases as less capacity is available which can be explained by the poor performance of a cargo first-come-first-served policy in case of insufficient capacity. Further, HBP's performance does also become worse as less capacity is available. Our explanation for this observation is that the inventory-insensitivity causes HBP to perform badly if capacity is scarce.

The numerical results for flights that offer too few passenger seats relative to demand as well as insufficient weight and volume are summarized in Figure 5.4. Here we keep weight and volume capacity constant ($\mathfrak{C}_w/\mathfrak{D}_w \approx \mathfrak{C}_v/\mathfrak{D}_v \approx$ 0.7) and let the number of available seats vary. We choose a situation where cargo capacity is scarce since otherwise cargo capacity control would not yield a benefit. Again HD3 demonstrates the best overall performance of all tested

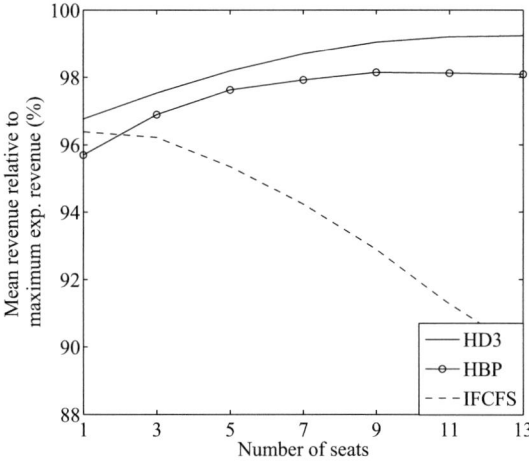

Figure 5.4: Heuristics' performance for weight, volume and passenger restricted flights (relative to maximum expected revenue)

heuristics with revenues very close to the maximum expected revenue. Another observation is that HD3 and HBP perform worse as fewer seats are available, whereas IFCFS performs better under such conditions. This is caused by the fact that IFCFS focuses on passenger capacity control, which is particularly important in case of an insufficient number of available seats. In this case, IFCFS can even balance the disadvantage from accepting cargo according to a first-come-first-served policy.

Tables 5.2 and 5.3 show the relative difference between z_{BP} and the maximum expected revenue for different capacity-demand ratios. For weight and

Total capacity			$\frac{z_{BP}}{Q_T V_T(\mathcal{C}_w,\mathcal{C}_v,\mathcal{C}_s)}$ %
$\mathcal{C}_w$	$\mathcal{C}_v$	$\mathcal{C}_s$	
4340	1970	13	113.44
3906	1773	13	111.63
3472	1576	13	111.25
3038	1379	13	111.07
2604	1182	13	109.98
2170	985	13	111.04
1736	788	13	111.29

Table 5.2: Upper bound quality depending on both available weight and volume (relative to maximum expected revenue)

volume restricted flights (see Table 5.2), observe that the upper bound's quality is relatively constant and even tends to become better if less capacity is available. Thus, the upper bound is quite a good approximation of the maximum expected revenue under these conditions. For a flight that is restricted in all capacity dimensions (see Table 5.3), the upper bound becomes less tight if fewer seats are available. In this situation, the maximum expected revenue decreases since very few profitable passenger requests can be accepted, and capacity has to be sold alternatively to cargo requests. (**BP**) sells this free capacity selectively to the most profitable cargo requests and thus achieves a higher revenue. This is in particular possible since parts of high-value requests can be accepted at the end of the booking horizon even if capacity is insufficient to accept entire requests.

Total capacity			$\dfrac{z_{BP}}{Q_T V_T(\mathfrak{C}_w, \mathfrak{C}_v, \mathfrak{C}_s)}$ %
$\mathfrak{C}_w$	$\mathfrak{C}_v$	$\mathfrak{C}_s$	
2400	1380	13	107.99
2400	1380	11	108.07
2400	1380	9	108.37
2400	1380	7	109.16
2400	1380	5	110.72
2400	1380	3	112.90
2400	1380	1	115.15

Table 5.3: Upper bound quality depending on available seats (relative to maximum expected revenue)

In summary, HD3 performs very well for all tested scenarios and achieves revenues that are very close to optimal. However, note that HD3 features the same shortcomings as HDP in the cargo capacity control experiments in case of volume restricted flights. On the other hand, it is particularly strong for weight-restricted flights. Further, HBP performs quite well if capacity is ample. IFCFS's performance is only comparable to the performance of the other heuristics if the number of total seats is very low or capacity is sufficient to accommodate expected demand. The upper bound we proposed demonstrates a good quality, especially if capacity is ample.

CHAPTER 6

Network Cargo Capacity Control

In Chapter 4, we already analyzed the single-leg cargo capacity control problem. Since we focused on simply structured policies of the basic problem, we neglected some practical challenges. In this chapter, we attempt to model a cargo capacity control problem that accounts for as many practical challenges as possible. This yields the following differences to the discussed single-leg model: First, we consider a network of flights rather than a single leg. Second, we allow for uncertain aircraft capacity and for an uncertain shipment capacity requirement. Third, in order to handle these uncertainties, we allow for overbooking. All these aspects imply a tremendous increase in complexity compared to the single-leg model, which is already computationally intractable for large problems. Therefore, our focus in this chapter is, on the one hand, on determining upper bounds on the maximum expected revenue, and on the other hand, on developing heuristics that determine feasible solutions to the decision problem.

In Section 6.1, we outline the network cargo capacity control model. In Section 6.2, we propose several bounds on the maximum expected revenue that are all based on linear programs. Section 6.3 provides an approximate dynamic programming approach to the network capacity control problem. An affine value function approximation and its structural properties as well as a piecewise linear approximation are proposed. As a further way of determining heuristic decision rules, a dynamic programming decomposition approach is discussed in Section

6.4. In Section 6.5, we assess the quality of the proposed bounds and the performance of the heuristics using numerical experiments.

The notation we use in this chapter deviates slightly from the notation we used in the previous chapters. First, we let the value function in this chapter be denoted by G since V represents the random volume requirement of shipments. Second, l represents a particular leg in this chapter, whereas it denoted a two-dimensional function in the third chapter.

6.1 Capacity Control Model

Consider a cargo carrier operating flights on a network. An aircraft's cargo capacity on each leg $l \in L = \{1, ..., \mathfrak{L}\}$ is represented by the random vector (K_l^w, K_l^v), in which K_l^w denotes the random variable describing the maximum weight that can be transported on leg l and K_l^v the maximum volume, respectively. Over a booking horizon of T time periods, the carrier may receive short-term booking requests for shipment classes $i \in I = \{0, ..., m\}$. Each class is characterized by its uncertain weight and volume requirement, its per unit contribution margin, and the legs it requests. We count time backwards with time period T denoting the first period of the selling process and $t = 0$ representing the departure of the freighters in the network. We assume that the arrival process follows a Poisson process, which is approximated by Bernoulli experiments. Choosing T as a sufficiently large number ensures that the probability of more than one arrival per time period can be neglected. In each period $t = T, ..., 0$, we denote the probability of an arrival of a booking request from class i by $q_{t,i} \geq 0$. The probability that no request arrives is given by $q_{t,0} = 1 - \sum_{i=1}^{m} q_{t,i} \geq 0$. We further define $q_{0,0} = 1$ and $q_{0,i} = 0$ for $i = 1, ..., m$. That means, no request arrives at $t = 0$. Like in the previous chapters, we make the following assumptions that are common in revenue management: First, customers do not behave strategically. Second, the decision maker is risk-neutral. Third, demand is independent between shipment classes and also independent of the availability of other classes.

In each period, in which a request is observed, a decision has to be made if the incoming request is accepted or rejected for transportation by the carrier. We assume that at the time the decision is made, the actual weight and volume of the requested class is only known in distribution. We denote the weight and volume that a class of type i requires at the time of departure by random variables W_i and V_i. It is common industry practice to only charge the weight and volume that were actually used. In particular, a contribution margin φ_i (which we hereafter refer to as revenue) is earned per chargeable weight unit of class i, and chargeable weight units are given by $\max\{W_i, V_i/\vartheta\}$, where ϑ is a constant representing the volume-weight ratio of a standard shipment. Rejected demand is lost. Class $i = 0$ represents the event of no arriving request, and we define $P(W_0 = 0) = 1$, $P(V_0 = 0) = 1$, and $\varphi_0 = 0$.

Note that we need to keep track of the number of accepted shipments of each booking class over time since their distribution of weight and volume might differ and realizations are only observed at departure. We denote the number of accepted class-i requests as $c_i \in \mathbb{N}_0$.

Since the capacity, the required weight, and the required volume by a class are uncertain, overbooking is allowed. Following Amaruchkul et al. (2007), we penalize overselling, i.e. the event that at the time of departure more weight or volume was sold than capacity became available, by non-negative per unit offloading cost ϕ_l^w and ϕ_l^v for oversold weight and volume on leg l, respectively. This approach is reasonable since a flight might be oversold in only one dimension, while units of the other dimension are still available. While this is a huge simplification of the actual offloading problem, Luo et al. (2009) report that this assumption can be found in cargo revenue management practice.

The objective of this decision problem is to identify an optimal control policy that maximizes the total expected revenue over the entire booking horizon. This can be reduced to solving the optimality equation of the following finite-horizon MDP $(T, S, E, A, p_t, r_t, \tilde{G}_0)$ with:

(i) *Planning horizon* $T \in \mathbb{N}_0$, indexed by t.

(ii) *State space* $S \times E = \mathbf{C_t} \times I$
   with $\mathbf{C_t} := \{(c_1, ..., c_m) \in \mathbb{N}_0^m : \sum_{i=1}^m c_i \leq T - t, \ \forall 0 \leq t \leq T\}$. The

state space comprises the number of accepted requests of each class as system states and the currently requested class as an environmental state. The upper bound of the state space is a consequence of the assumption that at most one request can be accepted per period. Thus, the sum of all accepted requests cannot be greater than the number of elapsed decision periods.

(iii) *Action space* $A \in \{0,1\}$ indicates whether a request is denied or accepted. The set of *admissible actions* is defined as $A(c,i) := \{0,1\}$ for all $c \in C_t$ and $i \in I$. Since the set of admissible actions is independent of the current state, we define $A(i) := A(c,i)$ for all $i \in I$ and $c \in C_t$.

(iv) *Transition law* $p_t(c,i,a,c+ae_i,i') = q_{t-1,i'}$
for all $t = T,...,1$, $c \in C_t$, $i,i' \in I$, and $a \in A(i)$. e_i is an m-dimensional vector, where the i-th entry is one and all other entries are zero. We define e_0 as the m-dimensional zero vector.

(v) *One-stage reward function*
$r_t(c,i,a) = a\mathbb{E}_{W_i,V_i}[\varphi_i \max\{W_i, V_i/\vartheta\}] =: a\rho_i$ for all $t = T,...,1$, $c \in C_t$, $i \in I$, and $a \in A(i)$.

(vi) *Terminal reward function*

$$\tilde{G}_0(c,i') = -\sum_{l \in L} \mathbb{E}_{W,V,K^w,K^v} \left[\phi_l^w \left(\sum_{i \in I(l)} W_i c_i - K_l^w \right)^+ + \phi_l^v \left(\sum_{i \in I(l)} V_i c_i - K_l^v \right)^+ \right]$$

for all $c \in C_0$ and $i' \in I$ with $I(l)$ denoting the set of classes that request leg l. We define $W = (W_1,...,W_m)$ and $V = (V_1,...,V_m)$ as the vector of random weight and volume requirement, respectively. Further, let K^w and K^v be a vector of capacities for weight and volume, respectively, on all legs $l \in L$. Note that we allow for any general distributions of actual weights, volumes, and capacities. In particular, weights and volumes might be dependent. However, we assume that capacity is independent of both weight and volume requirement.

Note that one could also account for additional loading restrictions, such as limited positions for certain pallets or containers, by introducing additional nondecreasing penalty functions per leg. For the sake of simplicity, we consider only weight and volume restrictions on a leg hereafter.

Let $\tilde{G}_t(\boldsymbol{c}, i)$ denote the maximum expected revenue that can be gained in periods t to departure by accepting additional requests given that $\boldsymbol{c} \in \boldsymbol{C}_t$ requests have already been accepted and class $i \in I$ is currently requested. This is the unique solution to the following optimality equation of the MDP:

$$\tilde{G}_t(\boldsymbol{c}, i) = \max_{a \in A(i)} \left\{ \rho_i a + \sum_{i' \in I} q_{t-1,i'} \tilde{G}_{t-1}(\boldsymbol{c} + a\boldsymbol{e}_i, i') \right\}. \qquad (6.1)$$

Accordingly, if a class-i request is accepted, a revenue ρ_i will be generated and the system state will increase by 1 in dimension i. If a request is rejected or no request arrives, no revenue will be generated and the system state will not change.

In order to reduce the MDP's large system state, we use the observable-disturbance form of (6.1) hereafter. We define $G_t(\boldsymbol{c}) := \sum_{i \in I} q_{t,i} \tilde{G}_t(\boldsymbol{c}, i)$ for all $t = T, ..., 0$ and $\boldsymbol{c} \in \boldsymbol{C}_t$ and write

$$G_t(\boldsymbol{c}) = \sum_{i \in I} q_{t,i} \max\{\rho_i + G_{t-1}(\boldsymbol{c} + \boldsymbol{e}_i), G_{t-1}(\boldsymbol{c})\}. \qquad (6.2)$$

If a booking request for shipment class $i \in I$ is accepted at time t, the expected revenue is $\rho_i + G_{t-1}(\boldsymbol{c} + \boldsymbol{e}_i)$. If the request is rejected, the expected revenue is $G_{t-1}(\boldsymbol{c})$. Accordingly, the optimal decision rule in t, in state $\boldsymbol{c} \in \boldsymbol{C}_t$, and if shipment class $i \in I$ is requested, is

$$f_t^*(c, i) = \begin{cases} 1 & \rho_i \geq G_{t-1}(c) - G_{t-1}(c + e_i) \\ 0 & \text{otherwise.} \end{cases} \qquad (6.3)$$

The difference $G_{t-1}(c) - G_{t-1}(c+e_i)$ can be interpreted as the opportunity cost of the cargo space a class-i request requires. It is the difference in the maximum expected revenue that can be gained by accepting additional requests in future time periods when a request for class i is rejected minus the maximum expected revenue when it is accepted. The decision rule says that a request should only be accepted if its revenue is at least as big as its opportunity cost.

In this setting $G_T(\mathbf{0})$ yields the maximum expected revenue that can be gained within the booking process if the freighter is initially empty. Although, in general, the initial state of freighters is given by the quantities sold through long-term contracts, we will assume that the freighters are empty when the booking process starts ($c = \mathbf{0}$). This is done for the ease of exposition only, an extension to a general initial state is straightforward.

Due to the curse of dimensionality, determining the exact values of $G_t(c)$, which are needed for finding out optimal decisions, is computationally infeasible. Even single-leg problems are intractable as we already showed in Chapter 4. In passenger network revenue management, several approaches to obtain heuristics and upper bounds on $G_T(\mathbf{0})$ are well known. In the following sections, we will discuss how and if results from this stream of literature carry over to cargo revenue management. In the next section, we apply linear programming approaches to our decision problem in order to determine upper bounds.

6.2 Upper Bounds based on Linear Programming

One rather crude simplification to make the above problem tractable would be to replace all random variables by their expected values (cf. heuristic HBP in Section 5.3). Instead of solving an MDP, the resulting problem would simply determine how many shipments of which class should be accepted under the condition that the number of accepted requests must be less than or equal to expected demand. The objective is to maximize expected revenue from accepted requests minus expected overbooking cost.

Allowing for partial (i.e. non-integer) acceptance of y_i requests from class $i \in I \backslash \{0\}$ yields the following optimization problem:

$$
\textbf{(DLP)} \quad \max_{y} \sum_{i=1}^{m} \rho_i y_i - \sum_{l \in L} \left[\phi_l^w \left(\sum_{i \in I(l)} \bar{w}_i y_i - \bar{k}_l^w \right)^+ \right.
$$
$$
\left. + \phi_l^v \left(\sum_{i \in I(l)} \bar{v}_i y_i - \bar{k}_l^v \right)^+ \right]
$$
$$
\text{s.t.} \quad y_i \leq \sum_{t=1}^{T} q_{t,i} \quad \forall i = 1, ..., m
$$
$$
y_i \geq 0 \quad \forall i = 1, ..., m
$$

with $\bar{w}_i = \mathbb{E}[W_i]$, $\bar{v}_i = \mathbb{E}[V_i]$, $\bar{k}_l^w = \mathbb{E}[K_l^w]$, and $\bar{k}_l^v = \mathbb{E}[K_l^v]$.

Although this problem is non-linear in the formulation given above, it can easily be transformed to a linear problem by introducing additional variables $\zeta_l^w \geq 0$ and $\zeta_l^v \geq 0$, replacing $\left(\sum_{i \in I(l)} \bar{w}_i y_i - \bar{k}_l^w \right)^+$ and $\left(\sum_{i \in I(l)} \bar{v}_i y_i - \bar{k}_l^v \right)^+$ respectively in (**DLP**), and adding the following constraints

$$
\sum_{i \in I(l)} \bar{w}_i y_i - \bar{k}_l^w \leq \zeta_l^w \tag{6.4}
$$

$$
\sum_{i \in I(l)} \bar{v}_i y_i - \bar{k}_l^v \leq \zeta_l^v \tag{6.5}
$$

for all legs $l \in L$.

Let z_{DLP} denote the maximum objective value of (**DLP**). This problem is a straightforward extension of the upper bound problem given in Proposition 2 of Amaruchkul et al. (2007) to a network model accounting for uncertain capacity. Amaruchkul et al. (2007) interpret the dual variables of (6.4) and (6.5) as the bid prices of one weight and volume unit, respectively, on leg l. We denote those values by λ_l^w and λ_l^v, respectively. Note that this problem is very similar to approaches for computing passenger bid prices based on solving a deterministic linear program, which is traditional in network revenue management (cf. Talluri & van Ryzin, 1998, pp. 93-95) and was recently extended to overbooking by Kunnumkal et al. (2012).

To incorporate stochastic information in the deterministic linear program, a randomized linear programming approach is common in passenger network revenue management and well known to provide a tighter bound than (**DLP**), see Talluri & van Ryzin (1999) and Kunnumkal et al. (2012). The underlying idea is that the expected values in (**DLP**) are replaced by random vectors. Let $\boldsymbol{D} = (D_{it})$ be a random matrix with $D_{it} \in \{0, 1\}$ describing the incoming requests of different classes over time with $P(D_{it} = 1) = q_{t,i}$. Denoting a realization of $\boldsymbol{D}$ by $\boldsymbol{d} = (d_{it})_{i=1,\dots,m,t=T,\dots,1}$, a value $d_{it} = 1$ indicates that a class-i request arrived at time t. By assumption, we have $\sum_{i=1}^m d_{it} \in \{0, 1\}$ for all t. We denote realizations of the random variables by their corresponding lower case letters. Then, the optimal control given a realization of demand, capacities, and capacity requirements is given by

$$\textbf{(RLP)} \quad \varrho(\boldsymbol{d}, \boldsymbol{w}, \boldsymbol{v}, \boldsymbol{k}^w, \boldsymbol{k}^v) = \max_{\boldsymbol{y}} \sum_{i=1}^m \varphi_i \max\{w_i, v_i/\vartheta\} y_i$$

$$- \sum_{l \in L} \left[\phi_l^w \left(\sum_{i \in I(l)} w_i y_i - k_l^w \right)^+ + \phi_l^v \left(\sum_{i \in I(l)} v_i y_i - k_l^v \right)^+ \right]$$

$$\text{s.t.} \quad y_i \leq \sum_{t=1}^T d_{it} \quad \forall i = 1, \dots, m$$

$$y_i \geq 0 \quad \forall i = 1, \dots, m.$$

Note that this problem represents a full information problem since complete knowledge about all incoming demand and capacities is used in the maximization. The maximum expected revenue under full information is then given by

$\mathbb{E}_{\boldsymbol{D},\boldsymbol{W},\boldsymbol{V},\boldsymbol{K}^w,\boldsymbol{K}^v}[\varrho(\boldsymbol{D},\boldsymbol{W},\boldsymbol{V},\boldsymbol{K}^w,\boldsymbol{K}^v)]$. Denote this quantity by z_{RLP}. Although z_{RLP} is difficult to calculate directly, it can easily be obtained, e.g. by Monte Carlo simulation (for an introduction to Monte Carlo simulation, see Rubinstein & Kroese, 2008).

In a passenger revenue management context, Kunnumkal et al. (2012) also introduce a partially randomized linear program, which only replaces a selection of expected values by their random variables. Let **(PLP)** be the problem with revenues, capacities, as well as required weights and volumes equal to their expected values and with a *random demand vector*, i.e.

$$\textbf{(PLP)} \quad \kappa(\boldsymbol{d}) = \max_{\boldsymbol{y}} \sum_{i=1}^m \rho_i y_i - \sum_{l \in L} \left[\phi_l^w \left(\sum_{i \in I(l)} \bar{w}_i y_i - \bar{k}_l^w \right)^+ \right. $$
$$\left. + \phi_l^v \left(\sum_{i \in I(l)} \bar{v}_i y_i - \bar{k}_l^v \right)^+ \right]$$
$$\text{s.t.} \quad y_i \le \sum_{t=1}^T d_{it} \quad \forall i = 1, \dots, m$$
$$y_i \ge 0 \quad \forall i = 1, \dots, m$$

and $z_{PLP} = \mathbb{E}[\kappa(\boldsymbol{D})]$.

The following theorem shows that all of the problems introduced above, z_{DLP}, z_{RLP}, and z_{PLP} give an upper bound on the maximum expected total revenue. Unlike in passenger revenue management, z_{RLP} does not always provide a tighter bound than z_{DLP}. But z_{PLP} can be shown to be tighter than z_{DLP}.

Theorem 6.1. $G_T(\boldsymbol{0}) \le z_{PLP} \le z_{DLP}$. *Further,* $G_T(\boldsymbol{0}) \le z_{RLP}$. *In general,* z_{RLP} *might be a tighter or a looser upper bound than* z_{DLP} *or* z_{PLP}.

Proof. Let $(A_{0t}^*, \dots, A_{mt}^*)$ denote the vectors maximizing the right hand side of (6.2) depending on the realization of $(\boldsymbol{D},\boldsymbol{W},\boldsymbol{V},\boldsymbol{K}^w,\boldsymbol{K}^v)$ at time t (we drop the direct dependence of A_{it}^* for notational simplicity). Given this, the total number of accepted requests from class $i \neq 0$ given those optimal actions is $\sum_{t=1}^{T} A_{it}^{*} D_{it}$.

Denote the optimal solution to (**PLP**) depending on (D) by Y_i^{PLP}. Given a realization of (D), $\sum_{t=1}^{T} A_{it}^{*} D_{it}$ is a feasible solution to (**PLP**). We combine this insight with Jensen's inequality. (In the context of probability theory, the latter states that if X is a random variable and f is a concave function, then $f(\mathbb{E}[X]) \geq \mathbb{E}[f(X)]$.) We have

$$G_T(\mathbf{0})$$

$$
= \mathbb{E}_{\boldsymbol{D},\boldsymbol{W},\boldsymbol{V},\boldsymbol{K}^w,\boldsymbol{K}^v} \left[\sum_{i=1}^{m} \varphi_i \max\left\{ W_i, \frac{V_i}{\vartheta} \right\} \sum_{t=1}^{T} A_{it}^{*} D_{it} \right.
$$

$$
- \sum_{l \in L} \left[\phi_l^w \left(\sum_{i \in I(l)} W_i \sum_{t=1}^{T} A_{it}^{*} D_{it} - K_l^w \right)^{+} \right.
$$

$$
\left. \left. + \phi_l^v \left(\sum_{i \in I(l)} V_i \sum_{t=1}^{T} A_{it}^{*} D_{it} - K_l^v \right)^{+} \right] \right]
$$

$$
= \mathbb{E}_{\boldsymbol{D}} \left[\sum_{i=1}^{m} \rho_i \sum_{t=1}^{T} A_{it}^{*} D_{it} \right]
$$

$$
- \sum_{l \in L} \mathbb{E}_{\boldsymbol{D},\boldsymbol{W},\boldsymbol{V},\boldsymbol{K}^w,\boldsymbol{K}^v} \left[\phi_l^w \left(\sum_{i \in I(l)} W_i \sum_{t=1}^{T} A_{it}^{*} D_{it} - K_l^w \right)^{+} \right.
$$

$$
\left. + \phi_l^v \left(\sum_{i \in I(l)} V_i \sum_{t=1}^{T} A_{it}^{*} D_{it} - K_l^v \right)^{+} \right]
$$

$$
\leq \mathbb{E}_{\boldsymbol{D}} \left[\sum_{i=1}^{m} \rho_i \sum_{t=1}^{T} A_{it}^{*} D_{it} - \sum_{l \in L} \left[\phi_l^w \left(\sum_{i \in I(l)} \bar{w}_i \sum_{t=1}^{T} A_{it}^{*} D_{it} - \bar{k}_l^w \right)^{+} \right. \right.
$$

$$
\left. \left. + \phi_l^v \left(\sum_{i \in I(l)} \bar{v}_i \sum_{t=1}^{T} A_{it}^{*} D_{it} - \bar{k}_l^v \right)^{+} \right] \right]
$$

$$\leq \mathbb{E}_{\boldsymbol{D}} \left[\sum_{i=1}^{m} \rho_i Y_i^{PLP} - \sum_{l \in L} \left[\phi_l^w \left(\sum_{i \in I(l)} \bar{w}_i Y_i^{PLP} - \bar{k}_l^w \right)^+ \right. \right.$$

$$\left. \left. + \phi_l^v \left(\sum_{i \in I(l)} \bar{v}_i Y_i^{PLP} - \bar{k}_l^v \right)^+ \right] \right]$$

$$= \mathbb{E}[\kappa(\boldsymbol{D})] = z_{PLP}.$$

Since $\kappa(\boldsymbol{d})$ is a concave function, Jensen's inequality yields

$$z_{PLP} = \mathbb{E}[\kappa(\boldsymbol{D})] \leq \kappa(\mathbb{E}[\boldsymbol{D}]) = z_{DLP}.$$

Summarizing the above, we have $G_T(\boldsymbol{0}) \leq z_{PLP} \leq z_{DLP}$. Now, consider the fully randomized linear program. We have

$$G_T(\boldsymbol{0})$$

$$= \mathbb{E}_{\boldsymbol{D},\boldsymbol{W},\boldsymbol{V},\boldsymbol{K}^w,\boldsymbol{K}^v} \left[\sum_{i=1}^{m} \varphi_i \max\{W_i, \frac{V_i}{\vartheta}\} \sum_{t=1}^{T} A_{it}^* D_{it} \right.$$

$$- \sum_{l \in L} \left[\phi_l^w \left(\sum_{i \in I(l)} W_i \sum_{t=1}^{T} A_{it}^* D_{it} - K_l^w \right)^+ \right.$$

$$\left. \left. + \phi_l^v \left(\sum_{i \in I(l)} V_i \sum_{t=1}^{T} A_{it}^* D_{it} - K_l^v \right)^+ \right] \right]$$

$$\leq \mathbb{E}_{\boldsymbol{D},\boldsymbol{W},\boldsymbol{V},\boldsymbol{K}^w,\boldsymbol{K}^v} \left[\sum_{i=1}^{m} \varphi_i \max\{W_i, V_i/\vartheta\} Y_i^{RLP} \right.$$

$$- \sum_{l \in L} \left[\phi_l^w \left(\sum_{i \in I(l)} W_i Y_i^{RLP} - K_l^w \right)^+ \right.$$

$$\left. \left. + \phi_l^v \left(\sum_{i \in I(l)} V_i Y_i^{RLP} - K_l^v \right)^+ \right] \right]$$

$$=\mathbb{E}_{D,W,V,K^w,K^v}\left[\varrho(D,W,V,K^w,K^v)\right]=z_{RLP}.$$

At this point, it is unclear if z_{RLP} is a tighter or a looser bound than z_{PLP} or z_{DLP}. To see that in general, z_{RLP} is neither tighter nor looser than the other two bounds, consider the following two examples.

Example 6.1. Take $T = 5$, $\mathfrak{L} = 1$, $m = 1$, $q_{t,1} = 1$ for $t = 1, ..., 5$, $\vartheta = 1$, $P(V_1 = 100) = 1$, $P(W_1 = 2) = 0.5 = 1 - P(W_1 = 98)$, $P(K_1^v = 100) = 1$, $P(K_1^w = 10) = 1$, $\varphi_1 = 1$, $\phi_1^v = 0$, $\phi_1^w = 100$ so that $\bar{w}_1 = 50$, $\bar{v}_1 = 100$, $\bar{k}_1^w = 10$, $\bar{k}_1^v = 100$. In this case, DLP and PLP solve

$$\max_{0 \le y \le 5} 100y - 100(50y - 10)^+$$

with $y^* = 1/5$ and $z_{DLP} = z_{PLP} = 100/5 = 20$.

RLP, on the other hand, solves the problem for two possible sample paths, each of which happen with a probability of 0.5. Simplifying the problems of those two sample paths gives:

Sample 1: $w_1 = 2$: $\quad\quad \max\limits_{0 \le \tilde{y} \le 5} 100\tilde{y} - 100(2\tilde{y} - 10)^+$

Sample 2: $w_1 = 98$: $\quad\quad \max\limits_{0 \le \hat{y} \le 5} 100\hat{y} - 100(98\hat{y} - 10)^+.$

We have $\tilde{y}^* = 5$ and $\hat{y}^* = 10/98$ giving $z_{RLP} = 0.5 \times 100 \times (5 + 10/98) > 20 = z_{DLP} = z_{PLP}$. As a consequence of this example, z_{RLP} can be even looser than z_{DLP}.

Example 6.2. To have an example showing that z_{RLP} might produce a bound that is tighter than z_{PLP} or z_{DLP}, take the data from Example 1 but change the booking horizon to $T = 1$ and the capacity for weight to $P(K_1^w = 50) = 1$, with $\bar{k}_1^w = 50$. In this case, DLP and PLP solve

$$\max_{0 \le y \le 1} 100y - 100(50y - 50)^+$$

with $y^* = 1$ and $z_{DLP} = z_{PLP} = 100$.

As before, RLP solves the problem for two possible sample paths, each of which happen with a probability of 0.5. This gives

Sample 1: $w_1 = 2$: $\max_{0 \le \tilde{y} \le 1} 100\tilde{y} - 100(2\tilde{y} - 50)^+$

Sample 2: $w_1 = 98$: $\max_{0 \le \hat{y} \le 1} 100\hat{y} - 100(98\hat{y} - 50)^+$.

We have $\tilde{y}^* = 1$ and $\hat{y}^* = 50/98$ giving $z_{RLP} = 0.5 \times 100 \times (1 + 50/98) < 100 = z_{DLP} = z_{PLP}$. As a consequence of this example, z_{RLP} can be tighter than z_{PLP}.

$\square$

We turn to an alternative, popular approach to determine upper bounds and bid prices in passenger revenue management, which is approximate dynamic programming.

6.3 An Approximate Dynamic Programming Approach

In this section, we propose an affine value function approximation in order to make the capacity control problem tractable. The approximation's structural properties are analyzed in Section 6.3.1. An enhanced approximation scheme that uses piecewise linear functions is proposed in Section 6.3.2.

A standard approach in approximate dynamic programming is to approximate the value function by a function that is affine in the state space. If we approximate the value of one unit of weight at time t on leg l by $\alpha_{l,t}^w$ and the value of one unit of volume at time t on leg l by $\alpha_{l,t}^v$, the approximation parameters can be interpreted as bid prices for weight and volume units on a particular leg and at a particular time. An intuitive decision rule would accept a class-i request if its revenue is at least as big as the sum of the bid prices of its requested weight and volume in the next period, i.e. $\sum_{l \in L(i)} [\alpha_{l,t-1}^w \bar{w}_i + \alpha_{l,t-1}^v \bar{v}_i]$, where $L(i)$ is the set of legs that are requested by class $i \in I$ (for $i = 0$, we define $L(i) = \emptyset$). This is in case of an arriving class-i request in period $t > 1$

$$f_t(i) = \begin{cases} 1 & \rho_i \geq \sum_{l \in L(i)} \left[\alpha_{l,t-1}^w \bar{w}_i + \alpha_{l,t-1}^v \bar{v}_i \right] \\ 0 & \text{otherwise.} \end{cases} \tag{6.6}$$

We refer to the sum of all bid prices of i, $\sum_{l \in L(i)} \left[\alpha_{l,t-1}^w \bar{w}_i + \alpha_{l,t-1}^v \bar{v}_i \right]$, as *approximated opportunity cost*. In order to obtain the decision rules in (6.6), we approximate $G_t(c)$ and $G_t(c + e_i)$ in (6.3) for all $t = T, ..., 1$ and $c \in C_t$ by

$$G_t(c) \approx \psi_t - \sum_{l \in L} \left[\alpha_{l,t}^w \sum_{i \in I(l)} c_i \bar{w}_i + \alpha_{l,t}^v \sum_{i \in I(l)} c_i \bar{v}_i \right], \tag{6.7}$$

with ψ_t as a constant offset in period t.

Offloading cost incurs in the last period only. To approximate the terminal values, we use the expected values of capacities and capacity requirements, i.e.

$$G_0(c) \approx - \sum_{l \in L} \left[\phi_l^w \left(\sum_{i \in I(l)} \bar{w}_i c_i - \bar{k}_l^w \right)^+ + \phi_l^v \left(\sum_{i \in I(l)} \bar{v}_i c_i - \bar{k}_l^v \right)^+ \right]. \tag{6.8}$$

Given optimality equations (6.2), we outlined in Section 3.3 that the maximum expected revenue at time T can be computed by solving the following LP:

$$(\tilde{\mathbf{P}}) \quad \min_{G_T(c),...,G_1(c)} G_T(\mathbf{0})$$

$$\text{s.t.} \quad G_t(c) - \sum_{i \in I} q_{t,i} G_{t-1}(c + a_i e_i)$$

$$\geq \sum_{i \in I} q_{t,i} \rho_i a_i \quad \forall c \in C_t, 1 \leq t \leq T, a \in A$$

$$G_t(c) \geq 0 \quad \forall c \in C_t, 1 \leq t \leq T,$$

where we define $\boldsymbol{a} := (a_0, a_1, ..., a_m)$ with a_i as the action depending on the requested class i. We further define $\boldsymbol{A} = A(0) \times ... \times A(m)$ with $A(0) = \{0\}$. Even though accepting or rejecting a request for $i = 0$ yields the same result, we set $A(0) = \{0\}$ in order to decrease the problem size. Further, note that we do not sum over all states in the objective function as done in Section 3.3 since we have an initial state and time-dependent states.

Plugging approximations (6.7) and (6.8) into ($\tilde{\mathbf{P}}$) yields

$$(\mathbf{P}_{AFA}) \quad \min_{\psi, \alpha^w, \alpha^v} \psi_T \tag{6.9}$$

$$\text{s.t.} \quad \psi_t - \psi_{t-1} + \sum_{i \in I} q_{t,i} a_i \left[\sum_{l \in L(i)} (\bar{w}_i \alpha_{l,t-1}^w + \bar{v}_i \alpha_{l,t-1}^v) - \rho_i \right]$$

$$- \sum_{l \in L} \left[(\alpha_{l,t}^w - \alpha_{l,t-1}^w) \sum_{i \in I(l)} c_i \bar{w}_i + (\alpha_{l,t}^v - \alpha_{l,t-1}^v) \sum_{i \in I(l)} c_i \bar{v}_i \right]$$

$$\geq 0 \quad \forall c \in C_t, 2 \leq t \leq T, \boldsymbol{a} \in \boldsymbol{A}$$
$$\tag{6.10}$$

$$\psi_1 - \sum_{l \in L} \left[\alpha_{l,1}^w \sum_{i \in I(l)} c_i \bar{w}_i + \alpha_{l,1}^v \sum_{i \in I(l)} c_i \bar{v}_i \right]$$

$$+ \sum_{i' \in I} q_{1,i'} \sum_{l \in L} \left[\phi_l^w \left(\sum_{i \in I(l)} (c_i + a_{i'} \mathbf{1}_{\{i=i'\}}) \bar{w}_i - \bar{k}_l^w \right)^+ \right.$$

$$\left. + \phi_l^v \left(\sum_{i \in I(l)} (c_i + a_{i'} \mathbf{1}_{\{i=i'\}}) \bar{v}_i - \bar{k}_l^v \right)^+ \right]$$

$$\geq \sum_{i \in I} q_{1,i} \rho_i a_i \quad \forall c \in C_1, \boldsymbol{a} \in \boldsymbol{A} \tag{6.11}$$

$$\psi_t, \alpha_{l,t}^w, \alpha_{l,t}^v \in \mathbb{R} \quad \forall 1 \leq t \leq T, l \in L. \tag{6.12}$$

The above problem still has the same amount of constraints as ($\tilde{\mathbf{P}}$) but only $T + 2\mathfrak{L} \times T$ variables. In order to analyze structural properties in more detail and to solve the problem via column generation, its dual formulation, ($\mathbf{D}_{AFA}$), is presented below.

$$
(\mathbf{D}_{AFA}) \quad \max_{X} \sum_{1 \le t \le T, c \in C_t, a \in A} X_{t,c,a} \sum_{i \in I} q_{t,i} \rho_i a_i
$$

$$
- \sum_{c \in C_1, a \in A} X_{1,c,a} \sum_{i' \in I} q_{1,i'} \sum_{l \in L}
$$

$$
\left[\phi_l^w \left(\sum_{i \in I(l)} (c_i + a_{i'} \mathbf{1}_{\{i=i'\}}) \bar{w}_i - \bar{k}_l^w \right)^+ \right. \tag{6.13}
$$

$$
\left. + \phi_l^v \left(\sum_{i \in I(l)} (c_i + a_{i'} \mathbf{1}_{\{i=i'\}}) \bar{v}_i - \bar{k}_l^v \right)^+ \right]
$$

s.t.
$$
\sum_{c \in C_t, a \in A} X_{t,c,a} \sum_{i \in I(l)} c_i \bar{w}_i
$$

$$
= \begin{cases} \sum_{c \in C_{t+1}, a \in A} X_{t+1,c,a} \sum_{i \in I(l)} (c_i + q_{t+1,i} a_i) \bar{w}_i & \forall l \in L, \\ & 1 \le t < T \\ 0 & \forall l \in L, t = T \end{cases}
$$

$$
\tag{6.14}
$$

$$
\sum_{c \in C_t, a \in A} X_{t,c,a} \sum_{i \in I(l)} c_i \bar{v}_i
$$

$$
= \begin{cases} \sum_{c \in C_{t+1}, a \in A} X_{t+1,c,a} \sum_{i \in I(l)} (c_i + q_{t+1,i} a_i) \bar{v}_i & \forall l \in L, \\ & 1 \le t < T \\ 0 & \forall l \in L, t = T \end{cases}
$$

$$
\tag{6.15}
$$

$$\sum_{c \in C_t, a \in A} X_{t,c,a} = \begin{cases} \sum_{c \in C_{t+1}, a \in A} X_{t+1,c,a} & \forall 1 \leq t < T \\ 1 & t = T \end{cases}$$

$$(6.16)$$

$$X_{t,c,a} \geq 0 \quad \forall 1 \leq t \leq T, c \in C_t, a \in A. \tag{6.17}$$

Note that the second part of constraints (6.14) and (6.15) can be eliminated since $C_T = \{0\}^m$. Further, constraint (6.16) can be replaced by

$$\sum_{c \in C_t, a \in A} X_{t,c,a} = 1 \quad \forall 1 \leq t \leq T. \tag{6.18}$$

Interpreting $X_{t,c,a}$ as state-action probabilities, constraint (6.14) enforces that the expected weight booked t time periods before departure equals the expected weight booked $t + 1$ time periods before departure plus the weight sold within that time period. Constraint (6.15) enforces the same for volume. This dual hence maximizes the expected revenue minus expected overbooking cost subject to flow balance constraints for weight and volume.

Strong duality ensures that the objective value of $(\mathbf{P}_{AFA})$ equals the objective value of $(\mathbf{D}_{AFA})$. We will denote this optimal value by z_{AFA}, which gives a tighter bound than the upper bound problem (**DLP**).

Theorem 6.2. *Any feasible solution to $(\mathbf{D}_{AFA})$ yields a feasible solution to (DLP) having a greater or equal objective value. Thus, $G_T(\mathbf{0}) \leq z_{AFA} \leq z_{DLP}$.*

Proof. The first inequality follows from Proposition 1 in Adelman (2007): One can show that any feasible solution to $(\tilde{\mathbf{P}})$ is an upper bound on the maximum expected revenue determined by (6.2). Since $(\mathbf{P}_{AFA})$ provides a feasible solution to $(\tilde{\mathbf{P}})$, we have $z_{AFA} \geq G_T(\mathbf{0})$. Thus, this approximate LP determines the lowest upper bound of the form (6.7) on the maximum expected revenue and the inequality follows.

In order to prove the second inequality, we define

$$y_i := \sum_{t>0, c \in C_t, a \in A} q_{t,i} a_i X_{t,c,a}$$

for all $i \in I$. Applying (6.18) to this definition yields

$$
\begin{aligned}
0 \le y_i &= \sum_{t>0, c \in C_t, a \in A} q_{t,i} a_i X_{t,c,a} \\
&= \sum_{t=1}^{T} q_{t,i} \sum_{c \in C_t, a \in A} a_i X_{t,c,a} \\
&\le \sum_{t=1}^{T} q_{t,i} \sum_{c \in C_t, a \in A} X_{t,c,a} \le \sum_{t=1}^{T} q_{t,i} \quad \forall i \in I.
\end{aligned}
$$

As a consequence, any feasible solution to $(\mathbf{D}_{AFA})$ gives a feasible solution to $(\mathbf{DLP})$. We will now show that the objective value of $(\mathbf{DLP})$ is greater than or equal to the objective value of $(\mathbf{D}_{AFA})$ for any feasible solution.

Considering the definition of y_i, the first term of (6.13) becomes

$$\sum_{i=1}^{m} y_i \rho_i.$$

Now consider the second term of (6.13) representing overbooking cost. Since $(\sum_{i \in I(l)} (c_i + a_{i'} \mathbf{1}_{\{i=i'\}}) \bar{w}_i - \bar{k}_l^w)^+$ and $(\sum_{i \in I(l)} (c_i + a_{i'} \mathbf{1}_{\{i=i'\}}) \bar{v}_i - \bar{k}_l^v)^+$ are convex in c and in a, and because $X_{t,c,a}$ as well as $q_{t,i}$ can be considered as probability distributions, we can repeatedly apply Jensen's inequality to obtain

$$
\sum_{c \in C_1, a \in A} X_{1,c,a} \sum_{i' \in I} q_{1,i'} \sum_{l \in L} \left[\phi_l^w \left(\sum_{i \in I(l)} (c_i + a_{i'} \mathbf{1}_{\{i=i'\}}) \bar{w}_i - \bar{k}_l^w \right)^+ \right.
$$
$$
\left. + \phi_l^v \left(\sum_{i \in I(l)} (c_i + a_{i'} \mathbf{1}_{\{i=i'\}}) \bar{v}_i - \bar{k}_l^v \right)^+ \right]
$$

$$\geq \sum_{c \in C_1, a \in A} X_{1,c,a} \sum_{l \in L} \left[\phi_l^w \left(\sum_{i \in I(l)} (c_i + q_{1,i} a_i) \bar{w}_i - \bar{k}_l^w \right)^+ \right.$$

$$\left. + \phi_l^v \left(\sum_{i \in I(l)} (c_i + q_{1,i} a_i) \bar{v}_i - \bar{k}_l^v \right)^+ \right]$$

$$\geq \sum_{l \in L} \left[\phi_l^w \left(\sum_{c \in C_1, a \in A} X_{1,c,a} \sum_{i \in I(l)} (c_i + q_{1,i} a_i) \bar{w}_i - \sum_{c \in C_1, a \in A} X_{1,c,a} \bar{k}_l^w \right)^+ \right.$$

$$\left. + \phi_l^v \left(\sum_{c \in C_1, a \in A} X_{1,c,a} \sum_{i \in I(l)} (c_i + q_{1,i} a_i) \bar{v}_i - \sum_{c \in C_1, a \in A} X_{1,c,a} \bar{k}_l^v \right)^+ \right].$$

$$(6.19)$$

Further, fixing i and summing constraint (6.14) over t yields

$$\sum_{t,c,a} X_{t,c,a} \sum_{i \in I(l)} c_i \bar{w}_i = \sum_{t,c,a} X_{t+1,c,a} \sum_{i \in I(l)} (c_i + q_{t+1,i} a_i) \bar{w}_i \quad \forall l \in L.$$

Rearranging terms yields

$$\sum_{c,a} X_{1,c,a} \sum_{i \in I(l)} c_i \bar{w}_i = \sum_{t,c,a} X_{t+1,c,a} \sum_{i \in I(l)} q_{t+1,i} a_i \bar{w}_i \quad \forall l \in L.$$

By applying the definition of y_i, we can write

$$\sum_{c,a} X_{1,c,a} \sum_{i \in I(l)} c_i \bar{w}_i = \sum_{i \in I(l)} y_i \bar{w}_i - \sum_{c,a} X_{1,c,a} \sum_{i \in I(l)} q_{1,i} a_i \bar{w}_i \quad \forall l \in L.$$

It follows that

$$\sum_{i \in I(l)} y_i \bar{w}_i = \sum_{c,a} X_{1,c,a} \sum_{i \in I(l)} (c_i + q_{1,i} a_i) \bar{w}_i \quad \forall l \in L. \qquad (6.20)$$

157

Similarly, constraint (6.15) yields

$$\sum_{i \in I(l)} y_i \bar{v}_i = \sum_{c,a} X_{1,c,a} \sum_{i \in I(l)} (c_i + q_{1,i} a_i) \bar{v}_i \quad \forall l \in L. \tag{6.21}$$

Using (6.20) and (6.21) gives that the last two lines in (6.19) are equal to

$$\sum_{l \in L} \left[\phi_l^w \left(\sum_{i \in I(l)} y_i \bar{w}_i - \bar{k}_l^w \right)^+ + \phi_l^v \left(\sum_{i \in I(l)} y_i \bar{v}_i - \bar{k}_l^v \right)^+ \right].$$

This proves that the objective of (**DLP**) cannot be lower than the objective value of ($\mathbf{D}_{AFA}$) for any feasible solution X. Accordingly, every feasible solution of ($\mathbf{D}_{AFA}$) can be transformed to a feasible solution of (**DLP**) yielding a greater or equal objective value. As a consequence, the maximization problem ($\mathbf{D}_{AFA}$) yields a lower upper bound. $\qquad\square$

We now analyze the structural properties of the approximation parameters.

6.3.1 Structural Properties

We motivated our approximation by arguing that $\sum_{l \in L(i)} \left[\alpha_{l,t-1}^w \bar{w}_i + \alpha_{l,t-1}^v \bar{v}_i \right]$ should approximate the opportunity cost of accepting a class-i request in period t. One can show that for an optimal solution, the approximated opportunity cost of a request is approximately constant in time.

Theorem 6.3. *For an optimal primal solution* $(\alpha^{w*}, \alpha^{v*}, \psi^*)$ *to* ($\mathbf{P}_{AFA}$), *we have for all* $1 < t \leq T$ *and* $i \in I$

$$\sum_{l \in L(i)} \left[\alpha_{l,t}^{w*} \bar{w}_i + \alpha_{l,t}^{v*} \bar{v}_i \right] \approx \sum_{l \in L(i)} \left[\alpha_{l,t-1}^{w*} \bar{w}_i + \alpha_{l,t-1}^{v*} \bar{v}_i \right] \gtrsim 0.$$

Proof. First, note that approximated opportunity cost of class $i' \in I$ in period $t > 1$ can be written as $\sum_{l \in L(i')} \left[\alpha_{l,t}^{w*} \bar{w}_{i'} + \alpha_{l,t}^{v*} \bar{v}_{i'} \right]$. On the other hand, we can plug approximation (6.7) into the right hand side of (6.2) for $G_t(\boldsymbol{c})$ and $G_t(\boldsymbol{c} + \boldsymbol{e}_{i'})$ and write approximated opportunity cost of class i' in period $t > 1$ as

$$
\begin{aligned}
0 \leq &G_t(\boldsymbol{c}) - G_t(\boldsymbol{c} + \boldsymbol{e}_{i'}) \\
\approx &\sum_{j \in I} q_{t,j} \max_{a \in A(j)} \left\{ a\rho_j + \psi_{t-1}^* \right. \\
&\left. - \sum_{l \in L} \sum_{i \in I(l)} (c_i + a\mathbf{1}_{\{i=j\}})(\alpha_{l,t-1}^{w*}\bar{w}_i + \alpha_{l,t-1}^{v*}\bar{v}_i) \right\} \\
&- \sum_{j \in I} q_{t,j} \max_{a \in A(j)} \left\{ a\rho_j + \psi_{t-1}^* \right. \\
&\left. - \sum_{l \in L} \sum_{i \in I(l)} (c_i + a\mathbf{1}_{\{i=j\}} + \mathbf{1}_{\{i=i'\}})(\alpha_{l,t-1}^{w*}\bar{w}_i + \alpha_{l,t-1}^{v*}\bar{v}_i) \right\} \\
= &\psi_{t-1}^* - \sum_{l \in L} \sum_{i \in I(l)} c_i(\alpha_{l,t-1}^{w*}\bar{w}_i + \alpha_{l,t-1}^{v*}\bar{v}_i) \\
&+ \sum_{j \in I} q_{t,j} \max_{a \in A(j)} \left\{ a\rho_j - a \sum_{l \in L(j)} (\alpha_{l,t-1}^{w*}\bar{w}_j + \alpha_{l,t-1}^{v*}\bar{v}_j) \right\} \\
&- \psi_{t-1}^* + \sum_{l \in L} \sum_{i \in I(l)} c_i(\alpha_{l,t-1}^{w*}\bar{w}_i + \alpha_{l,t-1}^{v*}\bar{v}_i) \\
&+ \sum_{l \in L(i')} (\alpha_{l,t-1}^{w*}\bar{w}_{i'} + \alpha_{l,t-1}^{v*}\bar{v}_{i'}) \\
&- \sum_{j \in I} q_{t,j} \max_{a \in A(j)} \left\{ a\rho_j - a \sum_{l \in L(j)} (\alpha_{l,t-1}^{w*}\bar{w}_j + \alpha_{l,t-1}^{v*}\bar{v}_j) \right\} \\
= &\sum_{l \in L(i')} (\alpha_{l,t-1}^{w*}\bar{w}_{i'} + \alpha_{l,t-1}^{v*}\bar{v}_{i'}).
\end{aligned}
$$

The inequality holds since $G_t(\boldsymbol{c})$ is non-increasing in c_i for all $i \in \{1,...,m\}$ (a proof can be done analogously to the one of Lemma 4.1). It follows that for all $1 < t \leq T$ and $i' \in I$, $\sum_{l \in L(i')} [\alpha_{l,t}^{w*} \bar{w}_{i'} + \alpha_{l,t}^{v*} \bar{v}_{i'}] \approx \sum_{l \in L(i')} [\alpha_{l,t-1}^{w*} \bar{w}_{i'} + \alpha_{l,t-1}^{v*} \bar{v}_{i'}]$. $\qquad\square$

In the remainder of this work, we assume exact rather than approximate time-independence of approximated opportunity cost. That is, for all $i \in I$ and $t = T, ..., 2$, we have $\sum_{l \in L(i)} \left[\alpha_{l,t}^{w*} \bar{w}_i + \alpha_{l,t}^{v*} \bar{v}_i \right] = \sum_{l \in L(i)} \left[\alpha_{l,t-1}^{w*} \bar{w}_i + \alpha_{l,t-1}^{v*} \bar{v}_i \right]$. A consequence of this assumption is that there exists an optimal solution featuring time-independent bid prices.

Theorem 6.4. *If an optimal solution with time-independent approximated opportunity cost exists, there also exists an optimal solution $(\alpha^{w*}, \alpha^{v*}, \psi^*)$ to $(\boldsymbol{P}_{AFA})$ with*

(i) $\alpha_{l,t}^{w*} = \alpha_{l,t-1}^{w*}$,

(ii) $\alpha_{l,t}^{v*} = \alpha_{l,t-1}^{v*}$,

(iii) $\psi_t^* \geq \psi_{t-1}^* \geq 0$

for all $1 < t \leq T$ and $l \in L$.

Proof. We first prove properties (i) and (ii) by showing that any optimal solution not satisfying the above structure can be altered to obtain an alternative optimal solution that satisfies those properties.

Consider an optimal primal-dual solution X^*, $(\alpha^{w*}, \alpha^{v*}, \psi^*)$. Let t' be the smallest $t > 1$ with $\alpha_{l,t}^{w*} \neq \alpha_{l,t-1}^{w*}$ or $\alpha_{l,t}^{v*} \neq \alpha_{l,t-1}^{v*}$. Now consider the alternative solution $(\alpha^{w\prime}, \alpha^{v\prime}, \psi')$ with

$$\alpha_{l,t}^{w\prime} = \begin{cases} \alpha_{l,t}^{w*} & \forall t \neq t', l \in L \\ \alpha_{l,t-1}^{w*} & t = t', l \in L \end{cases}$$

$$\alpha_{l,t}^{v\prime} = \begin{cases} \alpha_{l,t}^{v*} & \forall t \neq t', l \in L \\ \alpha_{l,t-1}^{v*} & t = t', l \in L \end{cases}$$

$$
\psi'_t = \begin{cases}
\psi^*_t & \forall t \neq t' \\[2ex]
\psi^*_t + \sum_{l \in L} \left[(\alpha^{w*}_{l,t-1} - \alpha^{w*}_{l,t}) \sum_{i \in I(l)} \bar{w}_i c_i \right. & \\[2ex]
\left. \qquad + (\alpha^{v*}_{l,t-1} - \alpha^{v*}_{l,t}) \sum_{i \in I(l)} \bar{v}_i c_i \right] & t = t'.
\end{cases}
$$

To see that $(\alpha^{w\prime}, \alpha^{v\prime}, \psi')$ is a feasible solution to $(\mathbf{P}_{AFA})$, note that the only constraints in (6.10) for which we altered any variables are those with $t = t'$ and $t = t' + 1$. Consider $t = t'$ first. For any $c \in \mathbf{C}_{t'}$ and $a \in \mathbf{A}$, this reads

$$
\psi'_{t'} - \psi'_{t'-1} + \sum_{j \in I} q_{t',j} a_j \left[\sum_{l \in L(j)} (\bar{w}_j \alpha^{w\prime}_{l,t'-1} + \bar{v}_j \alpha^{v\prime}_{l,t'-1}) - \rho_j \right]
$$

$$
+ \sum_{l \in L} \left[(\alpha^{w\prime}_{l,t'-1} - \alpha^{w\prime}_{l,t'}) \sum_{i \in I(l)} \bar{w}_i c_i + (\alpha^{v\prime}_{l,t'-1} - \alpha^{v\prime}_{l,t'}) \sum_{i \in I(l)} \bar{v}_i c_i \right]
$$

$$
= \psi^*_{t'} - \psi^*_{t'-1} + \sum_{j \in I} q_{t',j} a_j \left[\sum_{l \in L(j)} (\bar{w}_j \alpha^{w*}_{l,t'-1} + \bar{v}_j \alpha^{v*}_{l,t'-1}) - \rho_j \right]
$$

$$
+ \sum_{l \in L} \left[(\alpha^{w*}_{l,t'-1} - \alpha^{w*}_{l,t'}) \sum_{i \in I(l)} \bar{w}_i c_i + (\alpha^{v*}_{l,t'-1} - \alpha^{v*}_{l,t'}) \sum_{i \in I(l)} \bar{v}_i c_i \right] \geq 0,
$$

$$
(6.22)
$$

where the inequality follows from feasibility of $(\alpha^{w*}, \alpha^{v*}, \psi^*)$.

For $t = t' + 1$, (6.10) reads for any $c \in \mathbf{C}_{t'+1}$ and $a \in \mathbf{A}$

$$
\psi'_{t'+1} - \psi'_{t'} + \sum_{l \in L} \left[(\alpha^{w\prime}_{l,t'} - \alpha^{w\prime}_{l,t'+1}) \sum_{i \in I(l)} \bar{w}_i c_i + (\alpha^{v\prime}_{l,t'} - \alpha^{v\prime}_{l,t'+1}) \sum_{i \in I(l)} \bar{v}_i c_i \right]
$$

$$
+ \sum_{j \in I} q_{t'+1,j} a_j \left[\sum_{l \in L(j)} (\bar{w}_j \alpha^{w\prime}_{l,t'} + \bar{v}_j \alpha^{v\prime}_{l,t'}) - \rho_j \right]
$$

$$= \psi_{t'+1}^* - \psi_{t'}^* - \sum_{l \in L} \left[(\alpha_{l,t'-1}^{w*} - \alpha_{l,t'}^{w*}) \sum_{i \in I(l)} c_i \bar{w}_i + (\alpha_{l,t'-1}^{v*} - \alpha_{l,t'}^{v*}) \sum_{i \in I(l)} c_i \bar{v}_i \right]$$

$$+ \sum_{l \in L} \left[(\alpha_{l,t'-1}^{w*} - \alpha_{l,t'+1}^{w*}) \sum_{i \in I(l)} c_i \bar{w}_i + (\alpha_{l,t'-1}^{v*} - \alpha_{l,t'+1}^{v*}) \sum_{i \in I(l)} c_i \bar{v}_i \right]$$

$$+ \sum_{j \in I} q_{t'+1,j} a_j \left[\sum_{l \in L(j)} (\bar{w}_j \alpha_{l,t'-1}^{w*} + \bar{v}_j \alpha_{l,t'-1}^{v*}) - \rho_j \right]$$

$$= \psi_{t'+1}^* - \psi_{t'}^* - \sum_{l \in L} \left[(\alpha_{l,t'+1}^{w*} - \alpha_{l,t'}^{w*}) \sum_{i \in I(l)} c_i \bar{w}_i + (\alpha_{l,t'+1}^{v*} - \alpha_{l,t'}^{v*}) \sum_{i \in I(l)} c_i \bar{v}_i \right]$$

$$+ \sum_{j \in I} q_{t'+1,j} a_j \left[\sum_{l \in L(j)} (\bar{w}_j \alpha_{l,t'-1}^{w*} + \bar{v}_j \alpha_{l,t'-1}^{v*}) - \rho_j \right]$$

$$= \psi_{t'+1}^* - \psi_{t'}^* - \sum_{l \in L} \left[(\alpha_{l,t'+1}^{w*} - \alpha_{l,t'}^{w*}) \sum_{i \in I(l)} c_i \bar{w}_i + (\alpha_{l,t'+1}^{v*} - \alpha_{l,t'}^{v*}) \sum_{i \in I(l)} c_i \bar{v}_i \right]$$

$$+ \sum_{j \in I} q_{t'+1,j} a_j \left[\sum_{l \in L(j)} (\bar{w}_j \alpha_{l,t'}^{w*} + \bar{v}_j \alpha_{l,t'}^{v*}) - \rho_j \right]$$

$$+ \sum_{j \in I} q_{t'+1,j} a_j \left[\sum_{l \in L(j)} (\bar{w}_j \alpha_{l,t'-1}^{w*} + \bar{v}_j \alpha_{l,t'-1}^{v*}) - \sum_{l \in L(j)} (\bar{w}_j \alpha_{l,t'}^{w*} + \bar{v}_j \alpha_{l,t'}^{v*}) \right]$$

$$= \psi_{t'+1}^* - \psi_{t'}^* - \sum_{l \in L} \left[(\alpha_{l,t'+1}^{w*} - \alpha_{l,t'}^{w*}) \sum_{i \in I(l)} c_i \bar{w}_i + (\alpha_{l,t'+1}^{v*} - \alpha_{l,t'}^{v*}) \sum_{i \in I(l)} c_i \bar{v}_i \right]$$

$$+ \sum_{j \in I} q_{t'+1,j} a_j \left[\sum_{l \in L(j)} (\bar{w}_j \alpha_{l,t'}^{w*} + \bar{v}_j \alpha_{l,t'}^{v*}) - \rho_j \right] \geq 0, \tag{6.23}$$

where the last equality follows from the assumption of time-independent approximated opportunity cost, and the last inequality follows from the feasibility of

$(\alpha^{w*}, \alpha^{v*}, \psi^*)$. We hence conclude that $(\alpha^{w\prime}, \alpha^{v\prime}, \psi')$ is a feasible solution to the problem $(\mathbf{P}_{AFA})$.

To see that it is an optimal solution, we check if complimentary slackness is preserved. To do this, we need to show that for every $c \in C_t$, $a \in A$, and $1 \leq t \leq T$ with $X'_{t,c,a} > 0$, condition (6.10) is active. Since we showed above that the reduced revenue is the same under $(\alpha^{w\prime}, \alpha^{v\prime}, \psi')$ as under $(\alpha^{w*}, \alpha^{v*}, \psi^*)$, it follows that the dual variables under both solutions are equal, i.e. $X'_{t,c,a} = X^*_{t,c,a}$ for all $c \in C_t$ and $a \in A$ and $t = t', t'+1$. Again, we only need to check (6.10) for $t = t'$ and $t = t' + 1$ since nothing changes in the other constraints.

Consider $t = t'$ first. From the optimality of $(\alpha^{w*}, \alpha^{v*}, \psi^*)$, we know that for $c \in C_{t'}$ and $a \in A$ with $X^*_{t',c,a} > 0$, (6.10) is active for the solution $(\alpha^{w*}, \alpha^{v*}, \psi^*)$. As $X'_{t,c,a} = X^*_{t,c,a}$, it follows from (6.22) that (6.10) is also active for the alternative solution. For $t = t' + 1$, we can draw the same conclusion from (6.23).

Following the same steps repeatedly for larger t's yields properties (i) and (ii).

To see (iii), choose $c_i = 0$ and $a_i = 0$ for all $i \in I$ in constraint (6.10). It follows immediately that $\psi^*_t \geq \psi^*_{t-1}$. Doing the same in constraint (6.11) yields $\psi^*_1 \geq 0$ and thus $\psi^*_t \geq 0$ for all $1 \leq t \leq T$. Note that this structure holds for all feasible solutions. $\square$

The result of time-independent bid prices is in contrast to the approximate dynamic programming formulation for passenger revenue management suggested in Adelman (2007) where optimal bid prices vary over time. The reason for this contrast is that we allow for overbooking within the network formulation.

Due to Theorem 6.4 and the assumption of time-independent approximated opportunity cost, we will drop the index t hereafter and let α^{w*}_l and α^{v*}_l be the optimal, time-independent bid prices. Intuitively, one might expect α^{w*}_l and α^{v*}_l to be positive, just like in the passenger counterpart in Adelman (2007). This need not be true in our cargo problem, however, as the following example shows:

Example 6.3. Consider a network that consists of three locations and two legs (see Figure 6.1). Both legs have the same expected capacity, i.e. $\bar{k}^w_1 = \bar{k}^w_2 = 40$ and $\bar{k}^v_1 = \bar{k}^v_2 = 20$.

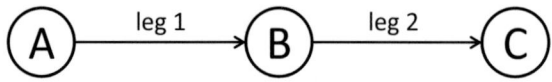

Figure 6.1: Two-leg example: Network

Over a booking horizon of $T = 3$ periods, requests for three different classes may arrive. The capacities of the carriers as well as the actual weight and volume of shipments of different classes equal their expected values. For simplicity take $\vartheta = 1$. The classes are characterized as outlined in Table 6.1.

Period	Class	Expected weight	Expected volume	Itine-rary	Revenue (per unit)	Revenue (total)	Proba-bility
t	i	$\bar{w}_i$	$\bar{v}_i$		φ_i	ρ_i	$q_{t,i}$
3	1	20	10	A-C	2.25	45	0.5
	2	10	10	A-B	2.5	25	0.3
	3	10	10	B-C	2.5	25	0.2
2	1	20	10	A-C	2.25	45	1.0
1	1	20	10	A-C	2.25	45	1.0

Table 6.1: Two-leg example: Classes and data

Classes 2 and 3 require only one leg, and class 1 requires both legs. Further, class 1 requires the same amount of volume as the other classes but twice the amount of weight. In period 3, requests for all classes may arrive. In each period 2 and 1, a request for class 1 arrives with probability 1. In each period, there may arrive at most one request in total. Further, for the sake of simplicity, we impose very high offloading cost (take e.g. $\phi = 5$) so that capacity is not overbooked.

Solving ($\mathbf{P}_{AFA}$) for this example yields $\alpha_1^{w*} = -4.5$, $\alpha_2^{w*} = 0$, $\alpha_1^{v*} = 9$, and $\alpha_2^{v*} = 4.5$ with $\psi_1 = \psi_2 = \psi_3 = 90$. Hence, we know that an upper bound is $z_{AFA} = \psi_3 = 90$.

Using these bid prices, we obtain approximated opportunity cost for class 1 of $-4.5 \times 20 + (9 + 4.5) \times 10 = 45$. Since $\rho_1 = 45$, our decision rule accepts a class-1 request. The approximated opportunity costs for classes 2 and 3 are computed as $-4.5 \times 10 + 9 \times 10 = 45$ and $4.5 \times 10 = 45$. Since $\rho_2 = \rho_3 = 25$, our decision rule rejects requests for both classes.

It is easy to verify that the expected revenue from following this policy is 90 and hence equal to the upper bound, z_{AFA}. We can conclude that it is optimal. In this example, the optimal policy cannot be obtained if we restricted the bid prices to non-negative values. To see this, note that one would need values that satisfy $20(\alpha_1^w + \alpha_2^w) + 10(\alpha_1^v + \alpha_2^v) \leq 45$ for class 1, $10\alpha_1^w + 10\alpha_1^v > 25$ for class 2, and $10\alpha_2^w + 10\alpha_2^v > 25$ for class 3, which is impossible.

Two things are important to remark here: First, one might argue that static bid prices of weight and volume capacity can also be obtained by determining the dual variables of (6.4) and (6.5) from (**DLP**). By definition, however, those values will be non-negative. In our example, the dual variables would be $\lambda_1^w = \lambda_2^w = 0$, $\lambda_1^v = 2.5$, and $\lambda_2^v = 2$. As argued above, an optimal policy cannot be obtained with those bid prices. The approximated opportunity cost for class 1 is $(2 + 2.5) \times 10 = 45$ but for classes 2 and 3, approximated opportunity cost is computed as 20 and 25, respectively. Consequently, the low revenue demand from classes 2 and 3 is not rejected.

Second, one might wonder why bid prices are non-negative in passenger revenue management. In contrast to passenger revenue management, cargo revenue management considers two dimensions and acceptance of multiple units. As a result, the opportunity cost $G_t(c) - G_t(c + e_i)$ of a class i may be lower than the sum of the opportunity costs of two other classes even if these classes require the same resource and even less total capacity.

Such a situation cannot be observed in classical passenger network revenue management since all customers require the same amount of capacity on a flight. However, if customer choice behavior is accounted for, Chaneton & Vulcano (2011) report optimality of negative bid prices in passenger network revenue management. In this setting, negative bid prices serve to take advantage of the substitution behavior of customers. That means, if customers can choose between several legs, their demand is moved to the leg that is more profitable for the airline.

Next, we outline how time-independent bid prices are obtained. We apply a column generation procedure as already outlined in Chapter 4.

Solution Procedure

Using Theorem 6.4, ($\mathbf{P}_{AFA}$) reduces to

$$(\tilde{\mathbf{P}}_{AFA}) \quad \min_{\psi, \alpha^w, \alpha^v} \psi_T$$

$$\text{s.t.} \quad \psi_t - \psi_{t-1} + \sum_{i' \in I} q_{t,i'} a_{i'} \left[\sum_{l \in L(i')} (\bar{w}_{i'} \alpha_l^w + \bar{v}_{i'} \alpha_l^v) - \rho_{i'} \right]$$

$$\geq 0 \quad \forall 2 \leq t \leq T, a \in A$$

$$\psi_1 - \sum_{l \in L} \left[\alpha_l^w \sum_{i \in I(l)} c_i \bar{w}_i + \alpha_l^v \sum_{i \in I(l)} c_i \bar{v}_i \right] - \sum_{i' \in I} q_{1,i'} \sum_{l \in L}$$

$$\left[\rho_{i'} a_{i'} - \phi_l^w \left(\sum_{i \in I(l)} (c_i + a_{i'} \mathbf{1}_{\{i=i'\}}) \bar{w}_i - \bar{k}_l^w \right)^+ \right.$$

$$\left. - \phi_l^v \left(\sum_{i \in I(l)} (c_i + a_{i'} \mathbf{1}_{\{i=i'\}}) \bar{v}_i - \bar{k}_l^v \right)^+ \right]$$

$$\geq 0 \quad \forall c \in C_1, a \in A$$

$$\alpha_l^w, \alpha_l^v \in \mathbb{R} \quad \forall l \in L$$

$$\psi_t \geq 0 \quad \forall 1 \leq t \leq T.$$

While ($\tilde{\mathbf{P}}_{AFA}$) features only a small number of decision variables ($2 \times \mathfrak{L} + T$), the number of constraints is still very large (especially at $t = 1$). Thus, an appropriate solution approach is to solve its dual by column generation (the dual problem, $(\tilde{\mathbf{D}}_{AFA})$, is presented in Appendix B).

We consider the pricing subproblem **(S)** for a given $t = T, ..., 2$

$$\textbf{(S)} \quad \max_{a \in A} \psi_{t-1} - \psi_t - \sum_{i' \in I} q_{t,i'} a_{i'} \left[\sum_{l \in L(i')} (\bar{w}_{i'} \alpha_l^w + \bar{v}_{i'} \alpha_l^v) - \rho_{i'} \right]$$

For $t = 1$, the pricing subproblem is

$$\textbf{(S1)} \quad \max_{a \in A, c \in C_1} \sum_{i' \in I} q_{1,i'} \rho_{i'} a_{i'} - \psi_1 + \sum_{l \in L} \left[\alpha_l^w \sum_{i \in I(l)} c_i \bar{w}_i + \alpha_l^v \sum_{i \in I(l)} c_i \bar{v}_i \right]$$

$$- \sum_{i' \in I} q_{1,i'} \sum_{l \in L} \left[\phi_l^w \left(\sum_{i \in I(l)} (c_i + a_{i'} \mathbf{1}_{\{i = i'\}}) \bar{w}_i - \bar{k}_l^w \right)^+ \right.$$

$$\left. + \phi_l^v \left(\sum_{i \in I(l)} (c_i + a_{i'} \mathbf{1}_{\{i = i'\}}) \bar{v}_i - \bar{k}_l^v \right)^+ \right]$$

(S1) features a non-linear objective due to the piecewise linear structure of offloading cost. However, by introducing some auxiliary variables and constraints we obtain a linear objective.

$$\textbf{(S1*)} \quad \max_{a \in A, c \in C_1, \delta^w \geq 0, \delta^v \geq 0} \sum_{i' \in I} q_{1,i'} \rho_{i'} a_{i'} - \psi_1$$

$$+ \sum_{l \in L} \left[\alpha_l^w \sum_{i \in I(l)} c_i \bar{w}_i + \alpha_l^v \sum_{i \in I(l)} c_i \bar{v}_i \right]$$

$$- \sum_{i' \in I} q_{1,i'} \sum_{l \in L} (\phi_l^w \delta_{l,i'}^w + \phi_l^v \delta_{l,i'}^v)$$

$$\text{s.t.} \quad \delta_{l,i'}^w \geq \sum_{i \in I(l)} (c_i + a_{i'} \mathbf{1}_{\{i = i'\}}) \bar{w}_i - \bar{k}_l^w \quad \forall l \in L, i' \in I$$

$$\delta_{l,i'}^v \geq \sum_{i \in I(l)} (c_i + a_{i'} \mathbf{1}_{\{i=i'\}}) \bar{v}_i - \bar{k}_l^v \quad \forall l \in L, i' \in I$$

The column generation procedure is the same as outlined in Section 4.3.

When the time-independent bid prices are used in (6.3), the resulting state- and time-independent heuristic decision rule for $i \in I$ and $t > 1$ is

$$f(i) = \begin{cases} 1 & \rho_i \geq \sum_{l \in L(i)} [\alpha_l^w \bar{w}_i + \alpha_l^v \bar{v}_i] \\ 0 & \text{otherwise.} \end{cases}$$

In $t = 1$, a request is accepted if its revenue is at least as big as the associated increase in approximated overbooking cost. We refer to the heuristic applying this decision rule as *affine approximation heuristic* or AFA hereafter. While this decision rule is easy to implement, the approximated opportunity cost is time-independent. This implies that a request for a particular class is either accepted or denied in *every* decision period, which yields a static acceptance policy. Furthermore, the policy is inventory-insensitive since the decision rules do not consider current booking levels.

In the next section, we propose a value function approximation that attempts to overcome the affine approximation's shortcoming, which is time- and inventory-insensitive bid prices.

6.3.2 A Piecewise Linear Approximation

A straightforward way to improve the AFA heuristic and its bound z_{AFA} is to allow for a more general form of the value function approximation. One simple extension that would prevent excessive overbooking of AFA is to approximate the value of one weight and volume unit differently depending on the capacity that is booked on a leg. That is, if leg l *is not overbooked*, we approximate the value of one weight unit at time t by $\mu_{l,t}^w$ and the value of one unit of volume at time t by $\mu_{l,t}^v$. If leg l *is overbooked*, we approximate the value of one weight unit at time t by $\tilde{\mu}_{l,t}^w$ and the value of one unit of volume at time t by $\tilde{\mu}_{l,t}^v$. This gives us capacity- and time-dependent bid prices and corresponds to the following approximation of $G_t(\boldsymbol{c})$ in (6.2) for all $t = T, ..., 1$ and $\boldsymbol{c} \in \boldsymbol{C}_t$:

$$
\begin{aligned}
G_t(\boldsymbol{c}) \approx \psi_t - \sum_{l \in L} \Bigg[& \mu_{l,t}^w \min \left\{ \sum_{i \in I(l)} c_i \bar{w}_i, \bar{k}_l^w \right\} + \mu_{l,t}^v \min \left\{ \sum_{i \in I(l)} c_i \bar{v}_i, \bar{k}_l^v \right\} \\
& + \tilde{\mu}_{l,t}^w \left(\sum_{i \in I(l)} c_i \bar{w}_i - \bar{k}_l^w \right)^+ + \tilde{\mu}_{l,t}^v \left(\sum_{i \in I(l)} c_i \bar{v}_i - \bar{k}_l^v \right)^+ \Bigg].
\end{aligned}
$$

$$(6.24)$$

In $t = 0$, we approximate overbooking cost like we did in the affine-linear case. Approximation (6.24) is similar to existing piecewise linear approximation schemes, e.g. in Meissner & Strauss (2012). While these authors divide capacity into equidistant intervals and approximate the value function in each interval by a different linear function, we use expected capacities as the point where to switch from one linear function to the other in order to limit computational effort. Plugging approximation (6.24) into ($\tilde{\mathbf{P}}$) yields the linear problem ($\mathbf{P}_{PLA}$).

$$
(\mathbf{P}_{PLA}) \quad \min_{\psi, \mu^w, \mu^v, \tilde{\mu}^w, \tilde{\mu}^v} \psi_T
$$

$$
\begin{aligned}
\text{s.t.} \quad \psi_t - \psi_{t-1} - \sum_{l \in L} \Bigg[& \mu_{l,t}^w \min \left\{ \sum_{i \in I(l)} c_i \bar{w}_i, \bar{k}_l^w \right\} \\
& + \mu_{l,t}^v \min \left\{ \sum_{i \in I(l)} c_i \bar{v}_i, \bar{k}_l^v \right\} \\
& - \sum_{i' \in I} q_{t,i'} \Bigg[\mu_{l,t-1}^w \min \left\{ \sum_{i \in I(l)} (c_i + a_{i'} \mathbf{1}_{\{i=i'\}}) \bar{w}_i, \bar{k}_l^w \right\} \\
& + \mu_{l,t-1}^v \min \left\{ \sum_{i \in I(l)} (c_i + a_{i'} \mathbf{1}_{\{i=i'\}}) \bar{v}_i, \bar{k}_l^v \right\} \Bigg] \Bigg]
\end{aligned}
$$

$$-\sum_{l \in L}\left[\tilde{\mu}_{l,t}^{w}\left(\sum_{i \in I(l)}c_i\bar{w}_i-\bar{k}_l^w\right)^{+}+\tilde{\mu}_{l,t}^{v}\left(\sum_{i \in I(l)}c_i\bar{v}_i-\bar{k}_l^v\right)^{+}\right.$$

$$-\sum_{i' \in I}q_{t,i'}\left[\tilde{\mu}_{l,t-1}^{w}\left(\sum_{i \in I(l)}(c_i+a_{i'}\mathbf{1}_{\{i=i'\}})\bar{w}_i-\bar{k}_l^w\right)^{+}\right.$$

$$\left.\left.+\tilde{\mu}_{l,t-1}^{v}\left(\sum_{i \in I(l)}(c_i+a_{i'}\mathbf{1}_{\{i=i'\}})\bar{v}_i-\bar{k}_l^v\right)^{+}\right]\right]-\sum_{i' \in I}q_{t,i'}a_{i'}\rho_{i'}$$

$$\geq 0 \quad \forall \boldsymbol{c} \in \boldsymbol{C}_t, 1 < t \leq T, \boldsymbol{a} \in \boldsymbol{A}$$

$$\psi_1 - \sum_{l \in L}\left[\mu_{l,1}^{w}\min\left\{\sum_{i \in I(l)}c_i\bar{w}_i,\bar{k}_l^w\right\}+\mu_{l,1}^{v}\min\left\{\sum_{i \in I(l)}c_i\bar{v}_i,\bar{k}_l^v\right\}\right.$$

$$\left.+\tilde{\mu}_{l,1}^{w}\left(\sum_{i \in I(l)}c_i\bar{w}_i-\bar{k}_l^w\right)^{+}+\tilde{\mu}_{l,1}^{v}\left(\sum_{i \in I(l)}c_i\bar{v}_i-\bar{k}_l^v\right)^{+}\right]$$

$$+\sum_{i' \in I}q_{1,i'}\sum_{l \in L}\left[\phi_l^{w}\left(\sum_{i \in I(l)}(c_i+a_{i'}\mathbf{1}_{\{i=i'\}})\bar{w}_i-\bar{k}_l^w\right)^{+}\right.$$

$$\left.+\phi_l^{v}\left(\sum_{i \in I(l)}(c_i+a_{i'}\mathbf{1}_{\{i=i'\}})\bar{v}_i-\bar{k}_l^v\right)^{+}\right]-\sum_{i' \in I}q_{1,i'}a_{i'}\rho_{i'}$$

$$\geq 0 \quad \forall \boldsymbol{c} \in \boldsymbol{C}_1, \boldsymbol{a} \in \boldsymbol{A}$$

$$\psi_t, \mu_{l,t}^{w}, \mu_{l,t}^{v}, \tilde{\mu}_{l,t}^{w}, \tilde{\mu}_{l,t}^{v} \in \mathbb{R} \quad \forall 1 \leq t \leq T, l \in L.$$

The resulting price-directed heuristic accepts a request for class $i' \in I$ at time $t > 1$ if

$$
\rho_{i'} \geq \sum_{l \in L(i')} \left[\mu_{l,t-1}^{w} \left(\min \left\{ \sum_{i \in I(l)} (c_i + \mathbf{1}_{\{i=i'\}}) \bar{w}_i, \bar{k}_l^w \right\} \right. \right.
$$

$$
\left. - \min \left\{ \sum_{i \in I(l)} c_i \bar{w}_i, \bar{k}_l^w \right\} \right)
$$

$$
+ \mu_{l,t-1}^{v} \left(\min \left\{ \sum_{i \in I(l)} (c_i + \mathbf{1}_{\{i=i'\}}) \bar{v}_i, \bar{k}_l^v \right\} - \min \left\{ \sum_{i \in I(l)} c_i \bar{v}_i, \bar{k}_l^v \right\} \right)
$$

$$
+ \tilde{\mu}_{l,t-1}^{w} \left(\left(\sum_{i \in I(l)} (c_i + \mathbf{1}_{\{i=i'\}}) \bar{w}_i - \bar{k}_l^w \right)^{+} - \left(\sum_{i \in I(l)} c_i \bar{w}_i - \bar{k}_l^w \right)^{+} \right)
$$

$$
+ \tilde{\mu}_{l,t-1}^{v} \left(\left(\sum_{i \in I(l)} (c_i + \mathbf{1}_{\{i=i'\}}) \bar{v}_i - \bar{k}_l^v \right)^{+} - \left(\sum_{i \in I(l)} c_i \bar{v}_i - \bar{k}_l^v \right)^{+} \right) \right].
$$

In $t = 1$, a request is accepted if its revenue is at least as big as the associated increase in approximated overbooking cost (like in the affine-linear case). The heuristic that applies these decision rules is referred to as PLA hereafter. Using this piecewise linear approximation, the approximation parameters do, in general, vary in time. Hence, the above decision rule is time-sensitive. The approximation parameters can be determined by solving the dual of $(\mathbf{P}_{PLA})$, $(\mathbf{D}_{PLA})$ (presented in Appendix B), via column generation. However, many auxiliary variables and constraints are necessary to transform the non-linear subproblem into a linear one. This increases computational effort tremendously and only makes this problem solvable for relatively small problem instances. (Note that in contrast to passenger revenue management, the terminal condition increases computational effort even further.)

An important property of $(\mathbf{P}_{PLA})$ is that its optimal objective value, z_{PLA}, provides a bound that is at least as tight as z_{AFA}.

Theorem 6.5. $G_T(0) \leq z_{PLA} \leq z_{AFA} \leq z_{DLP}$.

Proof. Since $(\mathbf{P}_{PLA})$ provides a feasible solution to $(\tilde{\mathbf{P}})$, it follows that $z_{PLA} \geq G_T(0)$. Thus, this approximate LP determines the lowest upper bound of the form (6.24) on the maximum expected revenue.

In order to prove the second inequality, we show that $(\mathbf{P}_{AFA})$ is a special case of $(\mathbf{P}_{PLA})$. This is simply achieved by setting $\mu_{l,t}^w = \tilde{\mu}_{l,t}^w = \alpha_{l,t}^w$ and $\mu_{l,t}^v = \tilde{\mu}_{l,t}^v = \alpha_{l,t}^v$ for all $l \in L$ and $1 \leq t \leq T$. Then, $(\mathbf{P}_{PLA})$ reduces to $(\mathbf{P}_{AFA})$. Accordingly, any feasible solution of $(\mathbf{P}_{AFA})$ gives a feasible solution to $(\mathbf{P}_{PLA})$. Thus, an optimal solution to $(\mathbf{P}_{PLA})$ has an objective value which is not greater than z_{AFA}. $\square$

In the next section, we propose a further heuristic that is time- and inventory-sensitive like PLA. The difference is that this heuristic utilizes the time-independent bid prices from the affine-linear approximation.

6.4 Dynamic Programming Decomposition

A different approach of value function approximation, which is popular in passenger revenue management, is to use bid prices in a dynamic programming decomposition (cf. Talluri & van Ryzin, 2004, Section 3.4). We outline how this approach can be adapted to our cargo setting below.

The underlying idea of the dynamic programming decomposition heuristic is to decompose the network MDP into weight and volume subproblems for each leg. The combination of the one-dimensional value functions is then used to approximate the network value function for all $t = T, ..., 1$ and $c \in C_t$ as

$$G_t(c) \approx \sum_{l \in L} \left[G_{t,l}^w(w_l(c)) + G_{t,l}^v(v_l(c)) \right],$$

where $w_l(c) := \sum_{i \in I(l)} c_i \tilde{w}_i$ converts the vector of accepted requests into expected weight on leg l, and $v_l(c) := \sum_{i \in I(l)} c_i \tilde{v}_i$ does the same for volume.

In order to preserve integrality of the state space, we define $\tilde{w}_i := \lfloor \bar{w}_i \rfloor$ and $\tilde{v}_i := \lfloor \bar{v}_i \rfloor$ for all $i \in I$.

Denote the revenue from accepting a class-i shipment on leg l by $\rho_{l,i}^w$ in the weight subproblem and by $\rho_{l,i}^v$ in the volume subproblem. Now, consider the single-resource MDP for weight on leg l. In this subproblem, the maximum expected revenue, which can be obtained after w weight units have been accepted and t time periods remain until departure, is given by

$$G_{t,l}^w(w) = \sum_{i \in I} q_{t,i} \max_{a \in A_l(i)} \left\{ \rho_{l,i}^w a + G_{t-1,l}^w(w + a\tilde{w}_i) \right\}$$

with $G_{0,l}^w(w) := -\phi_l^w \mathbb{E}\left[(w - K_l^w)^+ \right]$, and with $A_l(i) := \{0, 1\}$ for $i \in I$ and $l \in L(i)$.

The volume problems are formulated likewise to obtain the maximum expected revenue that can be obtained after v volume units have been accepted on leg l at time t, $G_{l,t}^v(v)$, for all legs l and decision periods t.

Using this approximation in (6.3) gives the following heuristic decision rule depending on $t = T, ..., 1$, $c \in C_t$, and $i \in I$:

$$f_t(c, i) = \begin{cases} 1 & \rho_i \geq \sum_{l \in L(i)} \left[G_{t-1,l}^w(w_l(c)) + G_{t-1,l}^v(v_l(c)) \right. \\ & \left. \qquad -G_{t-1,l}^w(w_l(c) + \tilde{w}_i) - G_{t-1,l}^v(v_l(c) + \tilde{v}_i) \right] \\ 0 & \text{otherwise.} \end{cases}$$

$$(6.25)$$

Depending on how the revenues of the subproblems, $\rho_{l,i}^w$ and $\rho_{l,i}^v$ are chosen, different dynamic programming decomposition heuristics can be analyzed. Furthermore, the following theorem shows that as long as the class-i revenues are split across dimensions so that the revenues of all subproblems sum up to their true value ρ_i for all $i \in I$, $\sum_{l \in L}[G_{t,l}^w(w_l(c)) + G_{t,l}^v(v_l(c))]$ yields an upper bound on the maximum expected revenue.

Theorem 6.6. *Let $\rho_{l,i}^w$ and $\rho_{l,i}^v$ denote the class-i revenue in a leg-l weight and volume subproblem, respectively. If*

$$\sum_{l \in L(i)} \left[\rho_{l,i}^w + \rho_{l,i}^v\right] = \rho_i \quad \forall i \in I,$$

the sum of the maximum expected revenues of the subproblems provides an upper bound on the maximum expected revenue determined in (6.2), i.e.

$$\sum_{l \in L} \left[G_{t,l}^w(w_l(\boldsymbol{c})) + G_{t,l}^v(v_l(\boldsymbol{c}))\right] \geq G_t(\boldsymbol{c}) \quad \forall t = T, ..., 0, \boldsymbol{c} \in \boldsymbol{C}_t.$$

Proof. This proof is a straightforward extension of the proof of Proposition 1 in Amaruchkul et al. (2007). The proof follows by induction on t. In $t = 0$, it follows from Jensen's inequality that

$$G_0(\boldsymbol{c})$$

$$= -\sum_{l \in L} \mathbb{E}_{\boldsymbol{W},\boldsymbol{V},\boldsymbol{K}^w,\boldsymbol{K}^v} \left[\phi_l^w \left(\sum_{i \in I(l)} W_i c_i - K_l^w\right)^+\right.$$

$$\left. + \phi_l^v \left(\sum_{i \in I(l)} V_i c_i - K_l^v\right)^+\right]$$

$$\leq -\sum_{l \in L} \left[\phi_l^w \mathbb{E}\left[\left(\sum_{i \in I(l)} \bar{w}_i c_i - K_l^w\right)^+\right] + \phi_l^v \mathbb{E}\left[\left(\sum_{i \in I(l)} \bar{v}_i c_i - K_l^v\right)^+\right]\right]$$

$$\leq -\sum_{l \in L} \left[\phi_l^w \mathbb{E}\left[(w_l(\boldsymbol{c}) - K_l^w)^+\right] + \phi_l^v \mathbb{E}\left[(v_l(\boldsymbol{c}) - K_l^v)^+\right]\right]$$

$$= \sum_{l \in L} \left[G_{0,l}^w(w_l(\boldsymbol{c})) + G_{0,l}^v(v_l(\boldsymbol{c}))\right].$$

Now assume that the assertion holds for periods $0, ..., t$. Then, we have for period $t + 1$:

$$G_{t+1}(\boldsymbol{c})$$

$$= \sum_{i \in I} q_{t+1,i} \max_{a \in A(i)} \{a\rho_i + G_t(\boldsymbol{c} + a\boldsymbol{e}_i)\}$$

$$\leq \sum_{i \in I} q_{t+1,i} \max_{a \in A(i)} \left\{ a \sum_{l \in L(i)} [\rho_{l,i}^w + \rho_{l,i}^v] + \sum_{l \in L(i)} [G_{t,l}^w(w_l(\boldsymbol{c}) + a\tilde{w}_i) \right.$$

$$\left. + G_{t,l}^v(v_l(\boldsymbol{c}) + a\tilde{v}_i)] + \sum_{l \notin L(i)} [G_{t,l}^w(w_l(\boldsymbol{c})) + G_{t,l}^v(v_l(\boldsymbol{c}))] \right\}$$

$$\leq \sum_{i \in I} q_{t+1,i} \left[\sum_{l \in L(i)} \left[\max_{a \in A(i)} \{a\rho_{l,i}^w + G_{t,l}^w(w_l(\boldsymbol{c}) + a\tilde{w}_i)\} \right. \right.$$

$$\left. \left. + \max_{a \in A(i)} \{a\rho_{l,i}^v + G_{t,l}^v(v_l(\boldsymbol{c}) + a\tilde{v}_i)\} \right] + \sum_{l \notin L(i)} [G_{t,l}^w(w_l(\boldsymbol{c})) + G_{t,l}^v(v_l(\boldsymbol{c}))] \right]$$

$$= \sum_{l \in L} \sum_{i \in I} q_{t+1,i} \left[\max_{a \in A_l(i)} \{a\rho_{l,i}^w + G_{t,l}^w(w_l(\boldsymbol{c}) + a\tilde{w}_i)\} \right.$$

$$\left. + \max_{a \in A_l(i)} \{a\rho_{l,i}^v + G_{t,l}^v(v_l(\boldsymbol{c}) + a\tilde{v}_i)\} \right]$$

$$= \sum_{l \in L} [G_{t+1,l}^w(w_l(\boldsymbol{c})) + G_{t+1,l}^v(v_l(\boldsymbol{c}))].$$

The first inequality follows from the induction assumption, and the second inequality follows from the fact that a maximum is a subadditive function. The equality in the second last line holds since the definition of $A_l(i)$ allows us to sum over all legs rather than making a difference between legs that are requested and legs that are not requested. $\square$

Unfortunately, it is not possible to establish a connection between these bounds and z_{AFA} in general. Their performance highly depends on the revenues assigned to the subproblems. Below we propose a decomposition heuristic that does this assignment by means of the bid prices for weight and volume on each single leg.

Bid-Price Based Heuristic

Amaruchkul et al. (2007) examine three possibilities, how revenue can be distributed over the weight and volume dimension in a single-leg problem. Two of their heuristics put all the revenue on one dimension, another and best heuristic achieves a trade-off by splitting it as $\rho_i^w = \varphi_i \mathbb{E}[W_i]$ and $\rho_i^v = \rho_i - \varphi_i \mathbb{E}[W_i]$. (We dropped the index l since they consider a single-leg problem.)

While the authors argue that the latter heuristic is intuitive, it is unclear why such a splitting would perform well in scenarios where one capacity dimension is tighter than the other. Further, it is unclear how their ideas should be extended to a network setting.

This is why we suggest to assign the revenue across dimensions in a way that is proportional to their bid prices and capacity requirements. For the weight (volume) subproblem of leg $l \in L$, a request for a class $i \in I$ in time period $t = T, ..., 1$ is viewed as a request to ship a weight of $\tilde{w}_i$ (volume of $\tilde{v}_i$) if $l \in L(i)$. If $\sum_{l' \in L(i)} [\alpha_{l'}^w \tilde{w}_i + \alpha_{l'}^v \tilde{v}_i] > 0$ for $i \in \{1, ..., m\}$, the revenue from shipping $\tilde{w}_i$ weight units on leg l is given by

$$\rho_{l,i}^w = \rho_i \times \frac{\alpha_l^w \bar{w}_i}{\sum\limits_{l' \in L(i)} [\alpha_{l'}^w \bar{w}_i + \alpha_{l'}^v \bar{v}_i]} \qquad (6.26)$$

and the revenue from shipping $\tilde{v}_i$ volume units on leg l is given by

$$\rho_{l,i}^v = \rho_i \times \frac{\alpha_l^v \bar{v}_i}{\sum\limits_{l' \in L(i)} [\alpha_{l'}^w \bar{w}_i + \alpha_{l'}^v \bar{v}_i]}. \qquad (6.27)$$

If the opportunity cost of a class was 0, we take $\rho_i \bar{w}_i / \sum_{l' \in L(i)} (\bar{w}_i + \bar{v}_i)$ and $\rho_i \bar{v}_i / \sum_{l' \in L(i)} (\bar{w}_i + \bar{v}_i)$, respectively. For $i = 0$, we define $\rho_{l,i}^w = \rho_{l,i}^v = 0$. Note that we use $\bar{w}_i$ and $\bar{v}_i$ rather than $\tilde{w}_i$ and $\tilde{v}_i$ when determining revenues since integrality of weight and volume is not necessary at this point.

The intuition is that if capacity on a leg in one dimension is ample, its bid price will be 0 and no revenue is "needed" on this leg. More revenue should be allocated to legs and dimensions with positive bid prices, where capacity is tight.

We refer to the heuristic that applies decision rule (6.25) with the above outlined revenues per subproblem as DPD (dynamic programming decomposition).

Remember that in the network setting, the bid prices for weight or volume may be negative on some legs. While this might be desirable in an AFA control policy, as shown in Section 6.3.1, negative single-leg revenues tend to significantly loosen the upper bound given in Theorem 6.6. Hence, using (6.26) and (6.27) might not give a very tight upper bound.

This can be explained as follows: For a given class i, let $L^{w-}(i)$ and $L^{v-}(i)$ be the set of legs with negative revenues $\rho_{l,i}^w$ and $\rho_{l,i}^v$, respectively. Now consider a class $i \neq 0$ for which there is a leg $l \in L$ with $\rho_{l,i}^w < 0$ and/or $\rho_{l,i}^v < 0$. If we enforce $\sum_{l \in L(i)} [\rho_{l,i}^w + \rho_{l,i}^v] = \rho_i$, this implies that the sum of the bid-prices over the other legs, $\sum_{l \in L(i) \setminus L^{w-}(i)} \rho_{l,i}^w + \sum_{l \in L(i) \setminus L^{v-}(i)} \rho_{l,i}^v$ will exceed the true revenue ρ_i. On all weight subproblems with $l \in L^{w-}(i)$ and all volume subproblems with $l \in L^{v-}(i)$, a class-i request will always be rejected, and a revenue of 0 will be gained from this. If a class-i request is accepted on the other subproblems, the total revenue it brings will by far exceed its actual revenue ρ_i.

Note that this phenomenon cannot happen if we enforce $\rho_{l,i}^w, \rho_{l,i}^v \geq 0$ for all classes i and all legs $l \in L(i)$. As a consequence, we expect a bound based on revenues as given in (6.26) and (6.27) not to be tight in the presence of negative bid prices. We therefore suggest to scale bid prices to achieve non-negativity when this approach is used to obtain an upper bound and refer to this upper bound as z_{DPD}.

The following section assesses the quality of our proposed bounds and the performance of the heuristics by means of numerical experiments.

6.5 Numerical Experiments

In this section, our first intention is to demonstrate the quality of the upper bounds, z_{DLP}, z_{RLP}, z_{PLP}, z_{AFA}, z_{PLA}, and z_{DPD}, which we proposed earlier. Further, we assess how well the suggested heuristics, AFA and DPD, perform. Their performance will be compared to several other heuristics:

- FCFS: A first-come-first-served policy;

- DLP: A price-directed heuristic with the same decision rule as AFA but with parameters equal to the dual variables of (**DLP**), as suggested in Pak & Dekker (2004);

- DPD′: A decomposition heuristic with revenues split in proportion to the bid prices given by the dual variables of (**DLP**); this heuristic generates a bound $z_{DPD'}$;

- ACG: A decomposition heuristic for single-leg problems suggested in Amaruchkul et al. (2007), which splits revenue as $\rho_i^w = \varphi_i \mathbb{E}[W_i]$ and $\rho_i^v = \rho_i - \varphi_i \mathbb{E}[W_i]$ and does not consider uncertainty in capacity (cf. Section 4.3 where we called this heuristic HD). It determines an upper bound z_{ACG} (Amaruchkul, Cooper, and Gupta).

Other linear programs, such as (**PLP**) could, of course, also be used to determine bid-prices in the price-directed or decomposition heuristics we suggested. In our numerical studies, however, we found that the differences between different methods to obtain bid prices seem to be small. A comparison of the heuristics' achieved revenue to the lowest upper bound will give us information on the optimality gaps of the heuristics.

We first discuss a single-leg example and provide numerical results for a large-scale network problem afterwards. All experiments were conducted on an Intel Core2 Quad CPU at 2.83 GHz and 8 GB RAM. We used Gurobi 5.0 (Gurobi Optimization, 2012) for solving the LPs.

Single-Leg Experiments

To test our heuristics on a single-leg model, we consider an example with 24 shipment categories as shown in Tables 6.2 and 6.3 (taken from Amaruchkul et al., 2007). Shipments of category $b = 1, ..., 24$ require an uncertain weight W_b and volume V_b at the time of departure. We assume that W_b and V_b follow a joint normal distribution with $\mathbb{E}[W_b] = \bar{w}_b$, $\mathbb{E}[V_b] = \bar{v}_b$, coefficient of variation

Category b	1	2	3	4	5	6	7	8	9	10	11	12
Mean weight $\bar{w}_b$ (kg)	50	50	50	50	100	100	100	100	200	200	200	250
Mean volume $\bar{v}_b$ ($\times 10^4$ cm^3)	30	29	27	25	59	58	55	52	125	119	100	147

Table 6.2: Mean weight and volume of shipment categories (part 1)

Category b	13	14	15	16	17	18	19	20	21	22	23	24
Mean weight $\bar{w}_b$ (kg)	250	300	400	500	1000	1500	2500	3500	70	70	210	210
Mean volume $\bar{v}_b$ ($\times 10^4$ cm^3)	138	179	235	277	598	898	1488	2083	233	17	700	52

Table 6.3: Mean weight and volume of shipment categories (part 2)

of $CV_d = 0.25$ for both weight and volume, and coefficient of correlation of 0.8. Each category can be requested with a revenue per chargeable weight $\varphi \in \{0.7, 1.0, 1.4\}$. Viewing a class as a combination of category and revenue per chargeable weight, $3 \times 24 = 72$ different classes may be requested. The expected revenue associated with a request for a category b and revenue per chargeable weight φ is $\varphi \mathbb{E}_{W_b,V_b} [W_b, V_b/\vartheta]$ with $\vartheta = 0.6$.

We consider a booking horizon of $T = 60$ decision periods. In each time period t, either a shipment with revenue per chargeable weight φ or no shipment is requested. The probabilities for incoming requests with revenue per chargeable weight φ are given in Table 6.4. Given a shipment request, there is a probability of 0.072 for the event that the shipment belongs to category $b = 1, ..., 10$. It is 0.04 for categories $b = 11, ..., 16$; 0.009 for categories $b = 17, ..., 20$; and 0.001 for categories $b = 21, ..., 24$. We assume that the category is independent of the requested revenue per chargeable weight. As a consequence, the request probability for class $i = (b, \varphi)$ in time period t, $q_{t,i}$, equals the probability of observing a revenue per chargeable weight φ in time period t multiplied by the

179

probability of observing a category b request in this time period. For instance, the probability for an arrival of a class with $\varphi = 1.4$ and $b = 15$ at $t = 10$ is $0.7 \times 0.04 = 0.028$.

Revenue	Periods 1..20	Periods 21..40	Periods 41..60
0.7	0	0.4	0.7
1.0	0.2	0.2	0.2
1.4	0.7	0.4	0
no request	0.1	0	0.1

Table 6.4: Request probabilities for different revenues per chargeable weight

The weight and volume capacities of the freighter, K^w and K^v, are random variables that follow a joint normal distribution with means $\bar{k}^w$ and $\bar{k}^v$, coefficient of variation of $CV_k = 0.25$ for both weight and volume capacity and a coefficient of correlation of 0.8. We drop the leg index in this single-leg model in order to simplify notation.

The expected total demand in weight and volume is calculated as $\bar{d}^w := \sum_{t=1}^{T} \sum_{i \in I} q_{t,i} \bar{w}_i$ and $\bar{d}^v := \sum_{t=1}^{T} \sum_{i \in I} q_{t,i} \bar{v}_i$. Using our example data, the expected demand is $\bar{d}^w = 10740$ weight units and $\bar{d}^v = 7355$ volume units. In the experiments, we vary mean capacities $\bar{k}^w$ and $\bar{k}^v$ in order to create scenarios with a shortage of weight and/or volume capacity. These scenarios are $(\bar{k}^w/\bar{d}^w, \bar{k}^v/\bar{d}^v) \in \{(1.0, 1.0), (0.5, 0.5), (1.0, 0.5), (0.5, 1.0)\}$.

Per unit overbooking cost for both weight and volume units is assumed to be 1.2 times the expected revenue per unit of available capacity. Thus, total weight and volume offloading cost is $\phi^w = 1.2 \times \sum_{t=1}^{T} \sum_{i \in I} q_{t,i} \rho_i / \bar{k}_w$ and $\phi^v = 1.2 \times \sum_{t=1}^{T} \sum_{i \in I} q_{t,i} \rho_i / \bar{k}_v$, respectively.

Upper Bound Quality

We solved DLP to obtain z_{DLP} and used 20,000 samples to estimate z_{PLP} and z_{RLP}. To obtain z_{AFA}, we solved $(\tilde{\mathbf{P}}_{AFA})$ by means of column generation with an optimality tolerance of 1%. Run times were less than 10 minutes for all problem instances. We solved for z_{PLA} by means of column generation with the same optimality tolerance. Run times were significantly longer (between 2-3 hours) for the piecewise linear approximation.

The bid prices obtained by the affine approximation were used to compute the value functions of each subproblem of DPD, which gave us z_{DPD}. Using different weights, as outlined above, we further determined $z_{DPD'}$ and z_{ACG}. Table 6.5 displays the computed upper bounds (tightest bound in bold).

$(\bar{k}^w/\bar{d}^w, \bar{k}^v/\bar{d}^v)$	z_{RLP}	z_{PLP}	z_{DLP}	z_{AFA}	z_{PLA}	$z_{DPD'}$	z_{DPD}	z_{ACG}
(1.0,1.0)	11514.32	11972.94	12407.50	12296.80	11904.70	**10277.99**	10280.15	11214.86
(0.5,0.5)	7299.53	7431.58	7752.52	7687.26	7315.03	**5698.50**	5700.79	6931.63
(1.0,0.5)	8398.32	8427.68	8722.19	8651.99	8284.90	6612.95	**6611.50**	11030.13
(0.5,1.0)	7435.12	7437.52	7752.52	7687.70	7314.56	5707.35	**5704.46**	7116.37

Table 6.5: Upper bounds for the single-leg problem

As shown earlier, we have $z_{PLA} \leq z_{AFA} \leq z_{DLP}$ and $z_{PLP} \leq z_{DLP}$. In these examples, z_{RLP} is smaller than z_{PLP} although this need not be true in general. Furthermore, z_{RLP} is tighter than z_{PLA} in case of unrestricted as well as both weight and volume restricted flights. The tightest upper bounds, however, are z_{DPD} and $z_{DPD'}$ which are almost equal and both significantly lower than z_{PLA}. Both bounds are also tighter than z_{ACG} for all tested scenarios. Further, note that the quality of z_{ACG} varies significantly depending on whether weight or volume is the tighter dimension. This disadvantage of z_{ACG} is caused by the priority on weight when assigning revenues to the subproblems. In case of volume restricted flights, these revenues are miscalculated since the shortness of volume is not appropriately accounted for. Prioritizing the capacity dimension that is expected to be the bottleneck is reasonable; however, whether a flight will be either weight or volume restricted can hardly be determined several weeks before departure.

Heuristic Performance

In order to assess the performance of our heuristics, we repeatedly simulated the arrival process. In each simulation run, we tracked the number of accepted requests of each class for each heuristic and subtracted offloading cost from total revenue at the end of the booking horizon. In order to obtain reliable results, we simulated 20,000 booking processes.

Since the decision rules of FCFS, AFA, and DLP are capacity-independent, we prevent excessive overbooking by stopping acceptance when the expected capacity is reached. Table 6.6 reports the simulated average net revenues (best performance in bold), which is total revenue minus offloading cost.

$(\bar{k}^w/\bar{d}^w, \bar{k}^v/\bar{d}^v)$	FCFS	DLP	AFA	PLA	DPD$'$	DPD	ACG
(1.0,1.0)	8454.13	8882.10	8972.24	8810.37	**9433.74**	9432.92	9240.15
(0.5,0.5)	2264.57	4895.96	4676.93	4800.95	5144.33	**5146.07**	4644.28
(1.0,0.5)	3916.01	6216.62	6115.17	6158.16	6343.28	**6343.49**	4297.30
(0.5,1.0)	3114.46	5432.21	5457.68	5489.67	5607.55	**5608.73**	5411.23

Table 6.6: Simulated average net revenue in the single-leg problem

DPD and DPD$'$ feature almost equal revenues, and they outperform all other heuristics for all capacity-demand ratios. Possible explanations for the fact that both heuristics outperform ACG are, first, an improved assignment of revenues to subproblems, and second, the consideration of uncertain capacity. The performance of DPD and DPD$'$ is also better than the performance of the price-directed heuristic PLA even though the latter also features a time- and inventory-sensitive decision rule. In all scenarios, both DPD and DPD$'$ perform exceptionally well, with solution gaps between 1.7% and 9.7%.

AFA and DLP would excessively overbook if no external stopping rule was provided. The artificial booking stop we imposed is the reason why AFA outperforms PLA for $(\bar{k}^w/\bar{d}^w, \bar{k}^v/\bar{d}^v) = (1.0, 1.0)$; it would be worse without. Both bid-price heuristics perform approximately equally well in the single-leg case since both are based on non-negative static bid prices. Besides our artificial booking stop, another possible source of inaccuracy is the use of approximated bid prices in AFA which are obtained through column generation allowing for an optimality tolerance. Our numerical experiments showed that a small change in bid prices may affect the acceptance policy of AFA significantly. Note that FCFS performs relatively bad in the above scenarios since low-value requests tend to arrive before high-value requests in the booking process. That means, if expected demand is greater than expected capacity, FCFS yields acceptance of unprofitable requests and does not leave sufficient capacity for accepting more profitable requests.

Network Experiments

To extend our example to a network setting, we consider a hub-and-spoke network comprising one hub and four spokes as shown in Figure 6.2. We again consider a booking horizon of 60 decision periods. Demand is given by the same 72 classes, with the same expected weight and volume, same revenues, and same arrival probabilities per time period, as in the single-leg example. In contrast to the single-leg setting, the network setting requires to additionally specify the requested legs for each class. We therefore randomly assigned an origin-destination pair to each class. The detailed assignment can be found in Hoffmann (2013a, Appendix C). Again, weight and volume for a given class follow a joint normal distribution with a correlation of 0.8. To study the impact of increased variation in weight and volume, we consider both a "high demand variation" and a "low demand variation" scenario. The low demand variation scenario is characterized by a coefficient of variation equal to $CV_d = 0.1$ for all classes, and it is $CV_d = 0.4$ in the high demand variation scenario.

Similarly, the weight and volume capacity of a freighter on leg l follows a joint normal distribution with means $\bar{k}_l^w$ and $\bar{k}_l^v$ and a coefficient of correlation of 0.8. To vary the degree of capacity uncertainty, we consider a "high capacity variation" scenario with a coefficient of variation of $CV_k = 0.4$ for weight and volume on each leg and a "low capacity variation" scenario, where this coefficient of variation is $CV_k = 0.1$.

183

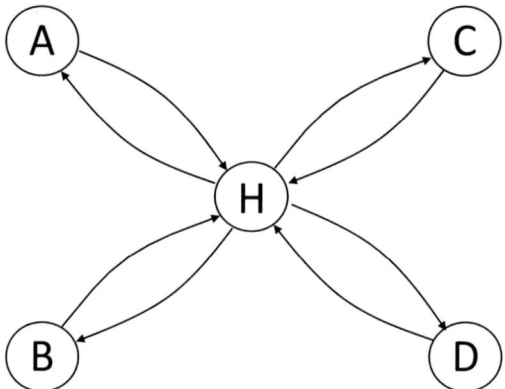

Figure 6.2: Hub-and-spoke network

Total expected demand on a particular leg in weight, $\bar{d}_l^w$, is between 1922 and 3566, and total expected demand on a particular leg in volume, $\bar{d}_l^v$, is between 1112 and 2063. We vary mean capacities in order to test scenarios with flights that are not restricted, both volume and weight restricted, only volume restricted, and only weight restricted. More specifically, we use $(\bar{k}_l^w/\bar{d}_l^w, \bar{k}_l^v/\bar{d}_l^v) \in \{(1.0, 1.0), (0.5, 0.5), (1.0, 0.5), (0.5, 1.0)\}$ for all $l \in L$. To limit the number of scenarios, we only consider extreme cases and use the same capacity-demand ratio on each leg. Thus, a capacity-demand ratio of 0.5 means that on *every* leg demand is twice as high as capacity. Offloading cost is calculated per leg in the same way as in the single-leg experiments.

Upper Bound Quality

Solving for the bid prices as dual variables of $(\tilde{\mathbf{P}}_{AFA})$ via column generation with an optimality tolerance of 1%, each problem instance was solved in less than 30 minutes. (The increased solution time is a result of the more expensive calculations to determine terminal cost in the network setting.) Restricting the solution time to 48 hours, we were not able to solve for z_{PLA} in this setting. We therefore do not report PLA results in this section. Table 6.7 gives an overview of the upper bounds z_{DLP}, z_{RLP}, z_{PLP}, z_{AFA}, $z_{DPD'}$, and z_{DPD}. We do not report z_{ACG} since the approach of Amaruchkul et al. (2007) covers only single-leg problems. Note that the tightest upper bound in each scenario is highlighted in bold font.

CV_d	CV_k	$(\bar{k}_l^w/\bar{d}_l^w, \bar{k}_l^v/\bar{d}_l^v)$	z_{RLP}	z_{PLP}	z_{DLP}	z_{AFA}	$z_{DPD'}$	z_{DPD}
0.1	0.1	(1.0,1.0)	10270.04	10442.16	13369.70	13096.40	10420.36	**9216.71**
		(0.5,0.5)	6934.23	7072.59	8594.52	8457.70	5890.76	**5808.90**
		(1.0,0.5)	7132.73	7161.55	8648.54	8568.05	**6013.23**	6098.43
		(0.5,1.0)	7105.64	7149.68	8623.46	8507.07	**5967.83**	6083.72
	0.4	(1.0,1.0)	8813.01	10442.07	13369.70	13046.70	9439.57	**7026.91**
		(0.5,0.5)	5924.81	7069.30	8594.52	8457.62	3929.17	**3435.29**
		(1.0,0.5)	6423.34	7166.02	8648.54	8568.04	4243.35	**4049.13**
		(0.5,1.0)	6408.16	7145.72	8623.46	8507.07	4192.30	**4006.96**
0.4	0.1	(1.0,1.0)	10652.70	11020.21	14152.80	13854.60	10852.01	**9709.01**
		(0.5,0.5)	7162.12	7470.33	9099.83	8973.35	6202.05	**6113.66**
		(1.0,0.5)	7613.72	7562.35	9150.54	9063.65	**6331.07**	6435.48
		(0.5,1.0)	7580.56	7565.32	9131.74	9008.53	**6297.65**	6545.49
	0.4	(1.0,1.0)	9229.54	11011.19	14152.80	13854.60	9698.76	**7444.93**
		(0.5,0.5)	6219.37	7475.03	9099.83	8973.35	4084.81	**3739.76**
		(1.0,0.5)	6860.47	7564.92	9150.54	9063.65	4460.41	**4251.57**
		(0.5,1.0)	6823.11	7558.53	9131.74	9008.53	4428.79	**4221.83**

Table 6.7: Upper bounds for the network scenarios

Again we have $z_{AFA} \leq z_{DLP}$ and $z_{PLP} \leq z_{DLP}$ as proven earlier. Further, the upper bound based on the randomized linear program, z_{RLP}, is tighter than z_{AFA} for all scenarios and even tighter than $z_{DPD'}$ if capacity is ample. Note that this cannot be guaranteed in general since it need not even be tighter than z_{DLP}. A further observation is that for low demand variability, we have $z_{RLP} \leq z_{PLP}$. For high demand variability, this is not always the case.

Across all scenarios, the tightest upper bound is given by either z_{DPD} or $z_{DPD'}$, where z_{DPD} is tightest in the majority of scenarios considered. Observe that all upper bounds tend to decrease if capacity uncertainty increases.

The reason for this observation is that overbooked situations occur more often if capacity uncertainty is high, which decreases total revenue. Observe further that the upper bounds increase as uncertainty in capacity requirement increases. The reason for this phenomenon is that the expected revenue of each request increases as the uncertainty in capacity requirement increases. This relationship is caused by the revenue depending on the maximum of weight and dimensional weight requirement. As weight and volume requirement are not perfectly correlated in our example, a higher variation yields a higher maximum of weight and dimensional weight causing higher revenues.

Heuristic Policy Performance

To determine the revenue performance of the heuristics, we repeatedly simulated request arrivals and tracked the number of accepted requests of each class for each heuristic. At the end of the booking horizon, we generated the random capacities for weight and volume of all flights and subtracted offloading cost.

In order to obtain reliable results, we ran again 20,000 simulations. Table 6.8 summarizes the average simulated net revenue for all tested heuristics (best performance in bold). Further, we report the solution gap, $(1 - \frac{max(DPD,DPD')}{min(z_{DPD},z_{DPD'})})$, for all scenarios. As we expected, the time- and inventory-insensitive heuristics AFA, DLP, and FCFS do not achieve a competitive performance. Observe that AFA tends to outperform DLP for low variation scenarios with $CV_k = CV_d = 0.1$. However, as uncertainty increases, DLP tends to outperform AFA. We conjecture that AFA's decision rule is more selective than DLP's decision rule since it uses negative bid prices (as shown in Example 6.3). This may be an advantage as long as capacity and capacity requirement are not very volatile since the bid prices are computed based on expected values. However, as uncertainty increases, this advantage may vanish.

The heuristics based on decomposition outperform all other heuristics, where DPD achieves the highest revenue in most tested scenarios. The solution gap of the best heuristic varies between 5% and 23% across scenarios. Observe that the solution gap is higher for scenarios with high uncertainty in capacity require-

CV_d	CV_k	$(\bar{k}_l^w/\bar{d}_l^w, \bar{k}_l^v/\bar{d}_l^v)$	FCFS	DLP	AFA	DPD'	DPD	Gap (in %)
0.1	0.1	(1.0,1.0)	8384.69	8392.73	8537.10	8688.48	**8728.49**	5.30
		(0.5,0.5)	4378.65	4746.81	4855.73	5309.28	**5329.22**	8.26
		(1.0,0.5)	4848.72	4773.65	4737.89	**5654.19**	5644.61	5.97
		(0.5,1.0)	4782.51	4999.00	5014.52	5620.25	**5621.97**	5.80
	0.4	(1.0,1.0)	5416.76	5413.94	5636.22	6254.07	**6364.06**	9.43
		(0.5,0.5)	-269.09	1780.78	1861.69	2936.11	**2945.38**	14.26
		(1.0,0.5)	2092.29	3200.44	3158.94	3709.77	**3720.58**	8.11
		(0.5,1.0)	2044.54	3315.53	3308.29	3723.08	**3736.55**	6.75
0.4	0.1	(1.0,1.0)	8262.05	8203.87	8227.76	8580.46	**8610.03**	11.32
		(0.5,0.5)	3169.96	3972.44	3965.41	4628.77	**4685.06**	23.37
		(1.0,0.5)	4414.66	4669.19	4675.46	**5393.97**	5356.15	14.80
		(0.5,1.0)	4313.90	4520.81	4450.87	**5319.98**	5269.81	15.52
	0.4	(1.0,1.0)	5402.38	5517.91	5512.03	6406.37	**6482.04**	12.93
		(0.5,0.5)	-1024.56	1936.22	1595.60	2911.58	**2914.57**	22.07
		(1.0,0.5)	1838.03	3237.42	3140.36	3707.96	**3720.39**	12.49
		(0.5,1.0)	1760.32	3172.07	3155.03	3700.83	**3711.32**	12.09

Table 6.8: Simulated average net revenue in the network scenarios

ment. Uncertainty in capacity has a smaller effect on the policy performance and likewise on the solution gap. The reasons why the decomposition heuristics can handle a high CV_k better than a high CV_d is that they take into account random capacity in terminal cost. Random capacity requirement is not accounted for since the state space of both decomposition heuristics represents the expected rather than random booked capacity. Naturally, the heuristics perform worse in scenarios with highly variable capacity requirements.

In summary, the decomposition heuristics outperform all other tested heuristics, both on single-leg and on network problem instances. Further, our experiments reveal that a heuristic using the time- and inventory-sensitive decision rule of the piecewise linear approximation does not perform as good as the decomposition heuristics. This highlights the quality of the decomposition heuristics in combination with static bid prices. All other price-directed heuristics using static bid prices do not achieve a competitive performance. Further, all proposed linear programs as well as the affine and the piecewise linear approximation provide an upper bound on the maximum expected total revenue. However, the sum of the maximum expected revenues of all subproblems of the decomposition heuristics give the tightest upper bound for most tested instances.

CHAPTER 7

Conclusions

We have pointed out that, in the airline industry today, profitability issues are omnipresent. Hence, airlines are struggling to detect sources of cost cutting and revenue improvement. Since aircraft are capacity-constrained, a potential way to increase revenues is the application of revenue management techniques. Even though cargo traffic is predicted to increase tremendously, very little attention has been paid on applying revenue management methods in the air cargo industry. In the field of cargo capacity control, even less effort has been put on doing research. Thus, we carried out studies on different kinds of capacity control problems prevailing in air cargo revenue management. In this chapter, we conclude our work by summarizing the results and insights of our research. Further, we propose possible extensions of our ideas and suggest future research directions.

7.1 Research Findings and Insights

After having given an overview of air cargo revenue management, related literature, and the necessary theoretical concepts, we studied a single-leg capacity control model in Chapter 4. We showed that the basic decision problem, modeled as a Markov decision process, does not feature a monotone optimal control policy, owing to the fact that cargo requires multiple capacity units. Thus, we proposed two further decision models which allow for partially accepting requests.

189

This generalization of the decision model yields an optimal control limit policy, which is comprehensible for revenue managers.

In case requests are not allowed to be partially accepted, we proposed several heuristics that provide feasible solutions to the basic capacity control model, which suffers from the curse of dimensionality for large problems. One of the heuristics is based on decomposition and features a monotone switching curve policy. Another heuristic approximates the value function by means of piecewise linear functions and thereby obtains bid prices for weight and volume. Further, the maximum objective value of the linear program, which is used to determine the bid prices, provides an upper bound on the maximum expected revenue of the single-leg capacity control problem. In numerical experiments, the heuristic based on the piecewise linear approximation demonstrated the best overall performance. Further, for all tested scenarios, the upper bound given by the underlying linear program was quite close to the maximum expected revenue. If shipments with a non-standard capacity requirement were considered, the decomposition heuristic outperformed existing heuristic approaches. However, its performance is very sensitive to the availability of a particular capacity dimension. If it is not known in advance whether weight or volume will be short, the decomposition heuristic is not appropriate.

In Chapter 5, we examined the problem of integrated capacity control of passenger seats and cargo space. In particular, we formulated the single-leg decision problem as a finite-horizon Markov decision process and analyzed the structure of its optimal decisions. Due to the same reasons given in the case of cargo capacity control, the optimal decisions do not follow any monotone structure. Hence, we suggested a further decision model that considers cargo capacity as one-dimensional and allows for partially accepting cargo requests. This model features an optimal switching curve policy, which is very intuitive and also easy to implement.

The basic model, which considers two cargo dimensions and does not allow partial acceptance, suffers from the curse of dimensionality when applied to large problems. In order to provide feasible solutions, we proposed two different heuristics and one upper bound on the maximum expected revenue. One heuristic decomposes the MDP's state space into weight, volume, and seat sub-problems. The resulting heuristic policy is a structured policy with acceptance thresholds that depend on two capacity dimensions. The other heuristic determines bid prices based on a deterministic linear program as it is used in passenger network revenue management. The maximum objective value of the linear program provides an upper bound on the maximum expected revenue. In numerical experiments, the decomposition heuristic performed very well for all tested scenarios. However, the performance of the heuristic depends on the availability of a particular capacity dimension as in the pure cargo case. The bid price heuristic and the associated upper bound demonstrated a good performance if a flight is not heavily capacity-constrained.

We also carried out a study for a network formulation of the cargo capacity control problem. In our model, overbooking is allowed, and the resulting Markov decision process accounts for uncertainty in both demand and capacity. We suggested several upper bound problems based on linear and approximate dynamic programming. When approximating the value function by an affine function, we showed that the approximation parameters, which we interpret as bid prices for weight and volume on a leg, are approximately constant in time. A surprising insight is that bid prices, obtained by this affine approximation, might be negative. We showed that negative bid prices may result in better control policies than bid prices obtained through a deterministic linear problem, which was suggested in previous work on cargo revenue management. As the affine approximation's decision rule is time- and inventory-insensitive, we proposed decomposition heuristics which use static bid prices and offer a time- and inventory-dependent acceptance policy. Our numerical results show that these heuristics outperformed all other tested heuristics, both on single-leg and on network problem instances. Further, these heuristics have the potential to provide very tight bounds, especially in scenarios with low variation in required capacities of accepted shipments. We also proposed a piecewise linear value function approximation which explicitly accounts for the state of overbooking on each leg. However, the bid prices of this heuristic are very difficult to obtain. Furthermore, our experiments revealed that a heuristic using the time- and inventory-sensitive decision rule of the piecewise linear approximation does not perform as good as the decomposition heuristics. This highlights the quality of the decomposition heuristic when combined with static bid prices.

Further, both the linear programs as well as the affine and the piecewise linear approximation provide an upper bound on the maximum expected revenue. We proved that the partially randomized linear program generates a tighter upper bound than the deterministic linear program. We also proved that the bound given by the deterministic linear program is looser than the bound based on the affine approximation. The upper bound from the piecewise linear approximation is even tighter than the bound obtained by an affine approximation at the expense of increased computational complexity. Our numerical study showed, however, that the sum of the optimal expected revenues of all subproblems of the decomposition heuristic provides the tightest upper bound for almost all tested instances. However, the quality of this bound highly depends on the way revenues of classes are allocated to legs and cannot be shown to outperform other approaches in general.

7.2 Future Research Directions

Research on air cargo revenue management is still at an early stage. Therefore, there is a large number of potential future research directions. Below, we name several of them, according to the capacity control problems we analyzed.

Single-Leg Cargo Capacity Control

In order to obtain optimal structured control policies in our model, we had to assume partial acceptance is allowed. If this assumption is dropped, a promising path of future research would be to study whether certain conditions regarding the arrival process of cargo bookings can be found that ensure the existence of an optimal switching curve policy. If these conditions are met in reality, airlines would be more in favor of implementing a cargo revenue management system.

Overbooking, cancellations, and no-shows are not considered in our model. If these are accounted for, a potential future research direction might focus on analyzing optimal decisions. Further, a study on overbooking levels ensuring the existence of structured optimal decisions could be conducted. Furthermore, especially the heuristic based on the piecewise linear approximation would need to be adjusted to a setting with overbooking.

We focused solely on quantity-based decisions. An interesting path of research might be to apply dynamic pricing techniques to air cargo. Even though this contradicts today's business practice, low cost carriers, which already apply dynamic pricing in passenger revenue management, may do the same for cargo.

It is common in cargo revenue management that expected revenue is maximized. However, large freight forwarders have a significant buying power and, if requests are rejected frequently, might just switch to a different airline. Thus, future work might incorporate the decisions' long-term value into the decision model. This topic has already been addressed in passenger revenue management, but its impact is much greater in the cargo business.

Integrated Capacity Control of Cargo Space and Passenger Seats

All future research directions for the single-leg model apply as well to the integrated model. Further, particularly interesting might be to extend the integrated capacity control model to a network of flights. Since, in practice, passenger revenue management is applied at a network level, an integrated model would probably find a higher acceptance if it is also done at a network level. This would require powerful heuristics in order to overcome the significantly increased curse of dimensionality.

A further promising path of research would be to approximate the value function of the integrated problem (either for a single-leg or a network formulation). Determining the approximation parameters via simulation or linear programming would give bid prices for weight, volume, and passenger seats. By means of this information, a price-directed heuristic could be constructed, which may yield better results than the price-directed heuristic based on the deterministic linear program that we proposed.

Network Cargo Capacity Control

Our numerical examples showed a superiority of the decomposition heuristic's bound which we could not prove analytically. Future work might be aimed at finding revenue allocations for the decomposition heuristic that can be proven to provide tight bounds and good heuristics.

One of the greatest challenges in our dynamic programming approximations is to efficiently solve the linearized subproblems in the column generation procedure. Future research might focus on developing advanced solution techniques for tackling this kind of problem, which arises due to the penalty cost's piecewise linear structure. Once this is done, one could also allow for random capacities within the approximation, which should improve performance.

Another promising path for future research would be to extend the Lagrangian relaxation techniques, suggested for passenger revenue management, to derive alternative, and possibly tighter upper bounds and better heuristics for air cargo network revenue management.

We assumed that the route a shipment travels is uniquely defined by the request. This is true for small carriers, but it need not hold for large airlines. Thus, future work could address the challenge of incorporating routing options into the decision problem while still applying revenue management techniques that are well studied.

We did not account for the availability of container positions in our model. Future research might analyze how such restrictions can be considered when controlling capacity. A promising way is to account for them in the terminal cost function. This would require new heuristics for solving the decision problem.

The network capacity control problem is quite similar to the capacity control problem of cruise lines. The number of sold cabin categories is usually modeled as the system state and capacity is given by the number of cabins and lifeboat seats. Thus, future research might study if our proposed heuristics and bounds would carry over to cruise line revenue management.

Proofs

Proof of Lemma 4.2. (i) Fix some $s \in \mathbb{N}_0$ and $a^* := f(s)$. Then, we have for all $a \in A(s)$ and $a < a^*$,

$$r(a) + \tilde{h}(s - a) \leq r(a^*) + \tilde{h}(s - a^*),$$

and together with concavity of $\tilde{h}$

$$r(a^*) - r(a) \geq \tilde{h}(s - a) - \tilde{h}(s - a^*)$$
$$\geq \tilde{h}(s + 1 - a) - \tilde{h}(s + 1 - a^*).$$

Since $n_1(s) \leq n_1(s + 1)$, it follows that

$$r(a) + \tilde{h}(s + 1 - a) \leq r(a^*) + \tilde{h}(s + 1 - a^*)$$

for all $a \in A(s + 1)$ and $a < a^*$. Thus, we have $f(s) \leq f(s + 1)$.
  For all $a \in A(s)$ and $a > a^*$, it holds that

$$r(a) + \tilde{h}(s - a) \leq r(a^*) + \tilde{h}(s - a^*),$$

and together with concavity of r

$$\tilde{h}(s + 1 - (a^* + 1)) - \tilde{h}(s + 1 - (a + 1)) = \tilde{h}(s - a^*) - \tilde{h}(s - a)$$

$$\geq r(a) - r(a^*)$$
$$\geq r(a+1) - r(a^*+1).$$

Since $n_2(s+1) \leq n_2(s) + 1$, it follows that

$$r(a+1) + \tilde{h}(s+1-(a+1)) \leq r(a^*+1) + \tilde{h}(s+1-(a^*+1)),$$

for all $a+1 \in A(s+1)$ and $a+1 > a^*+1$. Thus, we have $f(s+1) \leq f(s)+1$.

(ii) We prove concavity of h by a case-by-case analysis:

$\underline{f(s+2) = f(s):}$

$$h(s+2) - 2h(s+1) + h(s)$$
$$= \tilde{h}(s+2-a^*) - 2\tilde{h}(s+1-a^*) + \tilde{h}(s-a^*) \leq 0.$$

$\underline{f(s+2) = f(s)+1:}$

Let $a^* < n_2(s)$. Due to monotonicity of n_2, we have $a^*, a^*+1 \leq n_2(s+1)$. If $a^* = n_2(s)$, it follows from $f(s+2) = a^*+1 \leq n_2(s+2)$ and from concavity of n_2 that $n_2(s) < n_2(s+1) \leq n_2(s+2)$. Again, we have $a^*, a^*+1 \leq n_2(s+1)$. Let now $a^* = n_1(s) + k$ for some $k \geq 0$. It follows from the assumption that $f(s+2) = a^*+1 = n_1(s) + k + 1 \geq n_1(s+2)$, and hence $k+1 \geq n_1(s+2) - n_1(s)$. From convexity of n_1, it follows that $n_1(s+1) - n_1(s) \leq \lfloor \frac{k+1}{2} \rfloor$, and thus $n_1(s+1) \leq n_1(s) + \lfloor \frac{k+1}{2} \rfloor \leq n_1(s) + k = a^*$. Therefore, we have $a^*, a^*+1 \in A(s+1)$, and it holds that

$$h(s+2) - 2h(s+1) + h(s)$$
$$\leq \tilde{h}(s+2-a^*-1) - \tilde{h}(s+1-a^*-1) - \tilde{h}(s+1-a^*) + \tilde{h}(s-a^*) = 0.$$

$\underline{f(s+2) = f(s)+2:}$

$$h(s+2) - 2h(s+1) + h(s)$$
$$= r(a^*+2) - 2r(a^*+1) + r(a^*)$$

$$+ \tilde{h}(s + 2 - a^* - 2) - 2\tilde{h}(s + 1 - a^* - 1) + \tilde{h}(s - a^*)$$
$$\leq 0.$$

Altogether, we have that h is concave. $\qquad\square$

Proof of Lemma 5.2. In order to prove this lemma, we propose an alternative formulation of the decision model which, however, does not change the value function's structure. First, we allow for negative capacities, that means we extend C to $\bar{C} = \{..., -1, 0, 1, ..., \mathfrak{C}\}$ and C_s to $\bar{C}_s = \{..., -1, 0, 1, ..., \mathfrak{C}_s\}$. Second, we define the set of admissible actions as $A'(c, c_s, i) = \{0, ..., \gamma_i\}$ for all $i \in \hat{I}, c \in \bar{C}, c_s \in \bar{C}_s$. Third, we define the terminal reward function as

$$\bar{V}_0(c, c_s, i) = \min\{c, 0\}\Phi + \min\{c_s, 0\}\Phi =: \Psi(c, c_s)$$

for all $c \in \bar{C}$, $c_s \in \bar{C}_s$, $i \in \hat{I}$, and with $\Phi := \max_{i \in \hat{I}}\{\gamma_i \varphi_i\} + 1$. Fourth, we define the value function for $\min\{c, c_s\} < 0$ as

$$\bar{V}_t(c, c_s, i) = \Psi(c, c_s) = \max_{a \in A'(c, c_s, i)} \{a\varphi_i + \tilde{Q}_{t-1}\bar{V}_{t-1}(c - a, c_s - a\sigma_i)\}$$

$$(A.1)$$

for all $t = T, ..., 1$ and $i \in \hat{I}$. Note that the action maximizing the right hand side in (A.1) is $a = 0$, and thus we have $\bar{V}_t(c, c_s, i) = \Psi(c, c_s)$. All other notations and definitions are the same as in $\tilde{M}$. We denote the maximum expected revenue in state (c, c_s, i) at time $t = T, ..., 0$ as $\bar{V}_t(c, c_s, i)$.

Before we prove multimodularity, we first show that $\bar{V}_t(c, c_s, i)$ is equal to $\tilde{V}_t(c, c_s, i)$ for all $c \geq 0$, $c_s \geq 0$, $i \in \hat{I}$ and that negative system states are never occupied. First, consider $\bar{V}_t(c, c_s, i)$ for $t = T, ..., 1$, $c \geq 0$, $c_s \geq 0$, and $i \in \{0, ..., m_1\}$. Then, we have

$$\bar{V}_t(c, c_s, i) = \max_{a \in \{0, ..., \gamma_i\}} \left\{a\varphi_i + \tilde{Q}_{t-1}\bar{V}_{t-1}(c - a, c_s)\right\}. \qquad (A.2)$$

If $\gamma_i \leq c$, it follows that $\bar{V}_t(c, c_s, i) = \tilde{V}_t(c, c_s, i)$ since the admissible actions are identical, and negative system states cannot be reached. Now assume $c < a^* \leq \gamma_i$ with a^* as the action maximizing the right hand side of (A.2). Then, we have

$$\bar{V}_t(c, c_s, i)$$
$$= a^*\varphi_i + \tilde{Q}_{t-1}\bar{V}_{t-1}(c - a^*, c_s)$$

$$=a^*\varphi_i + \Psi(c - a^*, c_s)$$
$$\leq a^*\varphi_i + (c - a^*)\Phi$$
$$\leq \gamma_i\varphi_i + (c - a^*)\Phi$$
$$\leq \gamma_i\varphi_i - \max_{i\in\hat{I}}\{\gamma_i\varphi_i\} - 1$$
$$<0.$$

On the other hand, if $a^* \leq c < \gamma_i$, we have

$$\bar{V}_t(c, c_s, i) = a^*\varphi_i + \tilde{Q}_{t-1}\bar{V}_{t-1}(c - a^*, c_s) \geq 0.$$

Accordingly, all actions a with $c < a \leq \gamma_i$ are suboptimal and can thus be neglected. Therefore, optimal actions are always in the set of admissible actions of $\tilde{M}$ for $i \in \{0, ..., m_1\}$. Further, since actions satisfying $c < a \leq \gamma_i$ are suboptimal, negative system states are never occupied if class $i \in \{0, ..., m_1\}$ is requested. Now consider $\bar{V}_t(c, c_s, i)$ for $t = T, ..., 1$, $c \geq 0$, $c_s \geq 0$, and $i \in \{m_1 + 1, ..., m_2\}$. In this case, the optimality equation is

$$\bar{V}_t(c, c_s, i) = \max_{a\in\{0,1\}}\left\{a\varphi_i + \tilde{Q}_{t-1}\bar{V}_{t-1}(c - a, c_s - a)\right\}. \qquad (A.3)$$

If $\gamma_i \leq c$ and $\gamma_i \leq c_s$, it follows that $\bar{V}_t(c, c_s, i) = \tilde{V}_t(c, c_s, i)$ since the admissible actions are identical, and negative system states cannot be reached. Now assume $\min\{c, c_s\} < a^* \leq \gamma_i$ (i.e. $a^* = 1$) and a^* maximizes the right hand side of (A.3). Then, we have

$$\bar{V}_t(c, c_s, i) = \varphi_i + \tilde{Q}_{t-1}\bar{V}_{t-1}(c - 1, c_s - 1)$$
$$= \varphi_i + \Psi(c - 1, c_s - 1) \leq \varphi_i - \Phi = \varphi_i - \max_{i\in\hat{I}}\{\varphi_i\} - 1 < 0.$$

If $a^* \leq \min\{c, c_s\} < \gamma_i$ (i.e. $a^* = 0$) and a^* maximizes the right hand side of (A.3), we have

$$\bar{V}_t(c, c_s, i) = \tilde{Q}_{t-1}\bar{V}_{t-1}(c, c_s) \geq 0.$$

Thus, if $\min\{c, c_s\} < \gamma_i$, action $a = 1$ is suboptimal. Therefore, if $i \in \{m_1 + 1, ..., m_2\}$, optimal actions are always in the set of admissible actions of $\hat{M}$. This also yields that negative system states are never occupied.

For $t = 0$, we have $\bar{V}_0(c, c_s, i) = 0$ for all $c \geq 0$, $c_s \geq 0$, and $i \in \hat{I}$. Thus, for these values, $\bar{V}_0(c, c_s, i) = \tilde{V}_0(c, c_s, i)$. Further, negative systems states are not occupied in the terminal state for the reasons given above.

In summary, we know that $\bar{V}_t(c, c_s, i) = \tilde{V}_t(c, c_s, i)$ for $t = T, ..., 0$, $c \geq 0$, $c_s \geq 0$, and $i \in \hat{I}$. Further, negative system states are not occupied. Thus, if $\bar{V}_t(c, c_s, i)$ is multimodular in c and c_s, it follows that $\tilde{V}_t(c, c_s, i)$ is also multimodular in c and c_s.

We now show that $\bar{V}_t(c, c_s, i)$ is multimodular in $c \in \bar{C}$ and $c_s \in \bar{C}_s$. First note that cargo space and passenger seats are complementary resources since they are required at the same time by a passenger request. Thus, multimodularity is defined by supermodularity and superconcavity. The proof follows by induction on t. We first show that $\bar{V}_0(c, c_s, i) = \Psi(c, c_s)$ is multimodular. For any $i \in \hat{I}$, $\bar{V}_0(c, c_s, i)$ is supermodular in c and c_s since

$$
\begin{aligned}
&\bar{V}_0(c, c_s, i) - \bar{V}_0(c - 1, c_s, i) \\
={}& \min\{c, 0\}\Phi - \min\{c - 1, 0\}\Phi \\
={}& \min\{c, 0\}\Phi + \min\{c_s + 1, 0\}\Phi - \min\{c - 1, 0\}\Phi - \min\{c_s + 1, 0\}\Phi \\
={}& \bar{V}_0(c, c_s + 1, i) - \bar{V}_0(c - 1, c_s + 1, i).
\end{aligned}
$$

$\bar{V}_0(c, c_s, i)$ is superconcave in c and c_s, which is shown next: For any $i \in \hat{I}$, we have

$$
\begin{aligned}
&\bar{V}_0(c, c_s, i) - \bar{V}_0(c - 1, c_s, i) \\
={}& \min\{c, 0\}\Phi - \min\{c - 1, 0\}\Phi \\
\leq{}& \min\{c - 1, 0\}\Phi - \min\{c - 2, 0\}\Phi \\
={}& \min\{c - 1, 0\}\Phi + \min\{c_s - 1, 0\}\Phi - \min\{c - 2, 0\}\Phi - \min\{c_s - 1, 0\}\Phi \\
={}& \bar{V}_0(c - 1, c_s - 1, i) - \bar{V}_0(c - 2, c_s - 1, i),
\end{aligned}
$$

where the inequality follows from concavity of $\bar{V}_0(c, c_s, i)$, which is given by its piecewise-linear structure. We further have

$$\bar{V}_0(c, c_s, i) - \bar{V}_0(c, c_s - 1, i)$$
$$= \min\{c_s, 0\}\Phi - \min\{c_s - 1, 0\}\Phi$$
$$\leq \min\{c_s - 1, 0\}\Phi - \min\{c_s - 2, 0\}\Phi$$
$$= \min\{c - 1, 0\}\Phi + \min\{c_s - 1, 0\}\Phi - \min\{c - 1, 0\}\Phi - \min\{c_s - 2, 0\}\Phi$$
$$= \bar{V}_0(c - 1, c_s - 1, i) - \bar{V}_0(c - 1, c_s - 2, i).$$

Therefore, $\bar{V}_0(c, c_s, i)$ is superconcave and hence multimodular in c and c_s for any $i \in \hat{I}$.

Now assume $\bar{V}_t(c, c_s, i)$ is multimodular in c and c_s for some $t \geq 0$ and $i \in \hat{I}$. Since supermodularity and superconcavity are preserved under convex combinations, $\tilde{Q}_t\bar{V}_t(c, c_s)$ is multimodular, too. Consider now the decision period $t + 1$. For $i \in \{0, ..., m_1\}$, $c \in \bar{C}$, and $c_s \in \bar{C}_s$, we have

$$\bar{V}_{t+1}(c, c_s, i) = \max_{a \in \{0, ..., \gamma_i\}} \{a\varphi_i + \tilde{Q}_t\bar{V}_t(c - a, c_s)\}.$$

This is of the form

$$U_j\tilde{l}(\boldsymbol{x}, \iota) = \max_{a \in \{0, ..., n_\iota\}} \{ar_\iota + l(\boldsymbol{x} - a\boldsymbol{e}_j)\}$$

for $j = 1$. Since we assume that $\tilde{Q}_t\bar{V}_t(c, c_s)$ is multimodular, it follows from Proposition 3.4 that $\bar{V}_{t+1}(c, c_s, i)$ is multimodular in c and c_s for $i \in \{0, ..., m_1\}$. For $i \in \{m_1 + 1, ..., m_2\}$, $c \in \bar{C}$, and $c_s \in \bar{C}_s$, we have

$$\bar{V}_{t+1}(c, c_s, i) = \max_{a \in \{0, 1\}} \{a\varphi_i + \tilde{Q}_t\bar{V}_t(c - a, c_s - a)\}.$$

This is of the form

$$U\tilde{l}(\boldsymbol{x}, \iota) = \max_{a \in \{0, 1\}} \{ar_\iota + l(\boldsymbol{x} - \boldsymbol{a})\}.$$

Here it follows from the induction assumption and from Proposition 3.3 that $\bar{V}_{t+1}(c, c_s, i)$ is multimodular in c and c_s for all $i \in \{m_1 + 1, ..., m_2\}$.

In summary, $\bar{V}_{t+1}(c, c_s, i)$ is multimodular in $c \in \bar{C}$ and $c_s \in \bar{C}_s$ for all $i \in \hat{I}$. Hence, we can conclude that $\tilde{V}_{t+1}(c, c_s, i)$ is multimodular in $c \in C$ and $c_s \in C_s$ for $i \in \hat{I}$. $\qquad\square$

Dual Problems

The dual of $(\tilde{\mathbf{P}}_{AFA})$ is $(\tilde{\mathbf{D}}_{AFA})$:

$$
\max_{X} \sum_{1 \le t \le T, c \in C_t, a \in A} X_{t,c,a} \sum_{i \in I} q_{t,i} \rho_i a_i - \sum_{c \in C_1, a \in A} X_{1,c,a} \sum_{i' \in I} q_{1,i'}
$$

$$
\cdot \sum_{l \in L} \left[\phi_l^w \left(\sum_{i \in I(l)} (c_i + a_{i'} \mathbf{1}_{\{i=i'\}}) \bar{w}_i - \bar{k}_l^w \right)^+ \right.
$$

$$
\left. + \phi_l^v \left(\sum_{i \in I(l)} (c_i + a_{i'} \mathbf{1}_{\{i=i'\}}) \bar{v}_i - \bar{k}_l^v \right)^+ \right]
$$

$$
\text{s.t.} \quad \sum_{c \in C_1, a \in A} X_{1,c,a} \sum_{i \in I(l)} c_i \bar{w}_i
$$

$$
= \sum_{1 < t \le T, c \in C_t, a \in A} X_{t,c,a} \sum_{i \in I(l)} q_{t,i} a_i \bar{w}_i \quad \forall l \in L
$$

$$
\sum_{c \in C_1, a \in A} X_{1,c,a} \sum_{i \in I(l)} c_i \bar{v}_i
$$

$$
= \sum_{1 < t \le T, c \in C_t, a \in A} X_{t,c,a} \sum_{i \in I(l)} q_{t,i} a_i \bar{v}_i \quad \forall l \in L
$$

$$\sum_{c \in C_t, a \in A} X_{t,c,a} = \begin{cases} \sum\limits_{c \in C_{t+1}, a \in A} X_{t+1,c,a} & \forall 1 \leq t < T \\ 1 & t = T \end{cases}$$

$$X_{t,c,a} \geq 0 \quad \forall 1 \leq t \leq T, c \in C_t, a \in A.$$

The dual of ($\mathbf{P}_{PLA}$) is ($\mathbf{D}_{PLA}$):

$$
\max_{X} \sum_{1 \leq t \leq T, c \in C_t, a \in A} X_{t,c,a} \sum_{i \in I} q_{t,i} \rho_i a_i - \sum_{c \in C_1, a \in A} X_{1,c,a} \sum_{i' \in I} q_{1,i'}
$$

$$
\cdot \sum_{l \in L} \left[\phi_l^w \left(\sum_{i \in I(l)} (c_i + a_{i'} \mathbf{1}_{\{i=i'\}}) \bar{w}_i - \bar{k}_l^w \right)^+ \right.
$$

$$
\left. + \phi_l^v \left(\sum_{i \in I(l)} (c_i + a_{i'} \mathbf{1}_{\{i=i'\}}) \bar{v}_i - \bar{k}_l^v \right)^+ \right]
$$

s.t. $\displaystyle \sum_{c \in C_t, a \in A} X_{t,c,a} \min \left\{ \sum_{i \in I(l)} c_i \bar{w}_i, \bar{k}_l^w \right\}$

$$
= \begin{cases} \displaystyle\sum_{c \in C_{t+1}, a \in A} X_{t+1,c,a} \sum_{i' \in I} q_{t+1,i'} \\ \quad \cdot \min \left\{ \displaystyle\sum_{i \in I(l)} (c_i + a_{i'} \mathbf{1}_{\{i=i'\}}) \bar{w}_i, \bar{k}_l^w \right\} & \forall l \in L, 1 \leq t < T \\ 0 & \forall l \in L, t = T \end{cases}
$$

$$
\sum_{c \in C_t, a \in A} X_{t,c,a} \min \left\{ \sum_{i \in I(l)} c_i \bar{v}_i, \bar{k}_l^v \right\}
$$

$$
= \begin{cases} \displaystyle\sum_{c \in C_{t+1}, a \in A} X_{t+1,c,a} \sum_{i' \in I} q_{t+1,i'} \\ \quad \cdot \min \left\{ \displaystyle\sum_{i \in I(l)} (c_i + a_{i'} \mathbf{1}_{\{i=i'\}}) \bar{v}_i, \bar{k}_l^v \right\} & \forall l \in L, 1 \leq t < T \\ 0 & \forall l \in L, t = T \end{cases}
$$

$$\sum_{c \in C_t, a \in A} X_{t,c,a} \left(\sum_{i \in I(l)} c_i \bar{w}_i - \bar{k}_l^w \right)^+$$

$$= \begin{cases} \sum_{c \in C_{t+1}, a \in A} X_{t+1,c,a} \sum_{i' \in I} q_{t+1,i'} \\ \quad \cdot \left(\sum_{i \in I(l)} (c_i + a_{i'} \mathbf{1}_{\{i=i'\}}) \bar{w}_i - \bar{k}_l^w \right)^+ & \forall l \in L, 1 \le t < T \\ 0 & \forall l \in L, t = T \end{cases}$$

$$\sum_{c \in C_t, a \in A} X_{t,c,a} \left(\sum_{i \in I(l)} c_i \bar{v}_i - \bar{k}_l^v \right)^+$$

$$= \begin{cases} \sum_{c \in C_{t+1}, a \in A} X_{t+1,c,a} \sum_{i' \in I} q_{t+1,i'} \\ \quad \cdot \left(\sum_{i \in I(l)} (c_i + a_{i'} \mathbf{1}_{\{i=i'\}}) \bar{v}_i - \bar{k}_l^v \right)^+ & \forall l \in L, 1 \le t < T \\ 0 & \forall l \in L, t = T \end{cases}$$

$$\sum_{c \in C_t, a \in A} X_{t,c,a} = \begin{cases} \sum_{c \in C_{t+1}, a \in A} X_{t+1,c,a} & \forall 1 \le t < T \\ 1 & t = T \end{cases}$$

$$X_{t,c,a} \ge 0 \quad \forall 1 \le t \le T, c \in C_t, a \in A.$$

References

Adelman, D. (2003). Price-directed replenishment of subsets: Methodology and its application to inventory routing. *Manufacturing & Service Operations Management*, *5*(4), 348-371.

Adelman, D. (2007). Dynamic bid prices in revenue management. *Operations Research*, *55*(4), 647-661.

Air Cargo World. (2012). Airfreight's top forwarders. *Air Cargo World*, *15*(8), 28-29.

Airbus. (2011). *Airbus cargo global market forecast 2011-2030*. http://www.airbus.com/company/market/forecast/cargo-aircraft-market-forecast. Accessed 21 September 2012.

Altman, E., Gaujal, B., & Hordijk, A. (2003). *Discrete-event control of stochastic networks : multimodularity and regularity*. Berlin: Springer.

Amaruchkul, K., Cooper, W. L., & Gupta, D. (2007). Single-leg air-cargo revenue management. *Transportation Science*, *41*(4), 457-469.

Amaruchkul, K., & Lorchirachoonkul, V. (2011). Air-cargo capacity allocation for multiple freight forwarders. *Transportation Research Part E: Logistics and Transportation Review*, *47*(1), 30-40.

Axsäter, S. (2006). *Inventory control* (2nd ed.). Berlin: Springer.

Badinelli, R. D. (2000). An optimal, dynamic policy for hotel yield management. *European Journal of Operational Research, 121*(3), 476-503.

Becker, B., & Dill, N. (2007). Managing the complexity of air cargo revenue management. *Journal of Revenue & Pricing Management, 6*(3), 175-187.

Becker, B., & Wald, A. (2008). Air cargo overbooking based on the shipment information record. *Journal of Revenue & Pricing Management, 7*(3), 242-255.

Becker, B., & Wald, A. (2010). Challenges and success factors of air cargo revenue management. *Journal of Revenue & Pricing Management, 9*(1), 171-184.

Bellman, R. E. (1957). *Dynamic programming.* Princeton, NJ: Princeton University Press.

Bellman, R. E. (1957). A Markovian decision process. *Journal of Mathematics and Mechanics, 6*, 679-684.

Belobaba, P. (1989). Application of a probabilistic decision model to airline seat inventory control. *Operations Research, 37*(2), 183-197.

Belobaba, P. (Ed.). (2009). *The global airline industry.* Chichester: Wiley.

Benjaafar, S., ElHafsi, M., & Huang, T. (2010). Optimal control of a production-inventory system with both backorders and lost sales. *Naval Research Logistics, 57*(3), 252-265.

Bertsekas, D. P. (2005). Dynamic programming and suboptimal control: A survey from ADP to MPC. *European Journal of Control, 11*(4-5), 310-334.

Bertsekas, D. P., & Tsitsiklis, J. N. (1996). *Neuro-dynamic programming.* Belmont, Massachusetts: Athena Scientific.

Bertsimas, D., & Tsitsiklis, J. N. (1997). *Introduction to linear optimization.* Belmont, Massachusetts: Athena Scientific.

Billings, J. S., Diener, A. G., & Yuen, B. B. (2003). Cargo revenue optimisation. *Journal of Revenue & Pricing Management, 2*(1), 69-79.

Bitran, G. R., & Caldentey, R. (2003). An overview of pricing models for revenue management. *Manufacturing & Service Operations Management, 5*(3), 203-229.

Bitran, G. R., & Mondschein, S. V. (1995). An application of yield management to the hotel industry considering multiple day stays. *Operations Research, 43*(3), 427-443.

Bitran, G. R., & Mondschein, S. V. (1997). Periodic pricing of seasonal products in retailing. *Management Science, 43*(1), 64-79.

Blake, T. (2010). *Air freight demand and passenger prices in the presence of capacity constraints.* Working Paper, University of California, Davis.

Boeing. (2012). *Commercial airplanes.* http://www.boeing.com/commercial/ 757family/pf/pf_200f_tech.html. Accessed 13 August 2012.

Boeing. (2013). *World air cargo forecast 2012-2013.* http://www.boeing.com/ commercial/cargo/wacf.pdf. Accessed 15 February 2013.

Boyd, A. (1998). Airline alliance revenue management. *OR/MS Today, 25*(5), 28-31.

Boyd, E. A., & Bilegan, I. C. (2003). Revenue management and e-commerce. *Management Science, 49*(10), 1363-1386.

Brumelle, S., & Walczak, D. (2003). Dynamic airline revenue management with multiple semi-Markov demand. *Operations Research, 51*(1), 137-148.

Carr, S., & Duenyas, I. (2000). Optimal admission control and sequencing in a make-to-stock/make-to-order production system. *Operations Research, 48*(5), 709-720.

Chaneton, J. M., & Vulcano, G. (2011). Computing bid prices for revenue management under customer choice behavior. *Manufacturing & Service Operations Management, 13*(4), 452-470.

Charnes, A., & Cooper, W. W. (1959). Chance-constrained programming. *Management Science, 6*(1), 73-79.

Chen, M., Tsai, H., & McCain, S.-L. C. (2012). A revenue management model for casino table games. *Cornell Hospitality Quarterly, 53*(2), 144-153.

Chen, S., Gallego, G., Li, M. Z., & Lin, B. (2010). Optimal seat allocation for two-flight problems with a flexible demand segment. *European Journal of Operational Research, 201*(3), 897-908.

Chiang, W.-C., Chen, J. C., & Xu, X. (2007). An overview of research on revenue management: Current issues and future research. *International Journal of Revenue Management, 1*(1), 97-128.

Cross, R. G. (1997). *Revenue management: Hard-core tactics for market domination.* New York: Broadway Books.

Deb, R. K., & Serfozo, R. F. (1973). Optimal control of batch service queues. *Advances in Applied Probability, 5*(2), 340-361.

De Farias, D. P., & Van Roy, B. (2003). The linear programming approach to approximate dynamic programming. *Operations Research, 51*(6), 850-865.

Denardo, E. V. (1982). *Dynamic programming: Models and applications.* Englewood Cliffs, NJ: Prentice-Hall.

Descartes. (2012). *GF-X Exchange: The world's leading online airfreight booking solution.* https://www.descartes.com/content/documents/pi_gfx_exchange.pdf. Accessed 20 September 2012.

Elmaghraby, W., & Keskinocak, P. (2003). Dynamic pricing in the presence of inventory considerations: Research overview, current practices, and future directions. *Management Science, 49*(10), 1287-1309.

Erdelyi, A., & Topaloglu, H. (2010). A dynamic programming decomposition method for making overbooking decisions over an airline network. *INFORMS Journal on Computing, 22*(3), 443-456.

Faruqui, A., Hledik, R., & Tsoukalis, J. (2009). The power of dynamic pricing. *The Electricity Journal, 22*(3), 42-56.

Feinberg, E. A., & Shwartz, A. (Eds.). (2002). *Handbook of Markov decision processes : Methods and applications.* Boston, London: Kluwer Academic.

Fiig, T., Isler, K., Hopperstad, C., & Olsen, S. S. (2012). Forecasting and optimization of fare families. *Journal of Revenue & Pricing Management, 11*(3), 322-342.

Gallego, G., & van Ryzin, G. J. (1994). Optimal dynamic pricing of inventories with stochastic demand over finite horizons. *Management Science, 40*(8), 999-1020.

Geraghty, M. K., & Johnson, E. (1997). Revenue management saves National car rental. *Interfaces, 27*(1), 107-127.

Ghoneim, H. A., & Stidham, S. (1985). Control of arrivals to two queues in series. *European Journal of Operational Research, 21*(3), 399-409.

Glasserman, P., & Yao, D. D. (1994). Monotone optimal control of permutable GSMPs. *Mathematics of Operations Research, 19*(2), 449-476.

Graff, J. (2008). Revenue management for the whole aircraft: Coordinating acceptance decisions for passengers and cargo transportation. *Journal of Revenue & Pricing Management*, 7(4), 397-401.

Green, L. V., Savin, S., & Wang, B. (2006). Managing patient service in a diagnostic medical facility. *Operations Research*, 54(1), 11-25.

Guadix, J., Onieva, L., Muñuzuri, J., & Cortés, P. (2011). An overview of revenue management in service industries: an application to car parks. *Service Industries Journal*, 31(1), 91-105.

Gupta, D. (2008). Flexible carrier-forwarder contracts for air cargo business. *Journal of Revenue & Pricing Management*, 7(4), 341-356.

Gurobi Optimization. (2012). *Gurobi optimizer reference manual.* http://www. gurobi.com. Accessed 20 July 2012.

Ha, A. Y. (1997a). Optimal dynamic scheduling policy for a make-to-stock production system. *Operations Research*, 45(1), 42-53.

Ha, A. Y. (1997b). Stock-rationing policy for a make-to-stock production system with two priority classes and backordering. *Naval Research Logistics*, 44(5), 457-472.

Ha, A. Y. (2000). Stock rationing in an M/Ek/1 make-to-stock queue. *Management Science*, 46(1), 77-87.

Haensel, A., & Koole, G. (2011). Estimating unconstrained demand rate functions using customer choice sets. *Journal of Revenue & Pricing Management*, 10(5), 438-454.

Haensel, A., Mederer, M., & Schmidt, H. (2012). Revenue management in the car rental industry: A stochastic programming approach. *Journal of Revenue & Pricing Management*, 11(1), 99-108.

Hajek, B. (1984). Optimal control of two interacting service stations. *IEEE Transactions on Automatic Control, 29*(6), 491-499.

Han, D. L., Tang, L. C., & Huang, H. C. (2010). A Markov model for single-leg air cargo revenue management under a bid-price policy. *European Journal of Operational Research, 200*(3), 800-811.

Hellermann, R. (2006). *Capacity options for revenue management : Theory and applications in the air cargo industry.* Berlin: Springer.

Helm, W. E., & Waldmann, K.-H. (1984). Optimal control of arrivals to multiserver queues in a random environment. *Journal of Applied Probability, 21*(3), 602-615.

Hendricks, G., & Kasilingam, R. (1993). *Cargo revenue management at american airlines cargo.* Presentation at the AGIFORS Cargo Study Group Meeting, Rome, Italy.

Hinderer, K. (1970). *Foundations of non-stationary dynamic programming with discrete time parameter.* Berlin: Springer.

Hinderer, K., & Waldmann, K. H. (2001). Cash management in a randomly varying environment. *European Journal of Operational Research, 130*(3), 468-485.

Hoffmann, R. (2013a). *Dynamic capacity control in air cargo revenue management.* Doctoral dissertation, Karlsruhe Institute of Technology, Germany, http://digbib.ubka.uni-karlsruhe.de/volltexte/1000033297.

Hoffmann, R. (2013b). Dynamic capacity control in cargo revenue management - A new heuristic for solving the single-leg problem efficiently. *Journal of Revenue & Pricing Management, 12*(1), 46-59.

Huang, K., & Chang, K.-c. (2010). An approximate algorithm for the two-dimensional air cargo revenue management problem. *Transportation Research Part E: Logistics and Transportation Review, 46*(3), 426-435.

Huang, K., & Hsu, W. (2005). Revenue management for air cargo space with supply uncertainty. In *Proceedings of the Eastern Asia Society for Transportation Studies.*

IATA. (2012). *Cargo 2000.* http://www.iata.org/whatwedo/cargo/cargo2000/Pages/index.aspx. Accessed 3 September 2012.

Ignall, E., & Kolesar, P. (1974). Optimal dispatching of an infinite-capacity shuttle: Control at a single terminal. *Operations Research, 22*(5), 1008-1024.

Karaesmen, I. Z. (2001). *Three essays on revenue management.* PhD Thesis, Columbia University.

Karmarkar, S., & Dutta, G. (2012). Multi-period revenue management model for internet advertising. *Journal of Revenue & Pricing Management, 11*(2), 225-239.

Karmarkar, S., Goutam, D., & Tathagata, B. (2011). Revenue impacts of demand unconstraining and accounting for dependency. *Journal of Revenue & Pricing Management, 10*(4), 367-381.

Kasilingam, R. (1996). Air cargo revenue management: Characteristics and complexities. *European Journal of Operational Research, 96*(1), 36-44.

Kasilingam, R. (1997). An economic model for air cargo overbooking under stochastic capacity. *Computers & Industrial Engineering, 32*(1), 221-226.

Kasilingam, R. (2011). Revenue management and air cargo. In I. Yeoman & U. McMahon-Beattie (Eds.), *Revenue management: A practical pricing perspective.* Basingstoke: Palgrave Macmillan.

Kimes, S. E. (1989). Yield management: A tool for capacity-considered service firms. *Journal of Operations Management, 8*(4), 348-363.

Kimes, S. E. (2005a). Restaurant revenue management: Could it work? *Journal of Revenue & Pricing Management, 4*(1), 95-97.

Kimes, S. E. (2005b). A strategic approach to yield management. In A. Ingold, U. McMahon-Beattie, & I. Yeoman (Eds.), *Yield management : Strategies for the service industries.* London: Thomson.

Klein, R., & Steinhardt, C. (2008). *Revenue Management : Grundlagen und Mathematische Methoden.* Berlin: Springer.

Kleywegt, A. J., & Papastavrou, J. D. (2001). The dynamic and stochastic knapsack problem with random sized items. *Operations Research, 49*(1), 26-41.

Korean Air. (2012). *2011 financial release.* http://www.koreanair.com/local/na/gd/eng/au/ir/eng_au_ir.jsp. Accessed 10 July 2012.

Kunnumkal, S., & Talluri, K. (2011). *Equivalence of piecewise-linear approximation and lagrangian relaxation for network revenue management.* Working Paper, Barcelona Graduate School of Economics.

Kunnumkal, S., Talluri, K., & Topaloglu, H. (2012). A randomized linear programming method for network revenue management with product-specific no-shows. *Transportation Science, 46*(1), 90-108.

LaDue, M. (2004). *Ten challenges in air cargo revenue management.* Presentation at the AGIFORS Cargo Study Group Meeting, Washington DC, USA.

LAN. (2012). *Annual report 2011.* http://memoria.marketinglan.com/pdf/memoria_2011-en.pdf. Accessed 10 July 2012.

Lan, Y., Ball, M. O., & Karaesmen, I. Z. (2011). Regret in overbooking and fare-class allocation for single leg. *Manufacturing & Service Operations Management, 13*(2), 194-208.

Lautenbacher, C. J., & Stidham, S. (1999). The underlying Markov decision process in the single-leg airline yield-management problem. *Transportation Science, 33*(2), 136-146.

Lee, T. C., & Hersh, M. (1993). A model for dynamic airline seat inventory control with multiple seat bookings. *Transportation Science, 27*(3), 252-265.

Levin, Y., Nediak, M., & Topaloglu, H. (2012). Cargo capacity management with allotments and spot market demand. *Operations Research, 60*(2), 351-365.

Levina, T., Levin, Y., McGill, J., & Nediak, M. (2011). Network cargo capacity management. *Operations Research, 59*(4), 1008-1023.

Lewis, M. E. (2001). Average optimal policies in a controlled queueing system with dual admission control. *Journal of Applied Probability, 38*(2), 369-385.

Lu, J., & Mazzarella, J. (2007). Application of modified nested and dynamic class allocation models for cruise line revenue management. *Journal of Revenue & Pricing Management, 6*(1), 19-32.

Lufthansa. (2012). *Lufthansa group reports an operating loss of EUR 381m in the first quarter of 2012.* http://presse.lufthansa.com/en/news-releases/ single-view/archive/2012/may/03/article/2144.html. Accessed 8 October 2012.

Lufthansa Cargo. (2012). *Lufthansa cargo achieves high load factor in a challenging market.* http://lufthansa-cargo.com/en_de/mainnav/company/traffic-figures/lufthansa-cargo-achieves-high-load-factor-in-a-challenging-market/. Accessed 18 September 2012.

Luo, L., & Shi, X. (2006). The stochastic model of multi-leg capacity allocation for air cargo revenue management. In *Proceedings of the international conference on service systems and service management.*

Luo, S., Cakanyildirim, M., & Kasilingam, R. (2009). Two-dimensional cargo overbooking models. *European Journal of Operational Research, 197*(3), 862-883.

Maddah, B., Moussawi-Haidar, L., El-Taha, M., & Rida, H. (2010). Dynamic cruise ship revenue management. *European Journal of Operational Research, 207*(1), 445-455.

Mardan, S. (2010). *Lumpy and late: The challenges in air cargo and scientific processes to handle them.* Presentation at the AGIFORS Cargo Study Group Meeting, New York, USA.

McGill, J. I., & van Ryzin, G. J. (1999). Revenue management: Research overview and prospects. *Transportation Science, 33*(2), 233-256.

Meissner, J., & Strauss, A. (2012). Network revenue management with inventory-sensitive bid prices and customer choice. *European Journal of Operational Research, 216*(2), 459-468.

Mentzer, J. T., DeWitt, W., Keebler, J. S., Min, S., Nix, N. W., Smith, C. D., et al. (2001). Defining supply chain management. *Journal of Business Logistics, 22*(2), 1-25.

MergeGlobal. (2008). End of an era? *American Shipper, 50*(8), 32-47.

Morton, A. (2006). Structural properties of network revenue management models: An economic perspective. *Naval Research Logistics, 53*(8), 748-760.

Moussawi, L., & Cakandyildirim, M. (2012). Optimal overbooking limits of a two-dimensional cargo problem: A profit maximization approach. *Journal of Revenue and Pricing Management, 11*(4), 453-476.

Nielsen, K. (2004). *Revenue management at virgin atlantic cargo.* Presentation at the AGIFORS Cargo Study Group Meeting, Washington DC, USA.

Pak, K., & Dekker, R. (2004). *Cargo revenue management: Bid-prices for a 0-1 multi knapsack problem* (Technical report). Rotterdam: Erasmus University, Erasmus Research Institute of Management.

Papastavrou, J. D., Rajagopalan, S., & Kleywegt, A. J. (1996). The dynamic and stochastic knapsack problem with deadlines. *Management Science, 42*(12), 1706-1718.

Parthasarathy, M. (2010). Cargo infusion. *Ascend, 1*, 44-45.

Patrick, J., Puterman, M. L., & Queyranne, M. (2008). Dynamic multiprior-ity patient scheduling for a diagnostic resource. *Operations Research, 56*(6), 1507-1525.

Pfeifer, P. E. (1989). The airline discount fare allocation problem. *Decision Sciences, 20*(1), 149–157.

Phillips, R. (2005). *Pricing and revenue optimization.* Stanford: Stanford University Press.

Pilarski, A. M. (2007). *Why can't we make money in aviation?* Hampshire: Ashgate.

Pilon, R. (2007). *Future opportunities & directions for air cargo revenue man-agement.* Presentation at the AGIFORS Cargo Study Group Meeting, Jeju Island, South Korea.

Pölt, S. (1998). *Forecasting is difficult - especially if it refers to the future.* Presentation at the Reservations and Yield Management Study Group Meeting, Melbourne, Australia.

Popescu, A. (2006). *Air cargo revenue and capacity management.* PhD Thesis, Georgia Institute of Technology.

Popescu, A., Keskinocak, P., Johnson, E., LaDue, M., & Kasilingam, R. (2006). Estimating air-cargo overbooking based on a discrete show-up-rate distribu-tion. *Interfaces, 36*(3), 248-258.

Powell, W. B. (2007). *Approximate dynamic programming : Solving the curses of dimensionality.* Hoboken, NJ: Wiley.

Puterman, M. L. (1994). *Markov decision processes : Discrete stochastic dy-namic programming.* New York: Wiley.

Rajan, A., Steinberg, R., & Steinberg, R. (1992). Dynamic pricing and ordering decisions by a monopolist. *Management Science, 38*(2), 240-262.

Rasekh, L., & Yihua, L. (2011). Golf course revenue management. *Journal of Revenue & Pricing Management*, *10*(2), 105-111.

Rathert, B. (2006). Revving up cargo. *Ascend*, *2*, 64-65.

Rinnooy Kan, A. H. G., Stougie, L., & Vercellis, C. (1993). A class of generalized greedy algorithms for the multi-knapsack problem. *Discrete Applied Mathematics*, *42*(2-3), 279-290.

Rubinstein, R. Y., & Kroese, D. P. (2008). *Simulation and the Monte Carlo method*. Hoboken, NJ: Wiley.

Sabre. (2010). *A look at cargo revenue management: A discussion of revenue management for air cargo businesses*. http://www.sabreairlinesolutions.com/ images/uploads/Cargo_Management_White_Paper.pdf. Accessed 20 September 2012.

Sandhu, R., & Klabjan, D. (2006). Fleeting with passenger and cargo origin-destination booking control. *Transportation Science*, *40*(4), 517-528.

Savin, S. V., Cohen, M. A., Gans, N., & Katalan, Z. (2005). Capacity management in rental businesses with two customer bases. *Operations Research*, *53*(4), 617-631.

Schäl, M. (1975). Conditions for optimality in dynamic programming and for the limit of n-stage optimal policies to be optimal. *Zeitschrift für Wahrscheinlichkeitstheorie und verwandte Gebiete*, *32*(3), 179-196.

Schweitzer, P. J., & Seidmann, A. (1985). Generalized polynomial approximations in Markovian decision processes. *Journal of Mathematical Analysis and Applications*, *110*(2), 568-582.

Sennott, L. I. (1999). *Stochastic dynamic programming and the control of queueing systems*. New York: Wiley.

Shaw, S. (2004). *Airline marketing and management*. Aldershot: Ashgate.

Slager, B., & Kapteijns, L. (2004). Implementation of cargo revenue management at KLM. *Journal of Revenue & Pricing Management, 3*(1), 80-90.

Smith, B. C., Leimkuhler, J. F., & Darrow, R. M. (1992). Yield management at American Airlines. *Interfaces, 22*(1), 8-31.

Stidham, S., & Weber, R. (1993). A survey of Markov decision models for control of networks of queues. *Queueing Systems, 13*(1-3), 291-314.

Talluri, K., & van Ryzin, G. J. (1998). An analysis of bid-price controls for network revenue management. *Management Science, 44*(11), 1577-1593.

Talluri, K., & van Ryzin, G. J. (1999). A randomized linear programming method for computing network bid prices. *Transportation Science, 33*(2), 207-216.

Talluri, K. T., & van Ryzin, G. J. (2004). *The theory and practice of revenue management.* New York: Springer.

Topaloglu, H. (2009). Using lagrangian relaxation to compute capacity-dependent bid prices in network revenue management. *Operations Research, 57*(3), 637-649.

Topaloglu, H., & Tong, C. (2011). *On approximate linear programming approach for network revenue management problems.* Working Paper, School of Operations Research and Information Engineering, Cornell University.

Topkis, D. M. (1978). Minimizing a submodular function on a lattice. *Operations Research, 26*(2), 305-321.

Veatch, M. H., & Wein, L. M. (1992). Monotone control of queueing networks. *Queueing Systems, 12*(3-4), 391-408.

Veatch, M. H., & Wein, L. M. (1994). Optimal control of a two-station tandem production/inventory system. *Operations Research, 42*(2), 337-350.

Vinod, B., & Narayan, C. P. (2008). On optimising cargo rates to improve the bottom line. *Journal of Revenue & Pricing Management, 7*(4), 315-325.

Walczak, D. (2001). *Dynamic modelling approaches to airline revenue management.* PhD Thesis, University of British Columbia. Vancouver, Canada.

Walczak, D. (2006). Modeling high demand variance in dynamic programming. *Journal of Revenue and Pricing Management, 5*(2), 94-101.

Waldmann, K.-H. (1981). *Über dynamische Optimierungsprobleme bei stochastisch variierenden Umwelteinflüssen.* Habilitation, Technische Hochschule Darmstadt.

Waldmann, K.-H. (1983). Optimal replacement under additive damage in randomly varying environments. *Naval Research Logistics Quarterly, 30*(3), 377-386.

Waldmann, K.-H. (1984). Inventory control in randomly varying environments. *SIAM Journal on Applied Mathematics, 44*(3), 657-666.

Waldmann, K. H. (1998). On granting credit in a random environment. *Mathematical Methods of Operations Research, 47*(1), 99-115.

Waldmann, K.-H., & Stocker, U. M. (2012). *Stochastische Modelle* (2nd ed.). Berlin: Springer.

Wang, Y.-J., & Kao, C.-S. (2008). An application of a fuzzy knowledge system for air cargo overbooking under uncertain capacity. *Computers & Mathematics with Applications, 56*(10), 2666-2675.

Weatherford, L. R., & Bodily, S. E. (1992). A taxonomy and research overview of perishable-asset revenue management: Yield management, overbooking, and pricing. *Operations Research, 40*(5), 831-844.

Weber, R. R., & Stidham, S. (1987). Optimal control of service rates in networks of queues. *Advances in Applied Probability, 19*(1), 202-218.

Weiss, H. J. (1979). The computation of optimal control limits for a queue with batch services. *Management Science, 25*(4), 320-328.

Westermann, D., & Lancaster, J. (2011). Improved pricing and integration with revenue management - the next step toward improved revenues. *Journal of Revenue & Pricing Management, 10*(3), 199-210.

White, D. J. (1985). Real applications of Markov decision processes. *Interfaces, 15*(6), 73-83.

White, D. J. (1988). Further real applications of Markov decision processes. *Interfaces, 18*(5), 55-61.

White, D. J. (1993). *Markov decision processes.* Chichester: Wiley.

Williamson, E. L. (1992). *Airline network seat inventory control: Methodologies and revenue impacts.* PhD Thesis, Massachusetts Institute of Technology.

Xiao, B., & Yang, W. (2010). A revenue management model for products with two capacity dimensions. *European Journal of Operational Research, 205*(2), 412-421.

Xiong, H., Xie, J., & Deng, X. (2011). Risk-averse decision making in overbooking problem. *Journal of the Operational Research Society, 62*(9), 1655-1665.

Yadin, M., & Naor, P. (1963). Queueing systems with a removable service station. *Operational Research Quarterly, 14*(4), 393-405.

Yeoman, I., & McMahon-Beattie, U. (Eds.). (2004). *Revenue management and pricing: Case studies and applications.* London: Cengage Learning.

Yeoman, I., & McMahon-Beattie, U. (Eds.). (2011). *Revenue management: A practical pricing perspective.* Basingstoke: Palgrave Macmillan.

Yeoman, I., McMahon-Beattie, U., & Ingold, A. (Eds.). (2001). *Yield management: Strategies for the service industries* (2nd ed.). London: Cengage Learning.

You, P.-S. (1999). Dynamic pricing in airline seat management for flights with multiple flight legs. *Transportation Science*, *33*(2), 192-206.

Zhang, D., & Adelman, D. (2009). An approximate dynamic programming approach to network revenue management with customer choice. *Transportation Science*, *43*(3), 381-394.

Zhang, M., & Bell, P. (2012). Price fencing in the practice of revenue management: An overview and taxonomy. *Journal of Revenue & Pricing Management*, *11*(2), 146-159.

Zhang, M., Bell, P., Cai, G. G., & Chen, X. (2010). Optimal fences and joint price and inventory decisions in distinct markets with demand leakage. *European Journal of Operational Research*, *204*(3), 589-596.

Zhuang, W., Gümüs, M., & Zhang, D. (2011). A single-resource revenue management problem with random resource consumptions. *Journal of the Operational Research Society*. (Advance online publication 14 December 2011, doi: 10.1057/jors.2011.129)

Zhuang, W., & Li, M. Z. (2010). A new method of proving structural properties for certain class of stochastic dynamic control problems. *Operations Research Letters*, *38*(5), 462-467.

Zhuang, W., & Li, M. Z. (2012). Monotone optimal control for a class of Markov decision processes. *European Journal of Operational Research*, *217*(2), 342-350.